MYSTERIES ARCTIC

Introduction by
STEPHEN LEACOCK

COLLIER BOOKS
NEW YORK, N.Y.

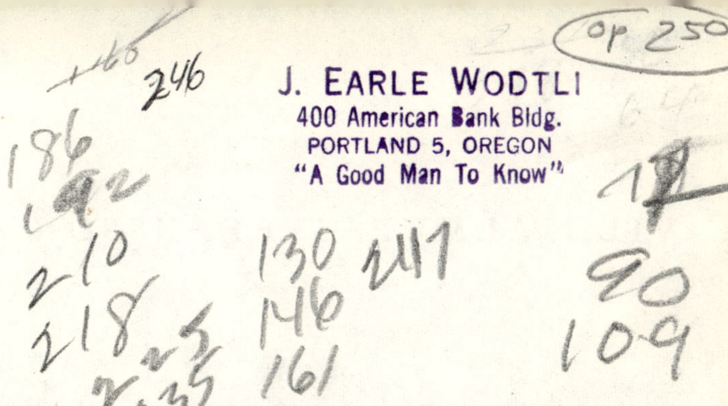

THE GREAT TRAGEDY of the first Atlantic crossing of Europeans to the New World was the disappearance of 9,000 people from their early American colony in Greenland. How and why did they disappear?

One of the most baffling problems of exploration is how Sir John Franklin and his party of over a hundred men died, apparently from hunger and malnutrition, in a district where several hundred Eskimos had been living comfortably for generations. How did the nineteenth-century English explorer and his party "contrive to die" of hunger when sufficient food was available?

Thomas Simpson, the explorer considered by some to be the discoverer of the Northwest Passage, was found dead of gunshot wounds. Was it murder or suicide? What were the real reasons for his mysterious death?

In the summer of 1930, the remains of S. A. Andrée and his party, who had vanished on a balloon voyage thirty-three years earlier, were found on one of the Spitsbergen Islands. What is the explanation of their disappearance and death?

Levanevsky, a famous Soviet airman, and his five companions, disappeared on a flight from Moscow to America over the North Pole in 1937. What happened to these six men?

VILHJALMUR STEFANSSON

UNSOLVED

OF THE

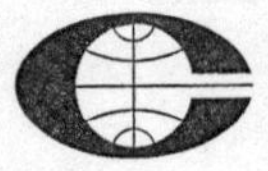

To

FANNIE

Introduction
(Telling How This Book Came to Be Written)

By STEPHEN LEACOCK

I AM VERY proud to think that I had some personal share in the initiation of the present volume. A few years ago, when all the world was reading of the discovery upon White Island of the remains of the ill-fated Andrée balloon expedition of 1897, speculation was rife and all kinds of guesses were hazarded as to the fate of the unfortunate Andrée and his companions. It seemed difficult to reconcile the obvious fact that they had escaped from the ice floes to a refuge on solid land, at a season not yet inclement, and apparently with abundant means of food, warmth and shelter, with the equally obvious fact that they had come to a sudden end. When the various guessers had had their say, Vilhjalmur Stefansson wrote in a current magazine article an explanation so lucid in its demonstration that the mystery cleared away from the scene as the Arctic mist from the ocean. When I read it I felt towards Stefansson that despairing admiration in which Dr. Watson lived towards Sherlock Holmes.

A little later, Stefansson was with me at my house here at Orillia and I broached to him an idea which I had been turning over in my mind ever since I had read the article on Andrée. It occurred to me that knowledge equally specialized and reasoning equally cogent might solve for us some long-standing mysteries which have intrigued all those who have followed Arctic exploration in person or from afar.

Among this last class I am proud to number myself. Arctic exploration, in so far as it can be carried out from an arm-chair before a winter fire, has long been for me a pursuit that verges on a passion. In this good cause I have spared neither hours nor effort. Let the hour be as late as it likes, let the snow beat at the window as it will, let the trees outside groan and creak with the frost. I can stand it. With the help perhaps of an odd glass of hot toddy kept warm on the hearth, I can face any Arctic winter that ever was. No igloo was ever snugger than my study-library on the Côte des Neiges road, with a volume of Arctic adventure to centre its warmth and comfort.

Under these circumstances of Arctic adventure I have penetrated into the remotest seas of either pole. I have been with Franklin on that famous journey to the Coppermine that was the prelude to his last and fatal adventure. I remember no more thrilling episode in my life than when Franklin and I—with Richardson and Back (later the Admiral) to support us—crossed the freezing Coppermine, running heavy with ice, in a craft made of willow sticks. Several times I had to stop reading and warm up.

In the same way I have been with Amundsen, with Shackleton, with Peary, with all those whose names constitute a beadroll of honour in the history of Arctic discovery. Nor is there any name more fit to rank on such a roll than that of Vilhjalmur Stefansson. For it has been his peculiar task and achievement to rob the northern lands and seas of the terror that hung over them.

It was through this attitude of his towards what he has called the "friendly Arctic" that I first came in touch with Vilhjalmur Stefansson many years ago. I had written, still from my armchair, a book called *Adventures of the Far North,* intended as a chronicle of the explorations of Arctic regions of Canada. What I lacked in knowledge, I undertook to supply by rhetoric. In this vein I wrote:

"For hundreds and hundreds of miles the vast fortress of ice rears its battlements of shining glaciers. The unending sunshine of the Arctic summer falls upon untrodden snow. The cold light of the aurora illumines in winter an endless desolation. There is no sound, save when at times the melting water falls from the glistening sides of some vast pinnacle of ice, or when the leaden sea forces its tide between the rock-bound islands. Here in this vast territory civilization has no part and man no place. Life struggles northward only to die out in the Arctic cold."

This seemed to me pretty fine stuff and I must confess that

in point of literary composition I am too fine an artist to worry about truth. But Stefansson is the other way. He has a weakness for fact. To him the Arctic is as full of life as Monte Carlo and has a social charm as high as that of Narragansett Beach. When I called it empty and lifeless he wrote to me in a tone of indignation which it grieves me to recall. His exact words, I do not remember; but the sense was that I might be a hell of a humorist but what I knew about the Arctic being lifeless would fill a book. And then he told me about the clouds of glorious mosquitoes on the barren lands and the bright flowers that carpet the Mackenzie delta. I wrote back meekly that I didn't mean *there,* that I meant farther north still: that the thing must stop somewhere. With which my soft answer turned away wrath and became the basis of a friendship which I have known and valued for twenty years.

For towards Stefansson I feel that peculiar gratitude which is shared by all Canadians who know his writings and particularly his glorious book called *The Northward Course of Empire*. More than any other man he has helped to dissipate the tradition of the "few acres of snow" that hemmed our reputation and impeded our advance. The vision of a vast northern empire, rigorous and stern to its children but kindly in its very rigour, rich in resources, not such as to fall into the idle hand and nourish the languor of inertia but such as come as the reward of effort and courage; this and the prospect of the intellectual culture that arises on such a foundation, is the view that he has held out for us.

For this present volume I can formulate no better wish than that it may share in the popularity and abiding merit of its predecessors.

    The Old Brewery Bay
        Orillia
      September, 1938

Acknowledgments

For the central idea of this book I am indebted to my old friend Stephen Leacock. The Introduction which he has honored me by writing gives the circumstances.

The volume is, too, a by-product of research done on behalf of certain departments of the United States Government and on behalf of Pan American Airways in connection with the need for information on northern history and conditions.

In the chapter about Thomas Simpson the list of people who have been helpful and friendly is much too long to print. It is with regret that we omit the names of many and single out Mrs. Douglas MacKay, editor of the Hudson's Bay Company magazine, *The Beaver*, who, in August, 1938, sent us galley proofs of the article by Mr. Lamb and Mr. MacKay which was to appear in the September issue; Will E. Ingersoll and the Macmillan Company of Canada, by whose permission we had access to the unpublished Ross correspondence; H. C. Knox, for his personal reminiscences; and Wm. Kaye Lamb, Librarian and Archivist of the British Columbia Provincial Library and Archives, for the thoughtful consideration of the problem as shown by his letters.

I am indebted to several personal friends and to many other scholars in several countries for help on specially doubtful questions. Thousands of books and other publications have been examined but only a few hundred contained material which appeared significant. A good many of those proved to be, in essence, duplicates; or else they were rewrites which seemed negligible in their contribution to our problems. Only a few score sources were actually used. Most of these are listed in the bibliographies for the various chapters.

Ten years spent in the Arctic and thirty devoted to northern literature have furnished a general background for these investigations. Much additional and special probing for the evidence upon which the separate studies are based has been done by my research associates, Mrs. Olive R. Wilcox and

Mrs. Genevieve N. Shipman. The manuscript has been prepared for the press by Mrs. Wilcox with the assistance of Miss Olga Dalman and seen through the press by Mrs. Wilcox.

Supplementary Note

It is a misfortune for our chapters on Franklin and on Simpson that all of the book except these acknowledgments had been set up before we received the first volume of what promises to be a monumental series of frontier records, the publications of The Hudson's Bay Record Society. In our paper on Thomas Simpson the character of George Simpson is of much consequence, and we now have new light on it through the *Journal of Occurrences in the Athabasca Department by George Simpson, 1820 and 1821, and Report* (London, 1938). The changes of view which might have been caused by a study of this document would be too complicated for brief statement here.

But a reference by George Simpson to Franklin is so pertinent and concise that we quote it in full: "Lieut. Franklin, the Officer who commands the party [Franklin's first expedition] has not the physical powers required for the labor of moderate Voyaging in this country; he must have three meals p diem, Tea is indispensible, and with the utmost exertion he cannot walk above *Eight* miles in one day, so that it does not follow if those Gentlemen are unsuccessfull that the difficulties are insurmountable."

Such contempt as Simpson here expresses for a tenderfoot weakling who required regular meals, and could not dispense with frills like tea and coffee, was still being expressed by the Hudson's Bay Company's servants on the Mackenzie River as late as 1908.

Vilhjalmur Stefansson

November 30, 1938

Contents

Unsolved Mysteries of the Arctic

Chapter 1

Disappearance of the Greenland Colony

THE GREAT ROMANCE of the Middle Ages was the first crossing of the Atlantic by Europeans, the unveiling of the New World. The great tragedy of the westward movement was the disappearance of 9,000 Europeans from their first American colony. The great mystery is how and why they disappeared.

It was seemingly the Irish, or at least people from the British Isles, who first crossed the main stream of the North Atlantic to discover Iceland some time before 795 A.D.—perhaps long before. Larger than Ireland, Iceland is the largest island known to have been discovered without aborigines by a European people. The Irish were for a time the only inhabitants. Norwegians began to reconnoitre the country around 850 and to colonize around 870. By 930 there were 50,000 Europeans in Iceland, a country wholly independent of all European nations. The language is Norse, but the blood, by varying estimates, is from 10 to 50 per cent Irish.

Iceland was the first European democracy north of the Alps, if you think of the country as European; the first American democracy if you think of it as part of the New World, which it geographically is. For you can see Greenland from Iceland, the next island in turn from Greenland and so till you reach the mainland of North America.

A Norwegian colonist, Gunnbjorn, on his way to a homestead in western Iceland, saw and reported Greenland around 900. In 982 a chieftain of the northwest coast of Iceland, Erik the Red, was outlawed for a period of three years. He decided to devote those years to the exploration of Greenland. He spent three winters there and examined the west coast several hundred miles northward, perhaps to Disko.

Erik liked the new country so well that he decided he

would urge its colonization when his exile was over. According to the saga, he called it "Green Land" because he thought people would colonize it more readily if it had an attractive name. But there may have been the other reason, too, that he found the districts green and beautiful, as travelers do now. For it is only in such literature as the kindergarten songs of our childhood that "in Greenland there is nothing green to grow."

The colonization propaganda took hold so readily in Iceland during the winter after Erik's return that he was able to start out the next spring with twenty-five ships carrying perhaps an average of thirty persons and a varying cargo of the Icelandic farm animals—horses, cattle, sheep, goats, pigs and fowl.

The ships met rough weather. Some of them were lost, and some turned back. Fourteen arrived in Greenland, therefore, with about four hundred people. This was in 986.

The colony developed at first chiefly along pastoral lines. However, as in northern European countries of the time, there was considerable reliance on fishing and hunting.

Immigration continued, chiefly from Iceland, and a government was formed similar to the Icelandic. By 990 the Greenlanders had their congress in session. This was America's first democracy, if we look upon Iceland as European.

In the year 1000 a citizen of the Greenland republic, Leif, the son of Erik the Red, saw the mainland of North America first in Labrador. During the next few years the Greenlanders tried to plant colonies on the mainland, and explored it southward. The discovery and exploration are not, as a share of the public still believes, a matter of dispute with historians. What they dispute is merely how far south the Greenlanders went. It is agreed they reached the St. Lawrence and Nova Scotia; many believe they reached Massachusetts or New York; a few think they attained Florida; and the suggestion has been advanced that the later Norse view of a connection between America and Africa was probably based on some voyage which discovered that the north coast of South America trends easterly and runs well toward Africa.

In the year 1000 parliament voted that Greenland should

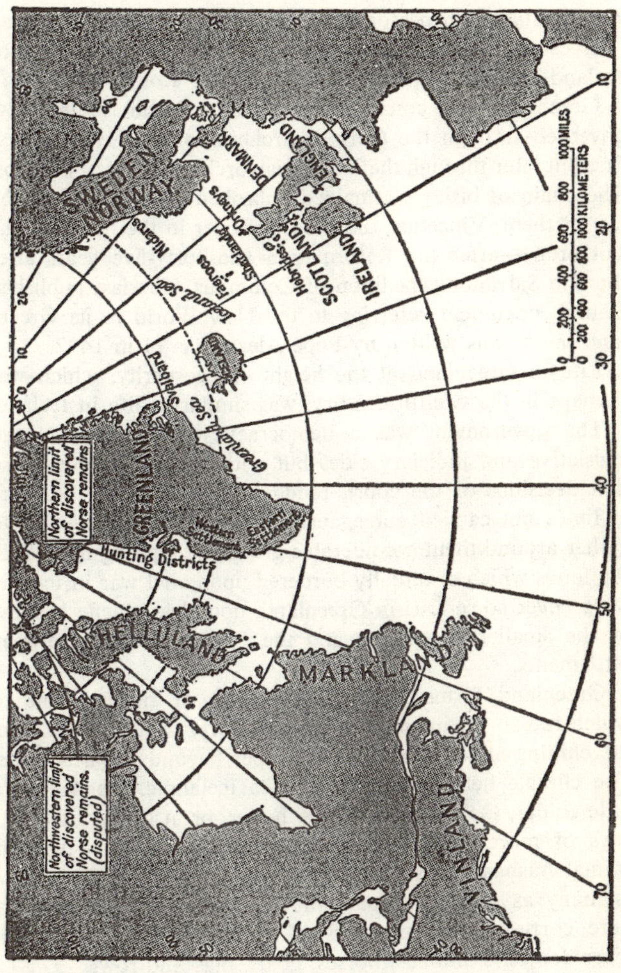

Map showing Icelandic settlements in Greenland, and countries explored from Greenland and Iceland during the Middle Ages. Compiled by Vilhjalmur Stefansson; drawn by William Briesemeister. Base map used by courtesy of the American Geographical Society, New York.

be Christian. Thenceforward we have two main European sources of the history of the New World, the literature of Iceland and the records of the Church of Rome.

Greenland was constituted a separate bishopric in 1124, governed through the German archbishopric of Hamburg at first but later through the Norwegian archbishopric of Nidaros. The chain of bishops remained unbroken till 1537, when the last of them, Vincetius, died as a prisoner in the hands of the Lutherans—after the Reformation and forty-five years after the San Salvador expedition of Columbus. The last published Church document referring to the New World in its Greenland sector was written by Pope Alexander VI in 1492.

Life in Greenland at the height of prosperity, which was perhaps in the twelfth century, was similar to life in Iceland.

The government was a democracy, with well developed legislative and judiciary sides but with a weak executive; so that decisions of the court, rendered according to law, were at times not carried out against chieftains who were able to gather around them considerable groups of fighting men. Still, the feuds which eventually bordered upon civil war in Iceland were never so serious in Greenland, doubtless chiefly because of the smaller population and the greater distance between settlements.

Greenland farms were at the heads of fjords, some of which run so far inland that you are thirty to fifty miles from the chilling effect of the ocean proper beyond the headlands. The climate here was similar to the Icelandic, the winters a little colder, the summers a little hotter, or at least with a few days of more extreme heat. The main dependence was on animal husbandry. Stables have been excavated which show as many as 104 stalls for cattle in a single barn, and there were corresponding numbers of sheep, with a few of the other domestic animals, horses, goats, pigs and fowl.

The houses were small. As in Iceland this was for two related reasons, that fuel was hard to come by, and that large timbers for building were scarce. The Icelanders got timber as driftwood, chiefly upon their own northern coast, and then by importation from Norway. The Greenlanders had driftwood, too, and doubtless made voyages north along the west Greenland coast to pick it up where it was more abundant. That is inference. What we know is that voyages were made across to Labrador where ships took on cargoes of timber that either were brought back to Greenland and used directly or were taken to Iceland where they were exchanged for European wares.

During the republic, Greenlanders had their own ships; but there were also trading and other vessels which came to Greenland from abroad, chiefly at first from Iceland but later from Norway and from other European countries. Through our knowldge of maritime developments, which has been corroborated by archaeological finds in Greenland, we can now see that by the fifteenth century a part, and likely enough the greater part, of the shipping was from the British Isles—from Bristol and Lynn. For instance, garments have been found preserved by the frozen ground of cemeteries that are cut in fashions which prevailed in Germany around 1450. It is likely that these fashions reached Greenland some decades later, perhaps around 1475. Their arrival probably depended on shipping from England.

The dress of Greenland in this late period, as well as in the earlier, was partly of imports and partly of cloth woven locally from the wool of Greenland sheep.

The exports with which Greenland paid for her imports were, in addition to the already mentioned timber from America, chiefly walrus and seal oil, the hides of these animals, wool, and perhaps dairy products. This is not so much known from direct commercial records as from statements on how Greenland paid tithes to Rome and taxes to Norway.

There were two luxury exports from Greenland, polar bears and falcons. The bears always, or nearly always, were presents or bribes for princes, secular or churchly. The falcons were sometimes gifts, but they were used in the payment of tithes or taxes and were regular exports.

During the late Middle Ages the sport of falconry had a hold on Europe such as not even baseball has on the American public now. Emperors and kings were passionate falconers, and so were nobility and gentry. There was a corresponding social gradation among falcons. Some species were so low, socially, that even peasants might use them.

One of the eagles was reserved for emperors. Second rank was held by the Greenland falcon, the hunting bird of kings and other royalty. That Greenland was the home of this bird of kings makes works on falconry sources of Greenland history. For instance, the Emperor Frederick II, King of Sicily and Jerusalem, says in his book *De Venandi cum Avibus* that Iceland is an island which lies in the sea between Norway and Greenland—showing that Greenland was even better known to the Mediterranean lands than Iceland. This book was written between 1244 and 1250.

In 1396 a son of the Duke of Burgundy was taken prisoner by the Saracens, who demanded twelve Greenland falcons for his return. That might seem a difficult ransom, for these birds were never domesticated—they had to be captured in their native country. The young nobleman, however, was ransomed. This means, among other things, that the Saracens knew enough about Greenland and its falcons to ask for the birds, and that either there were a dozen Greenland falcons in Europe where the Duke of Burgundy could get them, or else a special consignment of falcons was obtained from Greenland.

We have referred to the Christianizing of Greenland in the year 1000, to the establishment of the bishopric and the growth of the church thereafter. Its power seems to have been less in Greenland proportionately than in European countries. The bishops seem to have been men of influence rather than authority.

To the historian, the most important thing about the Greenland church is that through proclamations and other documents that come from the Popes themselves, and through various church records, we are able both to find direct information about how things were in Greenland and to check our other sources for reliability. These other sources are chiefly from Iceland.

In the early farming period, as we have implied, the European population of Greenland was concentrated at the heads of the fjords. From the start there must have been some dependence on hunting, and a greater dependence on fishing. We find archaeological confirmation of this, for in the farm refuse heaps the bones of game animals appear early. As time advanced there were more and more of these bones, showing an increasing dependence upon game.

But game is scarce in the farming districts, more abundant on the headlands. Then as now it was scarcer in the south of West Greenland than farther north, as a result of natural law. For the chief game animals are the seal, walrus and polar bear. Seals may be found where there is no ice, but they are usually more numerous among ice and much easier to secure, by Eskimo technique. The walruses, easier to kill than seals and bigger, are creatures of the ice. They are more numerous where there is more ice, and more readily secured on the ice than in the water. The polar bear, superficially a land animal, is really a sea beast. He, like the walrus, depends on the ice.

Accordingly, people from both the southern and the northern colony went for hunts north along the coast, well beyond the northern colony. These were at first summer journeys, made with tents; but there developed gradually a custom of spending the winter.

The most northerly evidence of European colonization in western Greenland, that is undisputed by everyone, is a runic stone which was found about four hundred and fifty miles north of the Arctic Circle, some twenty miles farther north than the present Upernivik. The inscription is signed by three men and is dated in April, which shows that these three men at least must have spent the winter in the vicinity. This gives the minimum extent of their ranging by 1300.

Folklore gathered by Knud Rasmussen indicates that the medieval Europeans went much farther north. They used to come sailing at least as far north as Etah, where Peary, centuries later, had winter base stations for his polar work. Here numerous European objects from the medieval Greenland period have been dug up within the last few years by archaeologists, some of them well north of Etah in the Inglefield Land section around 79° N.Lat., about eight hundred and fifty miles north of the Circle. It is disputed whether these articles show that Norsemen, or people of mixed Norse-Eskimo blood, were living in the Inglefield district. It may be that full-blooded Eskimos secured these articles by trade from the Norsemen of the more southerly coast.

Captain Gunnar Isachsen, second-in-command of the Sverdrup Expedition of 1898–1902, has written about what he thinks are Norse finds on the shores of Jones Sound—not in Greenland but in Canada, west of Melville Sound and six hundred miles north of the Circle. He identified there large numbers of stones placed in such a way that they must have been shelters for eider ducks.

When the Norwegians colonized Iceland in the ninth century they brought with them the custom of building eider-duck shelters. These are used in Iceland to this day without change of design (although new designs have also been introduced). The Icelanders would have taken the custom to Greenland when they colonized it.

Isachsen can have been mistaken in his identification; but that would be strange, for he is a Norwegian, used to seeing these shelters in his own country. Certainly nothing is more foreign to Eskimos than to build such shelters—unless, indeed, they had acquired this detail of European culture from the Norsemen.

Unless and until later students visit Jones Sound and show that Isachsen was mistaken, we must consider that Norsemen, of the centuries between the eleventh and the sixteenth, not only spread north along the Melville Sound coast of Greenland but also crossed the Sound and spread west into the Canadian islands.

The first premonitions of Greenland tragedy came in 1261, for in that year Greenland voluntarily ceased to be a republic and affiliated itself politically with Europe as a province of Norway, with a resulting decline in prosperity. It had been a republic since 990, or two hundred and seventy-one years —more than a hundred years longer than the United States has yet been a republic. During that period the country had been free to do the best it could for itself. Now, instead of receiving the expected favors from Norway, it became a stepchild, the victim of petty and major tyrannies, particularly of monopolistic trade.

Today most of us think of the America-facing coast of Greenland as running north and south where it really trends about northwest-southeast; Europe during the Middle Ages felt that it ran east and west. So we have the Icelandic, Norwegian, and other records speaking of the Eastern Settlement of Greenland where we would think of the Southern, and of the Western where we would speak of the Northern. The Eastern Settlement began near the south tip of Greenland and ran north along the West Greenland coast some one hundred miles, corresponding roughly to what now is the Julianehaab District. Then came the Uninhabited Coast, about one hundred and seventy miles to around Lat. 63° 45′ N. The section from there to about 65° N.Lat. was the Western Settlement, coinciding approximately with the present Godthaab District. Northwest from there, at least to three hundred miles beyond the Arctic Circle, ran the undefined stretch called the Northern Outposts (Nordurseta). At the height of prosperity during the twelfth and thirteenth centuries there were in the Eastern Settlement twelve churches, an Augustinian monastery, a Benedictine nunnery and about one hundred and ninety farms; the Western had four churches and some ninety farms.

The foremost historian of medieval Greenland was Professor Finnur Jonsson of the University of Copenhagen. In 1899 he estimated the population of the colony as never having exceeded 3,000; in a statement issued thirty years later he raised the estimate to 9,000. For meantime great numbers of ruins from the days of the republic had been excavated and a better basis for estimating had been gained.

Students who depended solely upon the direct literary sources of the history of the Greenland church and state, as found chiefly in Rome, Norway, and Iceland, have considered that the "last recorded voyage" to Greenland was either in 1410 or in 1448. They believed that even before this time all farms in the Western Settlement were tenantless, but considered that many if not most of the farms of the Eastern district were still occupied when this "last" contact with Europe took place.

Scandinavians reoccupied Greenland in 1721 with the support of a king who lived in Denmark, but under the leadership of Hans Egede, a missionary from Norway who had dedicated his life to the proposition that there still were Christian Scandinavians in Greenland whose faith needed rejuvenation. He was not the first to think and talk this way, for there had been through the centuries to 1492 a sequence of spokesmen, among them popes, who wanted the Roman Church strengthened in Greenland. After the Reformation there arose in Norway and elsewhere a desire to save the Greenlanders from the heresies of Rome and guide them toward the orthodoxy of Lutheranism.

In Egede's time it had come to be believed even by Icelanders, better informed than any other Europeans on these problems, that the Eastern Settlement, with which their ancestors had had continual relations from the tenth to the fourteenth century, had been on the east coast of Greenland; the Western Settlement, on the west coast. The ruins of churches and homes and the graveyards of Christians which Egede found in southwestern Greenland were to him, therefore, remains of the Western Settlement. It appeared to him that, but for these monuments, his departed countrymen had left no sign. He did not hear Norse words when he listened to the speech of the Eskimos. The customs of Europe and the religion of Christianity had left no traces that he could find.

Some years later, and particularly when Egede's children had secured a command of the Eskimo tongue, the missionaries began to pick up stories of how and why the Greenlanders had disappeared. Essentially these were that they had grown weak through the breakdown of commerce with Europe. They had not been able to secure iron for weapons, they had sickened because they had been deprived of those foods which are required for the health of Europeans. The weakened whites were then attacked by the Eskimos, not in any systematic way, but every now and then through specific quarrels. Finally the last small settlement was wiped out, the last white man destroyed.

Thus Egede and his successors in Greenland and the

scholars of Europe built up a consistent explanation of how and why the medieval Europeans had disappeared.

According to the theory developed, there had been ominous signs of the final tragedy from the start. For the Icelandic colonists who first settled Greenland, though they had seen no people, had found here and there on the coast remains, such as peculiar skin boats, which they afterwards recognized as proving that the same people had been ahead of them in this part of Greenland as those whom the Greenlandic explorers following the year 1000 had met in Labrador—Eskimos. But seemingly the Eskimos themselves were never seen in Greenland during the first generation or two of occupancy by the Europeans. Then the contact with the Eskimos began, and increased steadily. By the thirteenth century there were recurrent attacks by the natives; around 1345 the northern coloney of the Europeans, the Western Settlement, had been destroyed.

The account of the destruction of the northern colony we have from Ivar Bardarson, who was, from about 1341 to around 1360, manager of the farm attached to the Bishop's seat at Gardar, now called Egaliko, in the Julianehaab District. No news had been received from the Northern Settlement for several years and Bardarson organized a relief expedition. They sailed north along the coast, past an uninhabited stretch that separated the two colonies, and came to farmhouses. They were afraid to land. Spying from the boats they saw domestic animals grazing around the farms, but there were no people. Bardarson assumed they had all been killed by the Eskimos.

The main forces of destruction, scholars agreed, were malnutrition due to the lack of a mixed diet suited to Europeans, and decimation by attacks of savages healthy and aggressive on a meat diet.

The historians speculated as to subsidiary causes. The Black Death had swept over Norway in 1348–49. Although there had apparently been no sailings during the period 1346–55 from Bergen, which then by royal decree had a monopoly of the Greenland trade, this school believes that some ship finally carried the disease. Assuming, then, a mortality as in Norway, the Greenland colony would have been so weakened that the remnants became an easy prey to the Eskimos.

Forthright statements that the Greenland settlements were declining are found chiefly in certain papal documents. We give samples.

In 1276 Pope John XXI received a letter from the Archbishop of Nidaros. This has not been found in the Vatican archives, which are as yet barely touched in the search for pre-Columbian records of Europe's contact with America. However, the loss in this particular case is small, for the Pope summarized the Archbishop's letter in his reply.

The Pope has noted what the Archbishop says about Greenland being a remote country and about the difficulty in this instance of carrying out the instructions to visit personally all parts of the Kingdom of Norway for the purpose of collecting tithes. The diocese of Greenland is so far distant that one can scarcely reach those parts within the time appointed for the payment of the tithe. Moreover, when Greenland is reached, the farms are so far apart that one has to camp out between settlements. When finally, after great effort, the tithes have been collected, there may be no ship returning to Norway during the season. The Pope now understands, from the letter of the Archbishop, that it may require five years from the time that the Archbishop receives the instructions of his superiors to gather the tax and bring it back to Norway. Nevertheless the Pope commands the Archbishop to procure suitable men for this task and to give the collection of the tithes his own diligent solicitude.

In 1279 the Vatican had again received a letter from the Archbishop of Nidaros concerning the delay in collecting the Greenland taxes. Pope Nicholas III wrote on January 31, 1279, that the Vatican perhaps had been a little hasty in excommunicating the Greenlanders for being so slow in paying their tithes, and notified the Archbishop that the decree was lifted.

In 1282 Martin IV wrote that he understood from the Archbishop's letter that the recent consignment of the tithes consisted mainly of leather and of leather rope—commodities of which Norway itself produced an abundance, so that it was extremely difficult to sell them in the local market. The Archbishop wanted to know whether he should sell them for a nominal sum, hold them for a rise in the market, or ship the leather and ropes to Italy. The Pope agreed that the situation was difficult but thought that, everything considered, the Archbishop had better sell the leather for whatever he could get. And would he please hurry the proceeds along, for the Vatican was in desperate need of funds (to meet the bills of a projected crusade).

Nicholas V, in 1448, wrote to the Bishops of Iceland that he was saddened by the doleful story of the inhabitants of Greenland who for hundreds of years had been faithful to Holy Church. He had only now learned that these people had been attacked thirty years before by barbarians, who had devastated their homes, destroyed all but nine parochial churches, killed a large number of inhabitants, and carried many others away in captivity. The nine churches which were spared were those which "extend into the farthest districts, where they [the barbarians] could not approach conveniently because of the defiles of the mountains." At the same time that this news had reached the Pope there had come the further word that many of the captives had returned to their homes, making such repairs as they could and attempting to carry on divine worship. But their poverty was so great that for the entire thirty years they had been unable to support priests and a bishop, and had during this period been deprived of priestly guidance, except for a few who, after arduous travel, "had succeeded in reaching those churches which the barbarian hand had passed unhurt." The Greenlanders now were petitioning the Vatican to send a representative to minister to their spiritual wants. The Pope therefore commanded the Bishops of Iceland, "whom we understand to be one of the nearer bishops of the aforesaid island," to send to Greenland priests to govern the restored churches and administer the Sacrament. Also, if it seemed expedient, the Iceland Bishops were instructed to ordain some practical and able person as Bishop of Greenland.

In 1492 Alexander VI, who had just ascended the throne

of Peter, gave out a sort of letter of credit to Matthias, bishop-elect, who was about to devote himself to reviving the Church in Greenland. The Pope recites that when he was in minor orders (around 1456) he was already interested in the Greenland Church, and that when he was a bishop he participated in the election of their beloved brother Matthias to the bishopric of Greenland. Now that he is Pope he continues his interest and is concerned over the deplorable condition of the Greenlandic Church, which has had no resident priest for about eighty years—a period during which no ship has visited the country. The Greenlanders who "are accustomed to live on dried fish and milk for lack of bread, wine and oil," have as a result in many cases renounced their sacred baptismal vows.

The general idea that the European colony was destroyed through the breakdown of commerce with Europe, through the attack of "pirates" (as one letter calls them) who were Eskimos, with possible help from the Black Death, has been coaxed along right down to our own time, until in 1935 Poul Nörlund gives it the benefit and implications of what are to him the up-to-the-minute verdicts not merely of archaeology and geology but also of physiology and dietetics.

Nörlund and other somewhat less recent commentators have, then, added new trimmings to the Bardarson-Egede-Rink picture. One of them is that the climate of southwestern Greenland has deteriorated since the colonization, and that poverty and scarcity of food resulted in part from the growth of ice fields on land and the filling of the sea with drift ice, thus restricting the acreage of the grazing fields and meadows, decreasing their output through a shortening and chilling of the summer—rendering commerce less profitable to European ships because there were now fewer things for which to trade, and making navigation difficult because of the ice blockades.

This theory proceeds along the line that commerce declined through these natural causes and through the Norwegian monopoly of trade. There came, as a result, a physical deterioration which has been shown by archaeologists, particularly through skeletal proof of rickets and other deficiency diseases. It is no mere theory, says Nörlund, but is actually proven through the skeletons, that the people were weakened by malnutrition—the assumption being that, although Eskimos are healthy on a meat diet, Europeans cannot be; and that the cereal and other vegetal elements in the food of the Greenlanders became insufficient for health through the above mentioned decrease of commerce.

But whereas most of the school to which Nörlund belongs previously wanted to put the final extinction of the Norse colony fairly early in the fifteenth century, Nörlund concedes that evidence of many kinds makes it highly probable, if not certain, that European civilization was still being maintained by a people of Christian religion and blond complexion in southern west Greenland at least thirty years after Columbus.

We have now devoted all the space we can to what has long been the orthodox view. We turn to contrary views, which are frequently spoken of as new, but which have been maintained sporadically at least since 1776.

The main attack on the theory originated by the Norwegian Egede, and brought to full stature by the Dane Nörlund, came from the Norwegian Fridtjof Nansen at various times, but chiefly through the publication of the Norwegian original of the book which we have in two English volumes, called *In Northern Mists* (London and New York, 1911). However, in working out the chronology for the predecessors of Frobisher for the 1938 Argonaut edition of *The Three Voyages of Martin Frobisher,* we happened upon several predecessors of Nansen. We shall mention here only three. Two of these were apparently unknown to Nansen; for he was always meticulously fair in giving precedences and still does not mention them in his carefully documented two-volume work.

In 1774 the Icelandic missionary Egill Thorhallason was in Greenland and visited what we now know were both the Eastern and the Western Settlements, although he thought he had seen only the Western Settlement, the Eastern being still considered to be on the east coast. He was familiar with the views of Egede and his successors, and ridiculed them in an appendix to his *Rudera,* published in Copenhagen in 1776.

There are in literature few better examples of how clear

minds, even in different centuries, can arrive at the same conclusions from the same evidence, than the brief and trenchant appendix of Thorhallason compared with the lengthy and documented chapters of Nansen.

Thorhallason feels that perhaps most absurd of all the absurdities in the "orthodox" theory is the contention that the Black Death, introduced from Norway, so weakened the Europeans in Greenland that they fell a ready prey to the Eskimos. We know, says Thorhallason, that there was a great deal of contact between the Europeans and the Eskimos during the fourteenth century. What reason have we to think, he asks, that a plague coming from Europe would pick out only Europeans for destruction and leave the Eskimos in full number to strike down a few surviving whites? Thorhallason contends that the reverse would have been more likely; for European plagues, so far as he knows, are more deadly to American natives than to Europeans.

Thorhallason bears down on this argument and suggests that the Black Death, if it had reached Greenland, would have killed a higher percentage of Eskimos than of Europeans, reversing the strength ratio, if it was previously in favor of the Eskimos. He does not say so, but evidently means that if there had been a Black Death the next act would more reasonably have been an extermination of the few surviving Eskimos by the Europeans.

Next in absurdity, says Thorhallason, is the idea that the "barbarians" or "pirates" whom the Pope mentioned were Eskimos. What can be more ridiculous than to say that Eskimos were able, in their "ships," to attack only those Europeans who lived on promontories, but could not reach those who lived in the depth of the fjords? On the contrary, he says, the Eskimos would surely be able to ferret out any corner that was available to the whites. The barbarians to whom the Pope referred as taking prisoners on the forelands, and as being unable to reach the depth of the fjords, must have been Europeans in big ships. They had, perhaps, no local pilotage and so were timid about the narrow fjords.

Thorhallason takes up the Pope's statement that the barbarians took prisoners, whom they repatriated after several years. He thinks it absurd to believe that Eskimos would carry off captives. But this is just what you might expect from European pirates of the fourteenth century. Doubly illogical would it be for the Eskimos to repatriate captives; it would be logical for Europeans to do so.

Thorhallason feels that, if not absurd, it is scarcely reasonable to suppose that the Europeans and the Eskimos were hostile to each other in Greenland, and that the Eskimos were the aggressors. His whole knowledge of this people, he says, inclines him to believe that they would have been friendly, helpful, sympathetic. Thorhallason knew from the Icelandic sagas how arrogant the Norsemen had been in Europe. But he feels that in Greenland, facing new conditions, they would have acquired a humility and an adaptability that would make them almost as ready to be friends with the Eskimos as the Eskimos were to be friends with them.

Adoption of the Thorhallason view leads to a decision that Bardarson was wrong in thinking that the Eskimos had destroyed the Northern Settlement; that it is wrong to understand Vatican documents as saying (or is a mistake in the documents themselves) that the Greenlandic Europeans were attacked by Eskimos; and that everybody must have been wrong in thinking that the colony disappeared at all, in the sense of being exterminated. What happened was that, when European commerce declined, the European colonists gradually adopted an Eskimo culture, intermarried with the people, and disappeared only in the sense that their culture disappeared.

Seemingly unaware of Thorhallason, the Norwegian sociologist and historian Eilert Sundt, in a note to his edition of Hans Egede's diary (Kristiania, Norway, 1860) gives only about half of Thorhallason's reasoning but arrives at the same conclusion.

Sundt found that, among white families dwelling in Lapp districts of Norway, within a generation the tall and blond Norwegians begin to feel that the Lapps are a more successful and in that sense a better people, so that not only do the Norwegian men marry Lapp women but Norwegian girls come to prefer Lapp husbands, since they are more at home in the country and are better providers. And, queries Sundt, what reason have we to think that the modern Norwegian is different from the Norseman of the Middle Ages in Greenland? European culture would be less well adapted to Greenland conditions, and men would be the more successful, the better providers, the more nearly they adapted themselves to Eskimo ways. Thus, as among the Lapps whom Sundt knew personally, there would have been not only a marriage of Eskimo women to Norse men but also, by the choice of the women themselves, a deal of marriage between Norse women and Eskimo men.

Sundt closes by saying it is pathetic that Hans Egede, who longed for nothing so much as to discover in Greenland traces of the former Icelandic colonists, must have seen (without understanding what he saw) many who bore in their faces the clear proof that they were in part of European descent. Egede unknowingly revealed that he had seen European traits occasionally among the Greenland Eskimos of 1721 when he said: "Both the men and women . . . have broad faces and thick lips; they are flat-nosed and of a brown complexion. Still, some of them are attractive and of a fair complexion."

The question whether the European colony disappeared by extermination or amalgamation threatens to become an absurdly nationalistic issue. For most Danes favor the extermination theory, and most Norwegians the one of amalgamation. There are notable exceptions. For instance, the Dane Gustav Meldorf agrees (in 1906) with those writers who during the last one hundred and fifty years have held the opinion that the "barbarian" attacks upon the Greenlanders were made by European pirates or privateers. He considers that probably those Europeans who survived the pirate raids were befriended by the Eskimos and eventually amalgamated with them. He mentions Thorhallason and appears to have been acquainted with his view although he seems not to have read his appendix.

As said, the attack upon the extermination theory which the world has most noted was in Nansen's *In Northern Mists*. He uses the same arguments that Thorhallason and Sundt used, buttressing them with scholarship and adding a few details of his own. He makes it clear that there is no sound reason to believe that the medieval colony suffered from a change of climate. Besides, a chilling of the climate might have had effects that were on the whole good. An increase of ice in the sea, for instance, might have interfered somewhat with husbandry and with commerce, but it would have brought a compensating increase of game. For it is the veriest commonplace of northern countries that the more sea ice there is the more game there is, and the easier to secure. This, indeed, was one reason why the colonists, even during the early and largely pastoral stage of the settlement, used nevertheless to have their hunting outposts in the far north.

With greater scholarship, Nansen was better equipped than Thorhallason in at least one other way for tearing up the orthodox picture of how the Greenlanders disappeared. Thorhallason was a missionary from Iceland, where there are no big game animals. As a religious worker from a pastoral country he was doubly not a hunter. Nansen was an experienced hunter, well grounded in the lore of the chase.

As a practical hunter, and as one who knew Eskimo hunters, Nansen asks us to consider the facts on which Bardarson grounded his conclusion that the Europeans of the Northern Settlement were killed off by Eskimos.

Bardarson was not a Greenlander but a Norwegian temporarily resident there as superintendent of the bishop's farm in the southern district. His understanding of Greenland matters would be incomplete. The southern colony was little in touch with the Eskimos, as compared with the northern colony.

For several years none of the northern colonists had come south. They had no reason to come except for European wares, and we know that trade with Europe had sunk low before this period. On the other hand, they had a pressing reason for going north: they were more and more dependent upon hunting, less and less upon husbandry, and the hunting was better up north. Besides, traders usually visit their customers. Northerners who hoped for European trade would expect a visit from the south. They would not use up time on a southerly journey which was pressingly required for the northern hunt.

The southerners were curious to know how the northerners were getting on. Perhaps the new farm superintendent combined the traditional good Norwegian seamanship with the equally traditional Norwegian venturesomeness and a desire to see new countries. He made an occasion for going north, at once eager to see strange things and a bit fearful of the Eskimos who were supposed to be powerful in witchcraft, as were all similar people (for instance, the Lapps in northern Norway).

When the Bardarson party came opposite a farm of the Northern Settlement they pulled close inshore and had a good view of the house and of farm animals grazing about. But they saw no people. Doubtless they shouted, and probably they hovered about just offshore for a good while, finally convincing themselves that there was no human being anywhere near. They then returned to the southern colony and reported that the people of the Northern Settlement had been exterminated by the savages.

We have no information as to whether the southern colony accepted Bardarson's view that the northerners had been exterminated. The document we have is not even written by Bardarson himself. It was written in Norway after he had returned to his own country, his assignment to the Greenland job finished. Then apparently Bardarson gave verbal information to someone who knew how to write. There resulted the document we have, a memorandum by an unknown Norwegian of what Bardarson told him.

Nansen considers that Bardarson's interpretation of what he saw (perhaps rather the interpretation given in Norway to Bardarson's statement) is preposterous: that it shows a complete misunderstanding of the situation in Greenland, of hunting peoples in general and of the Eskimos in particular. He says it is easily possible that Eskimos, meeting domestic animals, might kill them as if they were a new kind of wild animal; or that, understanding them to be domestic and the property of a given person, they might nevertheless kill them.

Their purpose in killing, in either case, would be for eating. Eskimos might have killed farm animals without killing the people; but they certainly would not have killed the people without killing the farm animals.

The truth was that the northern colonists were now mainly devoted to hunting, but they had not yet wholly discontinued the breeding of sheep and cattle. It was mid-summer and the entire family were in one of the mountain valleys gathering eggs, catching salmon at a waterfall, or pursuing the caribou which, then as now, would have been hunted at this season.

Had Bardarson understood the conditions he would have inferred that all was well, from seeing the farm animals grazing about. The people, he would have known, were away because it was the hunting season.

There seems little doubt that, had Bardarson not been frightened by his misinterpretation of what he saw at the first farm, he would have gone on to other farms, eventually finding one where some at least of the family were not away hunting.

The records preserved from the time after Bardarson are mainly documents from Rome, of which we have given specimens. It is more than possible that communication between the north and south colonies was resumed after his time and was known in Iceland, even in Norway and at the Vatican, without documents surviving; and it is also probable that cataloguing and arranging of the Vatican archives will reveal further documents and make them fully available for study. However, if not at Bardarson's time, then perhaps not much later, the northern colonists gave up husbandry pursuits and went over completely to hunting. Thereupon they would naturally migrate northward, gradually or in a concerted movement of a large group. For it had now been known to them for centuries that the better hunting was in that direction.

Like Thorhallason, Nansen points out first that the Black Death may never have reached Greenland, and second that, if it did arrive, it must have killed natives as well as whites. He agrees that it was European pirates and not Eskimos that would have devastated the forelands without being able to reach the heads of the fjords. Like Thorhallason he says that for Eskimos to capture people for slavery is absurd, although for Europeans of the time it was logical. Doubly absurd would it be for the Eskimos (though logical for Europeans) to repatriate captured slaves, which the Pope says was done.

Thorhallason rested his argument about the pirates on common sense and a general knowledge of history. Nansen was able to document his conclusion; for he knew that in 1432 King Henry VI of England made an agreement with his royal uncle Eric of Pomerania, king of the Scandinavian countries, that English privateers should repatriate in dependencies of King Eric's realm prisoners who had been captured there. Among the dependencies were both Iceland and Greenland. So here you have a royal English promise that the very thing would be done by the pirates (or privateers) which Pope Nicholas V says was done by the "barbarians."

It is mainly through documentation that Nansen carries beyond Thorhallason the attack upon the contention, from Egede to Nörlund, that the blood of the European Greenlanders disappeared from Greenland. In this sphere the one thing which Nansen does not thoroughly demolish is Nörlund's contention that signs of rickets in the skeletons found at Herjolfsnes are proof that the medieval Norsemen disappeared from the whole of Greenland partly through malnutrition. So we follow that question beyond Nansen, aiming to show that while Nörlund is correct for Herjolfsnes, and for such trading centers as may have resembled Herjolfsnes, he is wrong in extending conclusions derived from a trading village to those hunting or farming communities which contained the larger part of the Greenland population during the centuries 1400 and 1500.

Nörlund's basic assumption is that Europeans will suffer malnutrition on an all-flesh diet, though Eskimos do not.

It was demonstrated by the Stefansson expeditions, through the experience of more than twenty non-Eskimos between the years 1906 and 1918, that everyone who tried it was as healthy on a diet consisting wholly of animal tissue and water as he had ever been on any diet. These men included not only more than half a dozen European nationalities but also

South Sea Islanders. It is known from other sources that Negroes do as well on an all-meat diet as Eskimos or whites.

A survey of the history of human diet through the resources of anthropology will show that in many different countries and climates, in the remote and recent past as well as in the present, large numbers of people have lived without malnutrition on diets where elements from the vegetable kingdom were either wholly absent or present in negligible quantity. No doctrine of that rapidly changing science, dietetics, is so surely on its way out as the notion that the only diet on which you can have normal health is one of elaborate and careful food mixture. The fact is, of course, as most anthropologists have long believed and as dietitians are now beginning to realize, that you can be healthy on a vegetarian diet, that you can be healthy on a flesh diet, and that you can be healthy on a blending of the two.

In any case, there is no evidence that people who live exclusively on flesh have a poorer chance of normal health than those who use, in addition to meat, such things as were imported from Europe to Greenland during the Middle Ages.

This is the general statement on health. The particular one concerning rickets is that an investigator of Nörlund's own nationality, Alfr. Bertelsen, has shown the disease is today fairly common in Greenland within the families of Danes who live mainly on food imported from Europe; and that rickets is practically unknown among those Eskimos in Greenland who still live on their native diet.

Dr. William A. Thomas of Chicago reported on deficiency diseases through the *Journal* of the American Medical Association from his observations in Greenland and northern Labrador. In Greenland he concluded that "among these primitive, carnivorous people there is neither scurvy nor rickets," thus confirming Bertelsen. In Labrador the natives have for so long been in contact with civilization that they have abandoned their primitive diet in favor of European foods. Among these Dr. Thomas found rickets to be "almost universal."

More recent Norwegian testimony confirms the Danish and American sources with regard to rickets. Dr. Arne Höygaard published at Oslo in 1937 "Some Investigations Into the Physiology and Nosology of Eskimos from Angmagssalik in Greenland: A Preliminary Statement." He says: "There was possibly slight rickets in the case of three small children in the colony, but none in the outlying district." The context shows the "slight rickets" to have been among families who lived partly on native and partly on European food; the absence of rickets was where European food was also absent.

While the most striking Nörlund argument is that the Europeans of Greenland during the Middle Ages suffered from rickets *because they had insufficient European food*, he also gives a picture of general physical breakdown. Such a breakdown would necessarily include tuberculosis. It is, therefore, pertinent that Dr. Höygaard writes (personal communication dated June 29, 1938) that he has been investigating the relation of tuberculosis to diet in east Greenland, and that he has found a better prognosis when the patients live in the primitive way than when they use, in addition to the meat, considerable amounts of a food rich in carbohydrates. Now grains (the only noteworthy source of carbohydrates available by European commerce to the medieval Greenlanders) rank high, if not at the top, among those food elements for the want of which Nörlund thinks the Europeans died out from Greenland during the Middle Ages. Thus he recommends for better health the very factors which Höygaard finds detrimental in the same climate.

True, Nörlund argues that carbohydrates are necessary for Europeans but not for Eskimos. However, as we have said, the existence of such a racial difference is a pure assumption. What little evidence we have tends in the opposite direction—the presence or absence of things like vitamins or carbohydrates apparently will have about the same physiological effect upon different races.

The place where Nörlund found the skeletons that showed rickets was the main trading station of south Greenland, Herjolfsnes, where people would have more European food than anywhere else in Greenland—partly because the ships arrived there and partly because the townspeople and the surrounding community made their living by dealing with these ships.

In other words, what Nörlund has really shown is only that dietetics and physiology were the same in Greenland during the Middle Ages as they now are in Greenland and in Labrador—that those who live on European foods, or on native foods handled in the European way, will develop rickets and other deficiency troubles.

So we can forecast with confidence that, whenever archaeological studies of Greenland are carried far enough, it will be established that skeletons show rickets where there are evidences, or at least probabilities, of a good deal of European contact; and that skeletons will not show rickets, nor marked signs of any of the deficiency diseases, where the evidence or the probabilities lead us to believe that the people were living chiefly on Greenland food prepared in the native Greenland way.

The medieval Europeans in Greenland needed for survival only the good sense to realize that they ought to change the European for the Eskimo way of life. Nansen puts it well where he says that he cannot think so badly of his own countrymen of the twelfth to the fifteenth century as to believe they were too stupid to learn that the road to salvation lay through shedding the customs they had brought with them and adopting those of their new country.

Nörlund has shown in our cited volume that the Europeans were still surviving as Europeans in Greenland to at least 1520.

The summer of 1578 Frobisher went ashore in Greenland and saw an encampment whose people had fled. He found there an iron trivet and things which showed that the people had "trade with some ciuill people, or else are in deede themselues artificiall workemen," and thus very different from the Eskimos, whom he knew in what we now call Baffin Island.

Nothing is clearer among students of the Eskimos than that a trivet has little or no place in their way of life, and that any piece of iron is sure to be cut up immediately into things for which they have use. It may seem strange to the casual reader, but is a fact widely attested, that things like rifle barrels or pieces of an anchor can be worked by Eskimos with Stone Age tools, and are shaped by them into knives, spearheads, arrow points, and particularly into needles.

Therefore, the people who left a trivet at their encampment, when they fled on the approach of Frobisher, either were not wholly Eskimo in their way of life or else were Eskimos who had such an abundant supply of iron that they could afford to leave some of it unused, in the shape of a trivet. In other words, you must choose one or the other theory: that this party were not wholly Eskimo, or that they were Eskimos who had had an extensive European contact of which we are unaware except through this evidence.

In 1586 John Davis found in Greenland a burial place of men who were dressed in skin, and who had no sign of European contact except that there was a cross laid upon the grave. The student of comparative religions, or of the history of religion, will consider nothing more reasonable than this discovery. For it is well known that the symbolism of a belief will survive longer than the belief itself. The people whose grave was found by Davis may not have been Christian in any other sense, but they still preserved the symbolism of the cross.

Seventy years after Davis we have a confirmatory statement from the Frobisher-Davis region. It comes to us round-about through a book on the West Indies. A Frenchman, Charles de Rochefort, in his *Histoire naturelle et morale des Iles Antilles de l'Amérique* (Rotterdam, 1658), digresses to include an account which he has received from Nicolas Tunes of Flushing. Tunes described a people he had found on his voyage of 1656 to Davis Strait, at 64° 10′ N.Lat., therefore in the vicinity of Gilbert Sound. De Rochefort says (pages 194-95): "Regarding the people who inhabited this country, our voyagers saw two sorts, who lived together with good relations and perfect amity. One sort had a very tall stature, well formed bodies, of a fairly white complexion. . . . The others were much smaller, of an olive complexion, well enough proportioned in their members except that their legs were short and thick."

Tunes, then, saw in 1656 two kinds of people in the district where, Nörlund concedes, European Greenlanders were living at least to 1520. One sort Tunes describes as if they might have been nearly or quite pure Eskimo; the other as if they could have been half or three-quarters European.

Both schools of thought with regard to the lost colony agree that, among the present 16,000 "Eskimos" in Greenland, few if any are without European blood, while some are so European in appearance that, conventionally dressed, they would pass unnoticed in any American or European gathering.

For this high percentage of European traits, including light eyes and hair, the two schools advance different explanations. Those who believe that there was extensive intermarriage between the two races during the Middle Ages, and that the civilization disappeared but not the blood, claim that these mixed people get half of their European traits through descent from the lost colony. Those who believe in the extinction of the medieval Europeans claim that all the European qualities, or practically all, are to be explained by mixture with Europeans since the time of Frobisher and Davis, chiefly through intermarriages since the Danes took over, following Egede in 1721.

Because the exterminationists have the advantage in point of numbers, we let the survivalists have the last say, through two quotations:

We repeat the statement of Hans Egede for what he saw in west Greenland during the years following 1721: "Both the men and women . . . have broad faces and thick lips; they are flat-nosed and of a brown complexion. Still, some of them are attractive and of a fair complexion."

To supplement Egede's statement we use a translation from the mentioned Norwegian sociologist and historian, Eilert Sundt, fellow countryman and admirer of Hans Egede. In his 1860 edition of Egede's diary, Sundt comments on the above passage: "Egede had probably expected to find recognisable countrymen; but the indefatigable way in which he took care of the 'savages' that he found there will please us still more when there is a reason to think that the remains of the Norwegian population really had assimilated with the Eskimos, so that he—though without understanding what he saw—had on his journey south [along the west coast of Greenland] a glimpse of his countrymen's fair hair and blue eyes."

Chapter 2

The Lost Franklin Expedition

ONE OF THE most baffling problems of Canadian exploration is how Sir John Franklin and his party of more than a hundred contrived to die to the last man, appearently from hunger and malnutrition, in a district where several hundred Eskimos had been living for generations, bringing up their children, and taking care of their aged. These Eskimos were of both sexes, all ages, and of every condition of health. Franklin's party, with the one exception of himself, were young men or in middle age, carefully selected for their good health and physical resourcefulness. They were, as John Brown says, "the elite of maritime England."

The Eskimos lived by hunting with weapons of the Stone Age; the British were armed with shotguns and muskets, not quite so good as ours today but certainly a lot more effective than the bows of the Eskimos. They must have had both hooks and nets for fish where the Eskimos had only hooks. They could have made for themselves harpoons from the wood and metal of their ships better than the ones which the Eskimos possessed, made of driftwood and native copper or bone.

We receive preliminary light on how one hundred and thirty Englishmen could manage to perish from hunger in a region well stocked with game by considering the record of British explorers of that period and particularly the record of Sir John Franklin himself.

Franklin entered the Navy in 1800 at the age of fourteen. Between that date and 1813 he was in the famous actions of Copenhagen, Trafalgar and New Orleans, besides many of less renown. Ships to which he was assigned took part in several blockades. His was the sort of life that develops discipline and courage rather than initiative or self-reliance. He had plenty of use for these virtues quite apart from naval encounters. He was only fifteen when he was assigned to H.M.S. *Investigator* for Australian and Antarctic exploration. Before the ship had been many days out she was known to be in poor condition, really unseaworthy. Her commander, Matthew Flinders, had chosen between a poor ship and none at all. There were hardships and trials a plenty.

In 1803 young Franklin was on the *Porpoise* which, in company with the *Cato* and the *Bridgwater,* was en route from Sydney to London. Both the *Porpoise* and the *Cato* struck reefs and foundered. The *Bridgwater* was in the clear, while the survivors of the other two ships were stranded on a reef which was 900 by 150 feet. There the *Bridgwater* left them and proceeded to Bombay where she reported both ships and all hands lost. No vessel therefore went to their rescue and it was not until two officers and twelve men had made the 750-mile trip to Sydney in an open boat that the eighty left on the reef were rescued.

In 1818 the Admiralty despatched an expedition for the North Pole in the ships *Dorothea* and *Trent*. David Buchan was commander. Franklin was in charge of the *Trent,* which, even before she left the harbor, developed a leak that was not satisfactorily repaired. Nevertheless the *Trent* came home from grueling struggles with the ice of the east Greenland sea in better condition than the *Dorothea.*

In 1819 Franklin was placed in charge of an overland expedition to northern Canada. He had with him three officers of the Royal Navy, Dr. John Richardson, George Back (who had been with him on the *Trent*) and Robert Hood. John Hepburn, an English seaman, was a sort of attendant. Back and Hood were midshipmen.

The expedition was in trouble from the start because of a local situation. The Hudson's Bay Company and the North West Company were engaged in their bitterest, and what was to prove their final, quarrel. Although Franklin and his party had letters to agents of both companies, they could get very little of the help which had been assured them in England. At the best agents of each company would explain why the other company should do the work. At the worst serious obstacles were thrown in their way by one agent to spite another. Franklin's personality here showed itself as one of great charm. He was tolerant, kindly and pious. He accepted the situation, and his *Narrative of a Journey to the Shores of the Polar Sea* glosses over the utter lack of discipline with which a disciplined man had to contend.

One way and another, chiefly by the exertions of a Hudson's Bay Company factor, John Bell, Franklin got together a party of fifteen native hunters, guides and interpreters (of whom eleven were Canadian *voyageurs*) and made, in 1821, his journey to the mouth of the Coppermine.

On August 25 of that year, the entire party were on the north coast of Canada east of the Coppermine and about three hundred miles west of where the men of his third expedition were destined to starve twenty years later. The freeze-up prevented further use of boats, and the party decided to march more than two hundred miles overland to Fort Enterprise, north of Slave Lake.

At first the native hunters were able to kill enough game to maintain the party, but their last caribou was secured on September 15.

Because we are looking for clues to how the Franklin men of the third expedition starved and died, we pay little attention to the dramatic narrative of the retreat toward Fort Enterprise but study the causes which made the drama tragic.

In the early stage of the journey the "hunters" were successful in getting caribou. The point which signifies is that the hunters were none of them Englishmen, not the lieutenant or two midshipmen from the Navy nor the surgeon—not even the sailor, Hepburn, though he is spoken of as a good marksman. The hunters were Indians or "Canadians" who were hired to hunt.

Why were the Englishmen, in self-help, a complete dead weight on the party? Was it beneath their dignity to co-operate in securing food? Was helping the workers, in their minds, detrimental to discipline? Whatever the reason, there is no sign either that they tried to assist in the hunting, or that they studied the methods of the hunt so as to be able to use them later.

We are already beginning to talk about the ability which British explorers of a hundred years ago demonstrated for not learning from their own experience, from the experience of fellow explorers or from the native people, the Eskimos. It is, therefore, pertinent to note that a hundred years later, in our own time, this situation has been reversed. We speculate here a little on how this came about.

Almost certainly, one of the main things which jolted the British out of their traditionalism was the startling and, to a few conservatives, definitely unwelcome success of Ernest Shackleton. Through a fault which became a merit, a quality of that buccaneering type to which he belonged, he outfitted his expedition of 1908 carelessly—partly, too, he was short both of money and of time for preparation. So his party found themselves in the Antarctic deplorably equipped in comparison with what was then orthodox, and in particular short of food. Because they did not have all the customary delicacies, nor even enough of the staple foods, they went out and slaughtered penguins and seals, living in good part on fresh meat—and discovering incidentally that they liked it. They came to the spring in such exuberant health that they made journeys which have never been equaled by sledging expeditions where the men themselves were the chief draft animals. Shackleton, who had grown weak through scurvy on his overland journey with Scott's first expedition, was strong as a horse on his own, his physical resilience matching the buoyancy of his mind.

If there was a contrast in good health with the previous Scott expedition, this was doubled when comparison was later made with Scott's second. Again Scott had secured the advice of British doctors and dietitians; again he had followed their every rule for feeding, clothing, housing, exercise, and what not. Again he depended on lime juice, lemon juice, fruit extracts, vegetables and the like, and again these failed him. His party developed scurvy on the way back from the South Pole. There are many ways of choosing the main cause for their heroic death. One of the most pertinent ways is to point out that early symptoms of scurvy are a mental and physical inability to face exertion. This accounted not merely for the breakdown but also for the short mileages of the last traveling days.

If we marvel how few there were who drew reasonable lessons from the British exploration of a hundred years ago, and how little attention was paid to the few who did draw them, we get, as said, a square contrast with the present leaders of British exploration. When men like Debenham, Priestley and Wordie, veterans of the Scott and Shackleton journeys, began to instruct and advise the younger men of Britain, there was developed a new school. In spite of their notable part in this, we are getting into the habit of calling it the Gino Watkins school, because he presented a brilliant example and also because he has died, his leadership acknowledged and his career finished.

These youngsters, chiefly from the universities, are showing themselves about the most adaptable travelers who have ever gone anywhere and have then told us what they did and how they did it. They analyze and study the records of previous explorers, they watch the Eskimos, and they borrow from whatever source both ideas and things. They eat, and they love to eat, caribou and seal, whale, walrus and fish. They use every method, European or Eskimo, for securing them. They use dogs and snowhouses. They dress in Eskimo clothes and take care of them in the Eskimo fashion. They out-Eskimo the Eskimo, as, for instance, when Augustine Courtauld, the winter 1930–31, spent several months alone on top of the Greenland Ice Cap, always mentally active, never lonesome, and in perfect health throughout.

Perhaps in this instance we may be giving Shackleton too much credit; perhaps the difference is in the spirt of our time. Englishmen are gentlemen still; but few of them confine themselves rigidly nowadays to merely being gentlemen, as the fashion was a hundred years ago.

Returning to Franklin, we find that game became more scarce as the party advanced from Coronation Gulf on the two-hundred-mile road to Fort Enterprise. There might have been recourse to fishing, at which the Englishmen, for aught we know, would have lent a hand. It did not come to that, for the porters had found the nets heavy, had surreptitiously left them behind, and had used the floats for a campfire. "Being thus deprived of our principal resource, that of fishing, and the men evidently getting weaker every day, it became necessary to lighten their burthens of everything except ammunition, clothing, and the instruments that were required to find our way."

The pemmican and portable soup gave out. Once in a while they managed to get a partridge. But in the main they subsisted on *tripe de roche* (a species of lichen), old shoes and scraps of leather, caribou skin and bones left by wolves after a kill.

The helplessness of these explorers would not be credible except that we know it from Franklin's and Richardson's own writings. It does not appear that they ever blamed themselves, or considered that anyone would blame them—indeed, we do not know from the literature of the time that anyone did blame them, in Britain at least.

Still harder to believe, but also forced upon us by the testimony of the men involved, is what they did to such food as they were able to secure.

The party had rather extraordinary luck in discovering the remains of caribou that had been killed and eaten by wolves. What the wolves had left was mainly skin and the bones. Now skin is as nourishing, weight for weight, as lean meat; but only if you eat it either raw or prepared in one of the ways which we know as ordinary cooking. What the Franklin party did was to scorch the leather till it was at least partly converted to the equivalent of charcoal. They ate the skin after burning some or all of the nourishment out of it!

Proceeding to the less and less easily credible things we are forced to believe, we come to what they did with the caribou bones. This was the autumn, when caribou are fat, which means that all the little chambers in the bones were filled with fat. The Franklin party had kettles, and there was plenty of firewood. There were stones lying about everywhere. If they had pounded the bones with stone hammers and boiled them, they would have had a rich, nourishing soup. They would have secured all the fat, which, of course, has more food value (caloric value) than anything else known to science.

What the Franklin party actually did was to hold the bones in the fire until they were "friable," whereupon they ate them—which means that they let most or all the food value go up in smoke and flame. Then they ate the charcoal.

Some things they did eat while they still had food value. For instance, we are told in one case that marrow was removed from a bone and eaten. It depends on various conditions whether wolves crack the long bones of caribou for marrow. Frequently they do, so that in all probability it was not often that the Franklin party had the chance which is mentioned in this instance. But they constantly had the chance to crush other bones and boil the fat out of them, as both Eskimos and Athapasca Indians customarily do.

As the party advanced it was the Indians and *voyageurs* who weakened first. More than half of them died on the return journey—two clearly from hunger and exhaustion, others exhausted but perhaps murdered, one shot by Richardson in self-defense—while none of the Englishmen died from hunger. This has been commented on as strange, it being assumed that the natives would have more strength. That Franklin shared this view is shown by his commenting, when he learned on September 26 that two of the men had stolen part of the officers' provisions: "This conduct was the more reprehensible, as it was plain that we were suffering, even in a greater degree than themselves, from the effects of famine, owing to our being of a less robust habit, and less accustomed to privations." On October 3 he tells of the weakened condition of the Englishmen, but says: "The voyagers were somewhat stronger than ourselves, but more indisposed to exertion on account of their despondency. . . . The officers were unable from weakness to gather *tripe de roche* themselves, and Samandrè, who had acted as our cook on the journey from the coast, . . . refused to make the slightest exertion. Hepburn, on the contrary, animated by a firm reliance on the beneficence of the Supreme Being, tempered with resignation to his will, was indefatigable in his exertions to serve us, and daily collected all the *tripe de roche* that was used in the officers' mess. . . ." For discipline, or because it was the right thing, the officers still had their own mess.

Just how equitably the loads were distributed among officers and men on the final stages of the journey is not clear. It is evident from the journal that on the trip north from Fort Enterprise most of the gear was carried by the men while the officers had comparatively light loads. The second day out, June 26, Franklin had to leave some things behind so that "the burthens of the men" might be lightened. He says: "The sufferings of the people in this early stage of our journey were truly discouraging to them, and very distressing to us, whose situation was comparatively easy."

There is a statement on August 31 that equipment was reduced to a mimimum so that "the men's burdens might be as light as possible." He lists the gear that had to be carried, including two canoes, and adds: "The officers carried such a portion of their own things as their strength would permit. . . ."

The morning of October 5, two days after Franklin had remarked, "The voyagers were somewhat stronger than ourselves, but more indisposed to exertion on account of their despondency," it was found that Crédit was so weak that it was necessary to reduce his load "to little more than his personal luggage." During that day's march Crédit and Vaillant could go no farther and the party were forced to leave them behind to die.

In the final stages of the journey, when little besides clothing and ammunition was retained, Franklin says: "I had only one blanket, which was carried for me, and two pair of shoes."

Is there a connection between the fact that it was the men who weakened first and the item of discipline or custom which required them to carry heavier loads than those carried by the officers?

Such a discipline was not exercised particularly by whites against natives but rather by officers against men of lower rank. There are cases in the history of British exploration in the Canadian Arctic where officers sat on the sledges while the men pulled. There are numerous cases where the officers walked in front or behind when the men were dragging the sledges. So far as these things have been explained it has been on the ground of discipline.

When the situation became desperate, Franklin sent Back ahead with one hunter-interpreter and two *voyageurs*. They were instructed to make all possible speed to Fort Enterprise, to search for the Indians who were supposed to be awaiting them there with supplies of game, and to make sure that things were in readiness for the arrival of the main party.

On cannibalism by at least one member of the expedition, there is little to be learned except from the direct statements on this subject by Franklin and Richardson. Their accounts of the tragic retreat were composed later, when they had arrived at definite conclusions; the printed narratives therefore do not contain the small but revealing details that would no doubt have been found in the diary entries themselves. It is Richardson's account that gives us most of our information on this gruesome aspect of the journey; but Franklin's narrative gives some indications.

Franklin relates that another splitting of the party became necessary on October 7, when it was apparent that Hood was too ill and weak to keep pace. Richardson and Hepburn volunteered to stay with him, while Franklin and the main group were to push on to Fort Enterprise and send back provisions. Ammunition was left with the rear party in the hope that "this deposit would be a strong inducement for the Indians to venture across the barren grounds to their aid."

But the men in Franklin's party were nearing exhaustion. The first evening out, J. B. Belanger and Michel arrived late at the camp, apparently exhausted. Both requested that they be permitted to drop back and join Richardson; they felt that they were too weak to reach Enterprise, and that their only chance was to stay at the tent site, which had been chosen because of there being a good supply of *tripe de roche* near by. Franklin reluctantly granted them the desired permission. "Having found that Michel was carrying a considerable quantity of ammunition, I desired him to divide it among my party, leaving him only ten balls and a little shot, to kill any animals he might meet on his way to the tent. This man was very particular in his inquiries respecting the direction of the house, and the course we meant to pursue; he also said, that if he should be able, he would go and search for Vaillant and Crédit; and he requested my permission to take Vaillant's blanket, if he should find it, to which I agreed, and mentioned it in my notes to the officers."

Franklin and his party then separated from Belanger and Michel, but they had gone only a few hundred yards when Perrault burst into tears and said he was too exhausted to go further. He, too, was allowed to keep his gun and ammunition, and he set off at once to join Belanger and Michel, who were still in camp and whose fire could be seen.

While all this was going on, Augustus the Eskimo interpreter became impatient and went on ahead, and was out of sight when the party resumed its march.

Only about two miles from where the other men had been left, Fontano, an Italian, became too weak to advance. He turned back; since there was a beaten trail to follow, it was hoped that he would be able to join the other men.

The party was thus reduced to five persons: Franklin, Adam, Peltier, Benoit, and Samandrè, all of whom succeeded in reaching Fort Enterprise, where they were later joined by the missing Augustus.

Turning from Franklin's testimony to Richardson's, we find that the day after the departure of the main party thick weather kept him, Hood and Hepburn from outside activity. They had no food and were ill but found the reading of religious books "of incalculable benefit."

On the morning of October 9, Michel, the Iroquois, arrived, bringing a note from Franklin which told of the decision of Michel and Belanger to return to the tent, and advising that they move their camp site to a clump of pines about a mile ahead. Michel explained his failure to arrive earlier by saying that he had become lost and had had to spend the night a mile or so from the camp. "Belanger, he said, being impatient, had left the fire about two hours earlier, and, as he had not arrived, he supposed he had gone astray.

It will be seen in the sequel, that we had more than sufficient reason to doubt the truth of this story."

At the time, however, Michel was welcomed heartily, particularly since he brought with him a hare and a partridge which he had secured that morning. The next day Michel led them directly to the pines, but it did not occur to them at the time that there was anything suspicious in this. "He [Michel] now informed us that he had, on his way to the tent, left on the hill above the pines a gun and forty-eight balls, which Perrault had given to him when with the rest of Mr. Franklin's party, he took leave of him. It will be seen, on a reference to Mr. Franklin's journal, that Perrault carried his gun and ammunition with him when they parted from Michel and Belanger."

That night Hepburn and Richardson returned to the tent, but Michel preferred to stay at the pines, keeping the hatchet with him. He was to join the others the next morning and assist in moving the remainder of the gear. He did not come, however, and when the two reached the pines, Michel was missing. He returned at dusk, when he reported that "he had been in chase of some deer . . . and although he did not come up with them, yet that he had found a wolf which had been killed by the stroke of a deer's horn, and had brought a part of it. We implicitly believed this story then, but afterwards became convinced from circumstances, the detail of which may be spared, that it must have been a portion of the body of Belanger or Perrault. A question of moment here presents itself; namely, whether he actually murdered these men, or either of them, or whether he found the bodies on the snow."

In the same paragraph Richardson presents the conclusions which he and Franklin later arrived at:

"Captain Franklin, who is the best able to judge of this matter, from knowing their situation when he parted from them, suggested the former idea, and that both Belanger and Perrault had been sacrificed. When Perrault turned back, Captain Franklin watched him until he reached a small group of willows, which was immediately adjoining to the fire, and concealed it from view, and at this time the smoke of fresh fuel was distinctly visible. Captain Franklin conjectures, that Michel having already destroyed Belanger, completed his crime by Perrault's death, in order to screen himself from detection. Although this opinion is founded only on circumstances, and is unsupported by direct evidence, it has been judged proper to mention it, especially as the subsequent conduct of the man showed that he was capable of committing such a deed. The circumstances are very strong. It is not easy to assign any other adequate motive for his concealing from us that Perrault had turned back, and his request overnight that we should leave him the hatchet; and his cumbering himself with it when he went out in the morning, unlike a hunter who makes use of his knife when he kills a deer, seems to indicate that he took it for the purpose of cutting up something that he knew to be frozen. These opinions, however, are the result of subsequent consideration. . . ."

In the following days Richardson and Hepburn were puzzled and annoyed by the erratic and surly behavior of Michel, but still their suspicions were not aroused. On several occasions Michel went out to hunt, always reporting failure on his return. Other days, however, he refused to hunt, and stayed in camp.

The morning of October 20, Hood and Michel were having an argument at the fire, outside the tent, while Richardson and Hepburn were engaged upon tasks at some distance. They heard the report of a gun, and when they arrived at the tent they found Hood dead, shot through the back of the head. Michel's actions immediately aroused suspicions, which were confirmed by a closer examination of the body and the position of the gun, which showed that it could not have been suicide. Michel insisted that he had been in the tent when the shot was fired, and that he did not know whether it had been fired by accident or by Hood deliberately. While talking to Richardson, he held a gun in his hands, so that Richardson did not dare voice his suspicions.

That afternoon Hood's body was removed to a clump of willows behind the tent. Returning to the fire, Richardson read the funeral service. The three men passed the night in the tent, none of them daring to go to sleep. Next morning they set out for the Fort.

During the two days which followed Michel stayed close to the two Englishmen, evidently wanting to prevent them from talking in private. Frequently he protested that he was incapable of committing murder. During this period Michel's surliness increased, with frequent threats and obscure hints. Richardson came to the conclusion that the only thing that restrained him from attacking the Englishmen was that he did not know the way to the Fort; that, when the party got near the Fort, they, in their turn, would be disposed of.

Michel was heavily armed—a gun, two pistols, an Indian bayonet and a knife—and Richardson and Hepburn felt they would be helpless in an open attack. They almost despaired of the chance to use strategy. Finally, October 23, the chance came:

"In the afternoon, coming to a rock on which there was some *tripe de roche*, he halted, and said he would gather it whilst we went on, and that he would soon overtake us. Hepburn and I were now left together for the first time since Mr. Hood's death, and he acquainted me with several material circumstances, which he had observed of Michel's behaviour, and which confirmed me in the opinion that there was no safety for us except in his death, and he offered to be the instrument of it. I determined, however, as I was thoroughly convinced of the necessity of such a dreadful act, to take the whole responsibility upon myself; and immediately upon Michel's coming up, I put an end to his life by shooting him through the head with a pistol. . . . Michel had gathered no *tripe de roche*, and it was evident to us that he had halted for the purpose of putting his gun in order, with the intention of attacking us, perhaps, whilst we were in the act of encamping."

It seems clear from the evidence that Michel killed one or more of the men he was suspected of killing; that important or chief in the motive for killing was that he was going to eat them; that his mysterious absences and his futile caribou hunts were visits to the places where he could eat human flesh; and that he had the hatchet with him for this purpose—north of Slave Lake at this time of year the frosts are hard and meat cannot be sliced with a knife.

The murder of Hood was no doubt chiefly so that the party would not have to stay in camp and nurse him but would be free to move ahead towards the Fort. As Richardson states, it was pretty clearly Michel's purpose to kill him and Hepburn and to arrive at the Fort as a sole survivor, free to explain how and why the others had dropped behind or died.

We have told that Franklin and his four companions succeeded in reaching Fort Enterprise, October 11; but their homecoming, which had been so eagerly anticipated, was instead a bitter disappointment. For the Fort was provisionless and deserted. A letter from Back awaited them there, saying that he was going on in search of Indians and that if unsuccessful he would continue on to Fort Providence, nearly two hundred and fifty miles to the south. His party was all in weakened condition, however, and he doubted that they could make Providence. Franklin considered that, even if they did, it would be too late to do either him or the Richardson party any good. Therefore he reached a decision to set out after Back; but weakness of all members of this group prevented this.

The only food possibility that Franklin could think of was some deerskins which they had discarded on their previous stay at the Fort. These were now retrieved, and the ash heap raked for bones.

On the 13th, Solomon Belanger, one of Back's *voyageurs*, stumbled exhausted into the Fort. They had seen no Indians, and Back wanted instructions. It was not until the 18th that Belanger was able to leave, with Franklin's instructions that Back was to join him at Reindeer Lake. After Belanger's departure, Franklin learned that he had attempted to entice Adam, the hunter, away, and that he had proposed to carry off the only kettle. Adam, however, was by this time too weak to move. Franklin found it hard to believe "a fact so derogatory to human nature" and mentions it to show the difficulties when distress warps feeling and understanding.

On October 20, Franklin, an interpreter and a *voyageur* set out for Reindeer Lake, having first emphasized to the three sick men they were leaving at Enterprise that any forthcoming help must be passed on to Richardson's party. An accident to Franklin's snowshoes forced his return. He sent the other two along with a note to Back telling why he was unable to keep the appointment.

At Enterprise all four men grew progressively worse, and were pulling down partitions for firewood, though other more suitable wood was only a few yards away.

Meantime Richardson and Hepburn were struggling towards Fort Enterprise. On October 26 a large herd of deer passed them. Hepburn, who "used to be considered a good marksman," tried to get one; but weakness made his hand unsteady, and he missed. On the 29th they again saw deer and Hepburn made another unsuccessful attempt. Richardson was almost completely exhausted and fell several times in the course of a day's march. On the same day they reached Fort Enterprise and Franklin's destitute party.

Badly off as were Richardson and Hepburn, they were stronger than any of Franklin's party, which now numbered four. Hepburn and Richardson both attempted to get game but were unsuccessful, although there were deer around them. Franklin's debility prevented his doing more than hunting for bones around the fort. The others were unable to leave their beds, and on November 1 two of them died. By November 7, the third man had sunk into apathy, while the British officers had only the consolation of religion to sustain them.

However, on that day a party of Indians with loaded sledges arrived. After Belanger had reported to Back on the state of affairs at Fort Enterprise, they had met a party of Indians and had told them of the distressing conditions. Some of the Indians then proceeded to Enterprise, took charge in a very competent way—declined to stay unless either the live bodies or the dead ones were put elsewhere and, after the dead had been hastily buried by Richardson, cleaned up the house, fixed up the sick men, and left two of their number to act as nurses. Since Back and his men, who had been subsisting on wolf leavings, were fed by the original party of Indians, and since Franklin and the rest were nursed back to health by a detachment from it, the day was saved.

We have already commented upon the fact that, until they were too weak to do it effectively, the Englishmen made no attempt to hunt. In explanation of this behavior we can think of nothing that is quite adequate—we must fall back on our conjecture that joining in the hunt, when they were accompanied by paid hunters, would have been beneath the dignity of officers of the British Navy, would have been detrimental to discipline. It may be said that the Britishers (except Hepburn, who is specifically called a good marksman) were inexperienced in hunting. But why should they be? Hunting, at least as a sport, is most respectable in England. Therefore, when they came to America, and their lives depended upon it, there should have been nothing in the way of a taboo to stop them. All five of them had, by 1821, been in America two winters.

Franklin's first expedition ended in 1822. His second was started in 1825, and Richardson was a member of it. So, also, was Back. These men, after suffering so much from dependence on their Indian hunters, had had three years in which to learn to hunt, or at least to shoot effectively. That they did not is indicated by the introduction to Franklin's book about the 1825-27 expedition, where he points out, among other things, that travelers in this part of America "must necessarily depend for subsistence on the daily supply of fish, or on the still more precarious success of Indian hunters." In other words, he had learned something—that the Indians' success was precarious; but he had not learned that it might be better to be able to rely on himself. He did, however, do the next best thing. In his previous journey he had come in contact with Peter Warren Dease, a chief trader of the North West Company, from whom he had received many valuable pointers. At the start of the second expedition he asked that Dease, now with the Hudson's Bay Company, since that alone was in the field, accompany him in charge of provisions and hunting.

Franklin's experiences on his second expedition, though somewhat different in detail, amount to the same as those of the first. He and his party now faced hunger and near starvation because of complete dependence on Dease.

Both of these expeditions were rewarded by promotion— Franklin was made a captain following the first, and was knighted following the second. The authorities could and did recognize courage, loyalty, energy and many other good qualities in Franklin. They either failed to see, or they generously overlooked, his inability to adapt himself to local conditions, his failure to profit by experience.

For a while at least Franklin's Arctic work was over. He was assigned to Mediterranean service in 1830; in 1837 he was appointed Lieutenant Governor of Van Dieman's Land. Here he established what later became the Royal Society of Tasmania, busied himself in improving the situation of convicts and contributed £500 towards starting a university, Lady Franklin giving 400 acres of land and a museum for the same purpose.

Under Franklin's administration, friction developed among the colonial officers, at first petty but later serious. Sir John was not happy in his post as governor of a colony part convict and part free, where each of the classes refused to have anything to do with the other. Jealousies culminated in Franklin's recall in 1843, a recall so abrupt that he had no indication of it until the new Governor arrived with the instructions.

Meanwhile George Back, who had been with Franklin on all the Arctic expeditions since the *Trent* in 1818, had been leading two expeditions of his own—the first in 1833–35 to search for Ross overland, the second in 1836–37 as an exploratory voyage in H.M.S. *Terror*. Seemingly, he had learned from his experiences even less than Franklin. He still placed dependence on native hunters during his overland journey, and he and his party were again in danger of starvation several times. During the *Terror's* wintering he made a record which we shall discuss later.

In 1845 the Admiralty was planning a new Arctic expedition, and Franklin, though fifty-nine years of age, asked for command of it. Two reasons have since been given for his strong desire to go—that he wanted to regain prestige lost in Tasmania; and that it was a deep desire of his heart to complete the Northwest Passage.

The command of the expedition was given to Franklin. Two ships, *Erebus* and *Terror,* were specially fitted out for the voyage. The personnel was hand-picked for qualities that would be useful, and no one was taken whose physique and mental attainments were not considered of the very best. In addition, the place of second in command was assigned to F. R. M. Crozier, who had been with Parry on two *Hecla* and *Fury* voyages and who was second in command of James Ross's Anarctic expedition of 1841. Graham Gore, another officer, had been in the Arctic with Back on the *Terror* voyage and in the Antarctic with James Ross. Thomas Blanky, one of the ice masters, had wintered four years in the Arctic with John Ross. Under Franklin, on the *Erebus* was James Fitzjames, who had seen tropical and semitropical service only but whose other qualities were thought to offset lack of polar experience. In writing to Lady Franklin, Sir John said: "S's remark is a just one that my officers are . . . better informed men than on any other expedition."

In May, 1845, the two ships, one hundred and twenty-nine officers and men, sailed from England with as high hopes for the discovery of the Northwest Passage and for general success as ever accompanied a northern expedition. They sent back their last mail two months later from Baffin Bay. Then they disappeared from the knowledge of the world for a decade.

There was, rightly, no worry for them at the end of the first year. There was too little worry at the end of the second; for England and Canada had many who knew how helpless men of the Franklin type would be if compelled to leave their ships and try to fend for themselves.

At first there were a few searchers and later there were many, so that in all forty expeditions engaged in the search through a decade, spending nearly $4,000,000. The expeditions were both government and private, chiefly British but also from the United States, and there were individual volunteer helpers from other countries.

The Franklin Search proved to be the greatest humanitarian effort of its kind in history. Incidentally it resulted in the discovery and exploration of many islands north of Canada and in much increase of knowledge. It did not, however, solve the mystery of what had happened to Franklin, beyond one scrap of information which was more tantalizing than anything else. In 1851 members of the Austin and Penny expeditions discovered that the ships had spent the winter 1845–46 at Beechey Island (south end of Wellington Channel) and that three men died who received Christian burial there. A pair of gloves, that had been weighted with stones and left to dry, was the only evidence of a hurried departure. This led to the conclusion that the "Island" (really a promontory) must contain cairns or records otherwise concealed; but no such records were found.

To illuminate what follows we quote one part of Franklin's instructions as issued by the Board of Admiralty May 5, 1845. There are twenty-three paragraphs, but we deal only with parts of two; that Franklin was to "continue to push to the westward without loss of time, in the latitude of about 74¼°, till you have reached the longitude of that portion of land on which Cape Walker is situated [i.e. Russell Island, north of Prince of Wales Island], or about 98° west. From that point we desire that every effort be used to endeavour to penetrate to the southward and westward in a course as direct towards Bhering's Strait as the position and extent of the ice, or the existence of land, at present unknown, may admit. . . . but should your progress in the direction before ordered be arrested by ice of a permanent appearance, and that when passing the mouth of the Strait, between Devon and Cornwallis Islands [i.e. Wellington Strait or Channel], you had observed that it was open and clear of ice; we desire that you will duly consider . . . whether that channel might not offer a more practicable outlet from the Archipelago, and a more ready access to the open sea. . . ."

For the conduct of the search suggestions and opinions of all kinds were offered—from that of William Parker Snow who wanted criminals to be sent out as they have "inexhaustible mental resources" to the reports of a séance in 1849 wherein the spirit of a four-year-old told another member of her family that the ships were in Victoria Strait, Point Victory, and that a channel which both Ross and Parry could not find existed and would lead to them. (This channel, says Skewes, was discovered in 1852 by Kennedy and Bellot, acting on the advice of the spirit of Weesy Coppin. It is now called Bellot Strait.)

Year after year the search expeditions worked east from Bering Sea and west from Greenland waters. They found no traces, beyond those of Beechey Island; they did not even meet Eskimos who had either seen or heard of Franklin, his ships, or his men.

Only one patch of the American Arctic was never searched: the mouth of Back River, the district between the islands Victoria and King William.

Beginning with 1847, Richard King, who had been with Back on his first expedition, agitated constantly for some party to go to Back River. King was not a naval officer; he had no standing with the Admiralty, and he had published accounts of the Back expedition which accused its commander of ineptness and blundering. Back, close friend of Franklin, now saw to it that no consideration was given King's proposal.

Most commentators agreed with Back that, since Franklin's instructions had been to sail southward and *westward* (or, alternatively, northward and westward) from Cape Walker, he could not possibly have reached the Back River area, which was southward and eastward. They urged that, no matter what the local conditions, Sir John would have held to his original orders from London. Richardson was among those who concurred, though for special reasons.

Year followed year in vain effort but with unabated zeal till there came the greater thrill and worry of the Crimean War. On January 19, 1854, the Government officially pronounced the men of the expedition dead. Nine years after they sailed from England their names were stricken from the rolls.

The unraveling of the mystery began with the close of the official search. In October, 1854, Dr. John Rae of the Hudson's Bay Company, who had accompanied Richardson on one of the official searching expeditions in 1848, arrived in London with fresh and startling news. His report to the Secretary of the Admiralty (dated Repulse Bay, July 29, 1854) says: ". . . during my journey over the ice and snow this spring, with the view of completing the survey of the west shore of Boothia, I met with Esquimaux in Pelly Bay, from one of whom I learnt that a party of 'white men' . . . had perished from want of food some distance to the westward. . . . Subsequently further particulars were received, and a number of articles purchased, which places the fate of a portion (if not of all) of the then survivors of Sir John Franklin's long-lost party beyond a doubt, a fate as terrible as the imagination can conceive.

"The substance of the information obtained at various times and from various sources was as follows:—

"In the spring, four winters past (spring of 1850), a party of 'white men' amounting to about forty, were seen traveling southward over the ice, and dragging a boat with them, by some Esquimaux who were killing seals near the north shore of King William's Land. . . . None of the party could speak the Esquimaux language intelligibly, but by signs the natives were made to understand that their ship, or ships, had been crushed by ice, and that they were now going to where they expected to find deer to shoot. From the appearance of the men, all of whom, except one officer, looked thin, they were then supposed to be getting short of provisions and purchased a small seal from the natives. At a later date the same season, but previous to the breaking up of the ice, the bodies of some thirty persons were discovered on the continent, and five on an island near it, about a long day's journey to the N. W. of a large stream, which can be no other than Back's Great Fish River. . . .

"Some of the bodies had been buried . . . some were in a tent, or tents, others under the boat, which had been turned over to form a shelter, and several lay scattered about in different directions. . . .

"From the mutilated state of many of the corpses, and the contents of the kettles, it is evident that our wretched countrymen had been driven to the last resource—cannibalism—as a means of prolonging existence.

"There appears to have been an abundant stock of ammunition. . . . There must have been a number of watches, compasses, telescopes, guns several (double-barrelled) &c, all of which appear to have been broken up [i.e., by the Eskimos, to make knives, needles and other tools]. . . .

"None of the Esquimaux with whom I conversed had seen the 'whites,' nor had they ever been at the place where the bodies were found, but had their information from those who had been there, and who had seen the party when travelling."

Rae purchased from the Eskimos a quantity of relics, mainly silverware. Some were identified as belonging to Franklin, Crozier, Gore, Goodsir, Peddie and McDonald.

One of the questions frequently raised is why Rae did not go to the locality reported by the Eskimos—a distance of some forty-five miles. Three explanations have been advanced besides Rae's own: that the delay would not permit him to return the same season; that he could not support his party on the game that was then in the country; and that he wanted to claim the £10,000 reward which had been offered "to any party or parties who, in the judgment of the Board of Admiralty, shall, by virtue of his or their efforts, first succeed in ascertaining their fate." Rae himself denies this last. The offer of a reward was first published March 7, 1850, but Rae affirms complete ignorance of it and says he returned in order that the Admiralty should have news as soon as possible.

Eventually the £10,000 was paid to Rae over the protests of Lady Franklin, who pointed out that the Eskimo story was of some thirty-five skeletons whereas there had been one hundred and twenty-nine men on the two ships, of whom only three were accounted for by the Beechey Island graves. Lady Franklin's contention—for which she had some support —was that others of the party might still be alive.

In his summary, Simmonds observes how curious it is that help should have been close so many times. In 1847 Rae was surveying Lord Mayor Bay and Committee Bay; in 1848 James Ross's party wintered at Port Leopold and traveled over North Somerset Island; in 1850 Austin was wintering at Griffith and Cornwallis islands, exploring around Cape Walker.

What now struck many was that if King's proposals had been accepted when he made them help would have come in time. Even a year later his party would have met the group whom the Eskimos reported en route to Back River. For his pains, King had been called presumptuous, egotistical and of warped judgment.

The report of cannibalism made by Rae immediately had repercussions. It was a serious assertion to make, particularly when neither he nor the Eskimos upon whom he relied had seen the bodies. Charges were made that the retreating party was murdered by Eskimos, that Rae was accepting the words of "balling and false savages." His reply, "The Lost Arctic Voyagers," printed by Charles Dickens in *Household Words* for March, 1855, is a painstaking analysis of why he believed the Eskimos and why he thought others should believe them.

In that same month, instead of the large naval expedition Lady Franklin had hoped for, further search for Franklin relics was placed in the hands of the Hudson's Bay Company. A canoe party under the leadership of James Anderson and J. G. Stewart went down the Great Fish River to the Arctic coast but, for various causes, spent only nine days in proper search. The official report, made by Chief Factor Hopkins, was dated LaChine, December 24, 1855, and reads: "The result of that Expedition [of Anderson and Stewart] has been the confirmation of the report conveyed to England by Dr. Rae last year. The coast and islands in the locality where the party of whites are reported to have perished in 1850, were carefully searched; and these, as well as from

Esquimaux in the neighbourhood, traces of the party were discovered, but no books or papers, nor human remains, although the exact spot was visited at which the natives told Dr. Rae they had seen the bodies, but being a low sandy spit, exposed to the sea, the probability is they were washed off, or buried in the sand.

"On the Montreal Island, as stated by the Esquimaux, small remains of a boat were found, having been cut up [i.e., by Eskimos] for the sake of the wood and nails. Among the chips and fragments, a piece of wood was discovered, with the word 'Terror' branded upon it; and another piece has 'Mr. Stanley' (? surgeon of the 'Erebus') cut on it with a knife. This last is part of a snowshoe. . . . These two relics, and a piece of rope, with a Government mark in it; the step of a boat-mast, shod with copper; a letter-clip, dated 1843; some pieces of bunting, and the remains of a thermometer, have been brought hither by Mr. Stewart. The more bulky articles Mr. Anderson has retained to be forwarded by another conveyance, consisting principally, I understand, of preserved meat cans, bar-iron, ash oars branded with the broad arrow, and some tools."

Anderson and Stewart offered large rewards for any papers or documents. The Eskimos understood what was wanted but could not produce anything.

On January 21, 1856, King made his fifth offer to conduct a search expedition down the Great Fish River, pointing out that he himself had left a cache on Montreal Island, that Franklin knew of the cache, and that if any of the party had been on that island, a record might have been left.

Again, no attention seems to have been paid to King's proposal.

Still refusing to accept the Rae verdict as final, Lady Franklin addressed Viscount Palmerston in July and December, 1856, renewing her plea for an expedition either to aid the survivors or to return the bones of those who, as Sir John Richardson had said, "forged the last link of the North West Passage with their lives." A Memorial attached to her letter was signed by more than fifty of the most illustrious scientific and naval men in England, many of them men who had been engaged in various expeditions of the search. The Admiralty, however, was presumably content with Rae's findings.

In the spring of 1857, therefore, Lady Franklin equipped an expedition in the screw yacht *Fox* and sent it out under command of Captain Leopold M'Clintock. Westbound that summer they were beset in Melville Bay and drifted around with the ice during the winter. They reached the search vicinity in 1858 and wintered at Port Kennedy, Bellot Strait, which is on the south coast of North Somerset, one hundred and fifty miles northerly from King William Island.

On April 20, 1859, M'Clintock and his party, with interpreter, met natives on the west side of Boothia who said two ships had been seen by the people of King William Island, that one had gone down in deep water while the other was forced on shore by the ice, where they supposed she still remained. From this ship they had taken most of their wood, and they identified its locality as Ootloolik. One man was mentioned as having been found dead on the ship—a large man with long teeth.

The ships, according to these Eskimos, were destroyed in August or September. They said that "all the white people went away to the 'large river' [Back River] taking a boat or boats with them, and that in the following winter their bones were found there."

En route from Matty Island to King William on May 7, other natives were interviewed. From them M'Clintock purchased silver spoons and forks, Eskimo bows and arrows of English woods, uniform and other buttons. These Eskimos reported that it was five days' journey to the wreck, though little was left of it now.

"There had been *many books* they said, but all have long ago been destroyed by the weather; the ship was forced on shore in the fall of the year by the ice. She had not been visited during this past winter, and an old woman and a boy were shown to us who were the last to visit the wreck; they said they had been at it during the winter of 1857–8.

"Petersen [the interpreter] questioned the woman closely, and she seemed anxious to give all the information in her power. She said many of the white men dropped by the way as they went to the Great River; that some were buried and some were not; they did not themselves witness this, but discovered their bodies during the winter following."

Montreal Island was thoroughly searched. It yielded no cairns, no bones, no relics of any kind beyond a piece of preserved meat tin, two pieces of iron hoop, some scraps of copper, and an iron-hoop bolt.

Crossing over to King William, the M'Clintock party was the first to search this island. On May 25, 1859, they came upon the first skeleton—a young man, a steward or officer's servant. Near him were a clothes brush and a pocket comb.

A search party of M'Clintock's expedition led by Lieutenant W. R. Hobson found a record at Point Victory, on the northwest coast of King William. It was on a printed form usually supplied to discovery ships, and read:

28 of May 1847 { H.M. Ships Erebus and Terror wintered in the ice in Lat. 70° 05′ N., Long. 98° 23′ W.

Having wintered in 1846–7 at Beechey Island in Lat. 74° 43′ 28″ N., Long. 91° 39′ 15″ W., after having ascended Wellington Channel to Lat. 77°, and returned by the west side of Cornwallis Island.

Sir John Franklin commanding the expedition.

All well.

Party consisting of 2 officers and 6 men left the ships on Monday 24th May 1847.

GM. GORE, *Lieut.*

CHAS. F. DES VOEUX, *Mate.*

M'Clintock points out that there is an error in the above document—since the ships were known to have wintered at Beechey Island in 1845–46.

Around the edges of the printed form is written a later and less cheerful message:

April 25, 1848. H.M. Ships Terror and Erebus were deserted on the 22nd April, 5 leagues NNW of this, having been beset since 12th Sept. 1846. The officers and crews consisting of 105 souls, under the command of Captain F. R. M. Crozier, landed here in Lat. 69° 37′ 42″ N., Long. 98° 41′ W. A paper was found by Lt. Irving under the cairn supposed to have been built by Sir James Ross in 1831, 4 miles to the northward—where it had been deposited by the late Commander Gore in June 1847. Sir James Ross' pillar has not however been found, and the paper has been transferred to this position which is that in which Sir J. Ross' pillar was erected. Sir John Franklin died on the 11th June 1847, and the total loss by deaths in the Expedition has been to this date 9 officers and 15 men.

JAMES FITZJAMES, Captain
H.M.S. Erebus

F. R. M. Crozier
Captain and Senior Officer
and start on tomorrow 26th
for Back's Fish River.

On May 30th, in the vicinity of Cape Crozier, Hobson found another relic—a boat mounted on a sledge, a total weight of fourteen hundred pounds. A quantity of tattered clothing was lying inside, as also were two skeletons, one of them wrapped in clothes and furs. Five watches and two double-barreled guns were also found. There were five or six small books, most of them religious; silk handkerchiefs, towels, soap, sponge, toothbrush, hair combs, twine, nails, saws, files, bristles, wax ends, powder, bullets, shot, cartridges, knives—in short, as M'Clintock puts it, "a quantity of articles of one description and another truly astonishing in variety and such as, for the most part, modern sledge travelers in these regions would consider a mere accumulation of dead weight, but slightly useful and very likely to break down the strength of the sledge crews." The only food was a little tea and some forty pounds of chocolate. There was more silver—eleven spoons, eleven forks and four teaspoons, twenty-six pieces of plate belonging to Franklin, Gore, Le

Vescomte, Fairholme, Couch, Goodsir, Crozier, Hornby and Thomas.

It has been considered one of the notable understatements of Arctic literature that M'Clintock says *modern* explorers would have left behind most of those things which, in pathetic fact, these men dragged along with them to where they died. He is further charitable when he accounts for the silver plate by saying that it must have been distributed to the men as the only means of saving it.

No iron utensils, such as sailors use, were found. Doubtless that was because most of them had been carried off by the Eskimos. There were discovered later on the island (around the cairn where the one record had been) cookstoves, pickaxes, shovels, iron hoops, old canvas, a copper lightning conductor, long hollow brass curtain rods, a small case of medicines and various scientific instruments.

Beyond the one record, no documents of any kind were found. Either the Eskimos or wind and water had destroyed them.

Neither Lady Franklin nor the Admiralty sent out further expeditions. England withdrew from the field. Interest and speculation continued, however, particularly in America.

In 1860–62, an American expedition under Charles Francis Hall was engaged in what he considered a Franklin search; for he was trying to complete the work of the earlier searching expeditions of the Americans DeHaven and Kane. Hall thought some of Franklin's men were probably still living, as Eskimos among Eskimos, and that he ought to do what he could to find them. He based his conviction on information from whalers that when whites lived Eskimo style they suffered no hardships. There was testimony confirming this from Hickey of the Kane expedition, who added that the native way of life maintained health and cured disease. It was Hall's own opinion that no Arctic explorer better knew the necessity for fresh meat than did Franklin; and if the party had been using plenty of meat they should have remained in good health and full strength. Hall supported his belief that Franklin's men would have provided themselves with plenty of fresh meat by quoting a report that Franklin had specifically told Captain Martin of the whaler *Enterprise*, when she met the Franklin ships in Greenland waters the summer of 1845, that shooting parties for the expedition had already been organized. (We shall discuss that report hereafter.)

Private capital and public subscriptions gave the money needed for a small-scale investigation. Hall left New London July 1, 1864, on the whaler *Monticello*, and on August 20th he and his supplies—fourteen hundred pounds in all—were landed at Depot Island. Here he began to recruit his "personnel," which finally consisted of one white man, Charles Rudolph (of the brig *Isabel*), and two Eskimos, Ebierbing and his wife Tookoolitoo, sometimes called Joe and Hannah. The party was then taken to "Wager River" by a tender of the *Monticello*—though the officer commanding the tender made a mistake as to position that cost Hall one year's extra work. Here the party settled down to live and travel Eskimo-style.

In a letter written from the west end of Rowe's Welcome, December 10, 1864, Hall has a startling tale. He has come upon some Eskimos who believe Crozier and two others are still alive. He says: "Crozier and three men with him were found by a cousin of *Ou-e-la* (Albert), *Shoo-she-ark-nook* (John), and *Ar-too-a* (Frank), while moving on the ice from one *igloo* to another; this cousin having with him his family and engaged in sealing. This occurred near Neitchille (Boothia Felix Peninsula). Crozier was nothing but 'skin and bones,' was nearly starved to death, while the three men with him were fat. The cousin soon learned that the three fat men had been living on human flesh, on the flesh of their companions who all deserted the two ships that were fast in mountains of ice; while Crozier was the only man that would not eat human flesh, and for this reason he was almost dead from starvation. This cousin . . . took Crozier and the three men at once in charge. He soon caught a seal, and gave Crozier quickly a little—a very little piece, which was raw— only one mouthful the first day. . . . By the judicious care of this cousin for Crozier, his life was saved. . . . When the cousin first saw Crozier's face, it looked so bad—his eyes all sunk in, the face so skeleton-like and haggard, that he did not dare to look upon Crozier's face for several days after; it made him feel so bad! This noble man . . . took care of Crozier and his three men, save one who died, through the whole winter. One man, however, died a short time after the cousin found them, not because he was starved, but because he was sick. In the spring, Crozier and the remaining two men accompanied this cousin on the Boothia Felix Peninsula to Neitchille. . . . Crozier and each of his men had guns and a plenty of ammunition, and many pretty things. . . . Here they lived with the Innuits (Eskimos) at Neitchille, and Crozier became fat and of good health. Crozier told this cousin that he was once at *Iwillik* (Repulse Bay), at Winter Island and Igloolik, many years before. . . . This cousin had heard of Parry, Lyon, and Crozier, from his Innuit friends . . . and therefore when Crozier gave him his name he recollected it. The cousin saw Crozier one year before he found him and the three men, where the two ships were in the ice. . . .

"Crozier and the two men lived with the Neitchille Innuits some time. The Innuits liked him (C.) very much. . . . At length Crozier, with his two men and one Innuit, who took along a *ki-ak* . . . left Neitchille to try to go to the *kob-luna*'s country, taking a south course.

". . . The Innuits never think they are dead—do not believe they are. Crozier offered to give his gun to the cousin . . . but he would not accept it. . . . Then Crozier gave him a long, curious knife (sword . . .), and many pretty things besides."

Traveling with his own Eskimos and another party, in April, 1866, Hall was making his fortieth encampment three miles from the coast and near Cape Beaufort, fifty miles south from eastern King William. Here other Eskimos visited him. We quote from Professor J. E. Nourse's *Narrative of the Second Arctic Expedition Made by Charles F. Hall* (Washington, 1879):

"*Kok-lee-arng-nun,* their head man, showed two spoons which had been given to him by *Ag-loo-ka* (Crozier), one of them having the initials F. R. M. C. stamped upon it. His wife, *Koo-narng,* had a silver watch-case. This opened up the way for immediate inquiries. Through Too-koo-li-too . . . it was learned that these Innuits had been at one time on board of the ships of *Too-loo-ark* (the great *Esh-e-mut-ta,* Sir John Franklin), and had their *tupiks* on the ice alongside of him during the spring and summer. They spoke of one ship not far from Ook-kee-bee-jee-lua (Pelly Bay), and two to the westward of Neit-tee-lik, near Ook-goo-lik . . . very many men from the ships hunted *took-too.* They had guns, and knives with long handles, and some of their party hunted the *took-too* [caribou] on the ice; killing so many that they made a line across the whole bay of Ook-goo-lik.

"The Pelly Bay men described the *Esh-e-mut-ta* as an old man with broad shoulders, thick and heavier set than Hall, with gray hair, full face, and bald head. . . . He was very kind to the Innuits;—always wanting them to eat something. . . . After the first summer and first winter, they saw no more of *Too-loo-ark* (Franklin); then *Ag-loo-ka* (Crozier) was the *Esh-e-mut-ta.*

"The old man and his wife agreed . . . that the ship on board of which they had often seen *Too-loo-ark* was over-whelmed with heavy ice in the spring of the year . . . the men all worked for their lives in getting out provisions; but, before they could save much, the ice turned the vessel down on its side, crushing the masts and breaking a hole in her bottom . . . she sank at once, and had never been seen again. . . . *Ag-loo-ka* and one other white man—the latter called 'Nartar' [Doctor?], a *pee-ee-tu* (steward)—started and went toward Oot-koo-ish-ee-lee (Great Fish or Back's River), saying they were going there on their way home. . . .

"The other ship spoken of as seen near Ook-goo-lik was in complete order. . . . For a long time the Innuits feared to go on board; but on the report by one of them that he had seen one man on the vessel alive, many of the natives visited it, but saw nothing of the man. They then rummaged everywhere, taking for themselves what they wanted, and throwing overboard guns, powder, ball, and shot.

"At an interview with the mother of *Too-shoo-art-thar-iu*

whose son saw *Ag-loo-ka* (Crozier) on the island of Ook-goo-lik, Hall was told that during the previous summer or winter, the Innuits of Ook-goo-lik had found two boats with dead *kob-lu-nas* in them—the boats on sledges; and that *Innook-poozh-e-jook* had one of them."

Difficulties in persuading the Eskimos to go on to King William then forced Hall's return to Repulse Bay where he spent his third winter.

Before the winter of 1867–68 closed, Hall had preparations complete for another journey on which he hoped to reach King William Island. However, he found it necessary to go to Melville Peninsula by reason of a story which natives had told him of seeing near Igloolik two white men, one tall, the other shorter. They also told of houses unlike those which they themselves built. Hall at first did not believe this. Later details convinced him that "it brought the story down as late as 1864, at which time some of Franklin's companions were alive near Fury and Hecla Strait."

He was further strengthened in what he thought was his duty by the remarks of Rae—that inexperienced men should have been deterred by the overland trip and should have made for and followed the well-known route to Fury Beach, southeastern Somerset Island, where an immense stock of provisions still remained at the place where the *Fury* was wrecked.

In April, Hall was on some islands which lie off Melville. The original reporter, Kia, was dead; but he learned from Koolooa that between Garry Bay and the northwest cape of Melville Peninsula he had seen a monument, which he was sure no Eskimo had built. He was with Kia when they saw the man—whom they at first took for an Indian. "He had a cap on his head, separate from his overcoat, which had a hood." They saw footprints "long and very narrow in the middle, with deep places at the heel. The tread of the footsteps was outward." This last would be significant—Eskimos do not toe out.

Hall's party found the monument. The site of the cache was covered with hard snow and it was necessary to camp beside it and work several days to uncover it. Cutting down to a depth of fifteen feet, they found nothing. The two Eskimo interpreters also brought them news of tent rings—one oblong and not built by Eskimos, the other the customary Eskimo style. Having failed to find the cache, Hall and his companions took down the monument "stone by stone." No record was inside of it. Hall, however, was satisfied that white men had camped there and had left the monument.

In May, 1868, he was en route to Tern Island. At Igloolik they met Kia's sister who told them the same story of the strange man. At Tern Island, another Eskimo, Kudloon, repeated the story. Hall and his party then returned to Repulse Bay.

In March, 1869, with an augmented party including Peter Bayne and five Eskimo men, three women and two chilren, Hall again started out for King William Island. In April he met a party of Pelly Bay natives who had utensils from the Franklin ships—a lamp, a snow shovel, a stone jug. Nourse says: *"Tung-nuk* told Hall that when the remains of the white men were discovered by Innuits on King William's Land, arms, legs, &c., were found cut off to be eaten, and the cut of the bone had always showed this to have been done by a saw. *Kob-big* said that all of the white men except two who were a long time ago at Ki-ki-tuk had perished. One of the two was *Ag-loo-ka* (Crozier), and both of these had certainly been seen by some of his (*Kob-big's*) friends. This last information made Hall greatly regret the absence of two of these, *Too-shoo-art-thar-iu* and *In-nook-poo-zhee-jook.* The former of these, who was said to have taken some care of Crozier and his men when nearly starving, was now in King William's Land. . . ."

In May, en route to King William, Hall met Innookpoozheejook. At this encampment there were many relics of the expedition which Hall bought. With Innookpoozheejook as guide, he next called at an encampment near Booth Point where more relics were found, among them a mahogany writing desk, eighteen inches long and ten wide. With the guide he then made a direct course for Todd Island, where five men were supposedly buried. He found part of a human thigh-bone, but the search was abandoned because of the snow which covered the island. *"Poo-yet-ta,* a native who had gone on with Hall from his last encampment to this island, now said that the remains were not buried when he first saw them, but were found lying down all close together, each fully dressed and unmutilated. In the pockets of one of the men a jack-knife had been found, and alongside of the remains, cans with meat in them which was eaten by the Innuits."

The next day Hall crossed to the mainland where he and his party found one unburied skeleton, and some other remains to which he gave burial. He thereupon concluded that he could account for probably seventy-nine out of the hundred and five men. However, Burwash, after his investigation of the King William district sixty-five years later, considered that only half the party had been accounted for.

Further information came from Ekkeepeerea, a Netsilik Eskimo, and Innookpoozheejook. When shown a chart, they pointed out the place where the Franklin ship sank—near O'Reilly (Ookjoolik) Island, between it and Wilmot and Crampton Bay. This ship had been sunk by Eskimos who were removing stores and who unwittingly damaged it—details given hereinafter. Inside the ship was a dead man whose body was large and heavy and whose teeth were long.

They also reported that near the head of Terror Bay was an encampment—a large tent in which there were blankets and bedding, tin cups, spoons, forks, knives, guns, pistols, ammunition, books and papers. As these last were good for nothing, the Eskimos threw them away or gave them to the children to play with. There were human bones, including skulls. Some bones looked as if they had been sawed off; some skulls had holes in them.

If it was true that bones had been cut with a saw, we have in that one fact almost certain proof of cannibalism. The only contrary possibility is that a frostbitten limb might have been amputated with a saw.

That Michel carried a hatchet when he absented himself from Richardson and Hood was taken by Richardson, and has always been taken since, to have meant that he was chopping up frozen bodies. There are only two ways—to use an axe or a saw; for a knife is not effective against hardened flesh, except to some extent when it is used as a pick.

The statement about holes in the skulls of the Franklin victims has been taken as further indication of cannibalism. This may well be, though probably not indicating that a man was killed to be eaten. For narratives of starvation usually show that the cannibals, rather than the victims of cannibalism, are the ones to die by gunshot. Those who do not play the game have to be killed by those who are trying to deal squarely with one another.

A man who uses tricks in dividing food so as to get a larger share for himself, a man who steals food, or one who surreptitiously digs up corpses that have been buried and eats of their flesh, is not merely to an extent antisocial to begin with but gradually, and perhaps rapidly, develops in that direction. His feeling of guilt tends to make him swagger and be insolent. He is stronger than the others and begins to feel his power over them. It is the rule, under such conditions, that the men who are weaker, because they have been sharing equitably, will plan and carry out the execution of the thief or cannibal.

We could take our examples from the history of starvation in many countries and climes but choose them from polar exploration.

The winter of 1883–84, the Greely expedition were at Cape Sabine on rations that meant slow starvation. One of the men was tricky in getting more than his share of the food. Later he began to steal outright. His health and strength were so much better than those of the others that they realized he would soon be in a position to do with them what he liked. It was agreed that he had to be executed. We do not know who fired the shots, for the party swore never to tell; but three shots were fired, and the skeleton of Private Charles B. Henry would likely enough show the mark of a bullet.

Our second case is from Franklin's own first expedition. We have given that story in detail and merely summarize here that when Michel seemed dangerous, and was found stronger than the rest through what they suspected was cannibalism, Richardson shot him through the head.

It is, then, correct to interpret bullet marks on the skeletons of Henry and Michel as evidence of cannibalism. Analogizing from these and many other cases, we would agree that holes in skulls of the Franklin party increase the presumption of cannibalism, although they do not necessarily indicate that the men shot were eaten.

Another Eskimo told Hall about Crozier's visit, seemingly in 1848. "The first time *Ag-loo-ka* came he did not come inside; next morning he entered one of the tents of the four families who were there encamped by the west shore of King William's Land, a little way above Cape Herschel (as pointed out on the chart) . . . *Ag-loo-ka* and his men had come along, the men dragging a large sledge laden with a boat and a smaller sledge with camp material and provision. Close by the Innuits they erected a tent; some of the men slept in the boat. . . . The time was late in the spring—July, Joe and Hannah [Hall's Eskimo interpreters] said it must have been, for the sea ice was nearly ready to break up. . . . *Tee-kee-ta* saw *Ag-loo-ka* kill two geese, and his men were busy shooting. . . . *Ag-loo-ka* tried very hard to talk to the Innuits, but did not say much to them. He had a little book as he sat in *Ow-er's* tent and wrote notes. . . . He ate a piece of seal raw, about as big as the fore and next fingers to the first joint. . . . He then said he was going to Iwillik (Repulse Bay). . . . One of his men was very fat, the others all poor. . . . The Innuits left them although supposing that they were abandoning starved men."

Hall reproved them for their behavior. Nourse, editing Hall, considers that so small a party of Eskimos might have feared the white men would starve them out.

Hall's next visit was to Inglis Bay where he found a piece of mast, oak and pine blocks, and part of a boat. He then returned to Repulse Bay. In a letter to Henry Grinnell dated June 20, 1869, Hall explains his reason for not staying: "Knowing as I now do the character of the Eskimos in that part of the country in which King William's Land is situated,

I cannot wonder at nor blame the Repulse Bay natives for their refusal to remain there. . . . How could we expect, if we got into straitened circumstances, that we would receive better treatment . . . than the 105 souls who were under the command of the heroic Crozier some time after landing on King William's Land? . . . Wherever the Eskimos have found the graves of Franklin's companions, they have dug them open and robbed the dead, leaving them exposed to the ravages of wild beasts. On Todd's Island, the remains of five men were *not* buried; but, after the savages had robbed them . . . their dogs were allowed to finish the disgusting work. The native who conducted my native party in its search over King William Land is the same individual who gave Dr. Rae the first information about white men having died to the westward of where he (Dr. Rae) then was (Pelly Bay) in the spring of 1854. His name is *In-nook-poo-zhee-jook*, and he is a native of Neitchille, a very great traveler and very intelligent. He is, in fact, a walking history of the fate of Sir John Franklin's Expedition."

One skeleton was brought south by Hall and sent to England. By a filling in a tooth it was identified as that of Le Vescomte. Interment was in Greenwich.

As we come to the end of these long and detailed statements we may gain something by an appraisal of Hall.

Hall was a Cincinnati blacksmith to whom the rescue of Franklin's survivors appealed as a religious call. At times he was the fanatic and mystic, to be discounted on that basis; but at other times, and frequently, he was level-headed and justly critical. He was always kind and generous except when his emotions were touched, particularly those that bordered on religion. He could understand sympathetically a difference between Eskimo and white views, but only if he felt them to be in the non-religious field. On the religious side he was violent and intolerant—as exemplified in our last quotation where he speaks of leaving the Franklin corpses "exposed to the ravages of wild beasts." In Eskimo thinking it is the same for a corpse to be eaten by a dog as it is with us for a corpse to decay. Most of the people of the north coast of North America lay out their own dead on hills and cover them either inadequately or not at all from carnivorous animals. This no more shows a lack of affection or of respect for the dead than our taking less pains than the Egyptians to embalm our loved ones.

If an Eskimo did exhume a corpse it would not be exactly with our purpose when we exhume a buried Pharoah; but to the people involved one exhumation is as justified as the other. The grounds are different, but have equal local validity.

We shall consider some items in the testimony of Hall later, but might say here that on the whole it would seem to be reliable. His interpreters, a man and wife who were long his affectionate and intimate companions, were good; for they spoke English fairly well and commanded an Eskimo dialect which differed but slightly from that of the King William neighborhood.

The next expedition to reach the Franklin district was that of Lieutenant Frederick Schwatka of the United States Army. With a party of three white men and Ebierbing, the Eskimo who had been with Hall, he set out in July, 1878, to search for Franklin records. The narrative of his expedition is written by one of Schwatka's companions, William H. Gilder. A prime reason for the journey was that Captain Thomas Barry had reported that, while wintering at Repulse Bay on a whaling voyage in 1871–73, he had heard from natives of a "stranger in uniform" who had visited them some years before and who was accompanied by many white men, all of whom had afterwards died; "but the chief had meanwhile collected a great quantity of papers. He had left these papers behind him in a cairn, where among other things, some silver spoons had since been found." In 1876, at Marble Island, Barry's ship had been visited by other natives who, on seeing his logbook, had remarked that the "great white man who had been among them many years before had kept a similar book."

The Schwatka expedition sailed with provisions for eighteen months for twelve men. On April 1, 1879, after a winter of preparation and of hunting, the party, now numbering four whites and thirteen Eskimos, began its march from

Hudson Bay toward King William Island. Their first news came at a Netsilik encampment west of Richardson Point where they obtained "a few unimportant relics." An old man, Seeuteetuar, told that he had seen a number of skeletons near the water line three or four miles west of the present encampment, and that books and papers were scattered around as were spoons, forks and watches. There was no sledge, but there was a boat which was afterwards broken up and taken away by the natives.

Another Eskimo, Toolooah, reported that as late as "last summer" (1878) he had picked up pieces of bottles, iron, wood and tin cans off Grant Point. He also declared he had seen traces of white men in the Ookjoolik country on the western coast of Adelaide Peninsula. A third Eskimo had seen traces near Cape Jane Franklin and along the coast to Cape Felix.

An old woman, Ahlangyah, "pointed out the eastern coast of Washington Bay where she, in company with her husband, and two other men with their wives, had seen ten white men dragging a sledge with a boat on it many years ago. . . . Five of the white men put up a tent on the shore and five remained with the boat on the ice." The Eskimos had camped near by and had sold the party some seals. At the end of five days both parties started for Adelaide Peninsula, but the white men did not travel as fast as the natives. Eventually rotten ice forced the Eskimos to return to Gladman's Point. They expected the white men to join them there but never saw them again.

"Some of the white men were very thin, and their mouths were dry and hard and black. They had no fur clothing on. . . . One of them was called 'Agloocar,' and another 'Toolooah.' . . . Another one was called 'Dok-took.' . . .

"The following spring . . . she saw a tent standing on the shore at the head of Terror Bay. There were dead bodies in the tent, and outside were some covered over with sand. . . . She saw nothing to indicate any of the party she met before. . . . There were knives, forks, spoons, watches, many books, clothing, blankets, and such things. . . . This was the same party of Esquimaux who had met the white men the year before. . . ."

Schwatka and his party crossed over to King William Island where they met a young man, Adlekok, who reported having found a new cairn. This they investigated, but it had been built by Hall.

Ogzeuckjeuwock, a Pelly Bay native, also had a story. At the boat place west of Richardson Point, "he saw books . . . in a tin case, about two feet long and a foot square, which was fastened, and they broke it open. The case was full. Written and printed books were shown him, and he said they were like the printed ones." Outside the boat he saw a number of skulls—more than four. "He also saw bones from legs and arms that appeared to have been sawed off. Inside the boat was a box filled with bones; the box was about the same size as the one with the books in it.

"He said the appearance of the bones led the Inuits to the opinion that the white men had been eating each other." He gave as a reason that "the bones were cut with a knife or saw. They found one big saw and one small one in the boat. . . . There was no cairn there. . . . Some of the books were taken home for the children to play with, and finally torn or lost, and others lay around among the rocks until carried away by the wind and lost or buried beneath the sand."

Combining the stories, Schwatka and Gilder concluded that these skeletons were the men seen by Ahlangyah and her friends on Washington Bay. They discount the fact that when confronted with both manuscript and printed books the Eskimo had chosen the printed books as resembling those of Franklin's party, and considered that the books in the tin box were records in charge of the chief surviving officers "as it is not probable that men who were reduced to the extremity that these were, and having to drag everything by hand, would burden themselves with general reading matter." Probably, however, it was not general reading matter. Englishmen of that period would carry Bibles at least as far as they did silver plate.

The Schwatka party, supporting itself by hunting, traveled

about the island, making observations and watching for cairns and records. En route from Franklin Point to Collinson Inlet they found graves of two white men, with other human bones on the ground above them. Around the Inlet itself they found nothing; but a mile and a half above their camp they came upon the camp made by Crozier when he and the men abandoned the ship. There were cookstoves, copper kettles, clothing, blankets, canvas, iron and brass implements and a quantity of cloth and brass buttons in an open grave. Upon one of the stones near the grave they found a silver medal, a mathematical prize awarded John Irving by the Royal Naval College in 1830. This enabled them to identify the skeleton as that of the third officer of the *Terror*. His bones were subsequently taken to Edinburgh for burial.

Two days were spent in further search of this locality and brought forth other relics—a brush with the name H. Wilks, a two-gallon jug, and several tin cans, sledge harness, etc. On a second visit they found a pile of stones which contained M'Clintock's record of May 7, 1859.

About three miles south of Cape Felix other material was found—canvas, red woolen cloth, blue cloth, a piece of an ornamented cup and cans of preserved potatoes.

En route to Cape Sidney, their hopes were raised by finding a well made cairn or pillar, seven feet high. They took it down, stone by stone, but no record was in it. They therefore left a record and rebuilt the cairn. Still continuing their travel day by day, they found another cairn, similar to the first one. The top had been taken down but a stone had preserved a fragment of paper. On this was carefully drawn a hand with the index finger pointing. The bottom of the paper had rotted away and with it any writing that may have been on it. They spent hours searching this locality but found nothing else.

On a point below Cape Maria Louisa they found a cache—built by Eskimos—containing a wooden canteen, barrel-shaped and marked on one side No. 3 and on the other G. B. under the British broad arrow. There were staves of another canteen, a small keg, a tin powder can, several red cans marked "Goldner's Patent," a narrow-bladed axe and several broken porter and wine bottles stamped "Bristol Glass Works."

In August they searched the neighborhood which Ahlangyah and others had spoken of as "the tent place." It was so close to the water that all traces had disappeared. The party buried all bones that they found (except Lieutenant Irving's). The only additional relic discovered was a pewter medal commemorating the launching of the steamer *Great Britain* in 1843.

By November the Schwatka party considered their work done and were on the mainland at Sherman Inlet. A piece of a boat was found there printed either 10 or OR with part of the R obliterated. Gilder points out that if the ships' blocks were printed with the name of the ship, this would indicate that it was the *Terror* which had drifted.

The expedition had traversed more than two thousand miles and had been absent from its base of supplies for eleven months and twenty days, living by hunting.

Gilder believes that the most important direct contribution to the Franklin search was the determination of what had happened to the records.

Schwatka did not stay in the United States long enough to write about Franklin, for news that De Long and the *Jeannette* were missing sent him off in search for them. Gilder would write the book. He had acted as correspondent for the *New York Herald,* and some of the material was published in that paper, including a mention of cannibalism. Once more this aroused a storm, which at one time threatened to develop in Britain into an anti-American wave. Like Rae before him, Gilder was forced to take notice of the attacks. But he refrained from choosing sides. He merely quoted a letter from Rae who believed the cannibalism stories, and one from Captain Sir G. H. Richards, another distinguished leader of the Franklin Search, who considered that if there was eating of human flesh the Eskimos did it.

A small search contribution was made by the Amundsen expedition which began in 1903 and which spent two winters in Gjoa Havn, King William Island. One skeleton (previously buried by Hall) was found by Hansen and the monument over it replaced. This party were not interested in the Franklin records, or at least they devoted little time to searching for them.

In 1923 Knud Rasmussen's Fifth Thule Expedition studied the Netsilik Eskimos. Seventy-five years had passed since Crozier wrote his record, and the stories were hearsay only. Rasmussen picked up tradition about Rae, Hall and Schwatka, all of whom were correctly identified. These stories appeared fairly accurate, and so Rasmussen gives what is now tradition of Franklin.

An old man told him: "My father Mangaq was with Tetqatsaq and Qablut on a seal hunt on the west side of King William's land when they heard shouts, and discovered three white men who stood on shore waving to them. This was in spring; there was already open water . . . and it was not possible to get in to them before low tide. The white men were very thin, hollowed-cheeked, and looked ill. They were dressed in white man's clothes, had no dogs and were traveling with sledges which they drew themselves. They bought seal meat and blubber, and paid with a knife. . . . The white men cooked the meat at once with the aid of the blubber, and ate it. Later on the strangers went along to my father's tent camp and stayed there the night before returning to their own little tent, which was not of animal skins but of something that was white like snow. At that time there were already caribou on King William's Land, but the strangers only seemed to hunt wildfowl; in particular there were many eider ducks and ptarmigan then. . . . Father and his people would willingly have helped the white men, but could not understand them; they tried to explain themselves by signs. . . . They had once been many, they said; now they were only few, and they had left their ship out in the pack-ice. They pointed to the south, and it was understood that they wanted to go home overland. They were not met again, and no one knows where they went to."

Another old man told: "Two brothers were once out sealing northwest of Qeqertaq (King William's Land). It was in the spring. . . . Far out on the ice they saw something black. . . .

They looked more closely and found that it was a great ship. They ran home at once and told their fellow-villagers of it, and next day they all went out to it. They saw nobody, the ship was deserted, and so they made up their minds to plunder it. . . ."

Going down into the ship, the Eskimos found dead men lying in their beds. "It was dark there. But soon they found tools and would made a hole in order to let light in. And the foolish people, not understanding white man's things, hewed a hole just on the water-line so that the water poured in and the ship sank. And it went to the bottom with all the valuable things, of which they barely rescued any.

"The same year, well into spring, three men were on their way from King William's Land to Adelaide Peninsula. . . . There they found a boat with the bodies of six men. In the boat were guns, knives, and some provisions. . . .

"There are several places in our country where we still see bones of these white men. I myself have been at Qavdlunar-siorfik, a point on Adelaide Peninsula. . . . Up to only a few years ago we used to go over there to dig for lead and pieces of iron. . . .

"That is all I know about the . . . white men who once visited our country and who were lost without our forefathers being able to help them."

In 1928-29, Major L. T. Burwash was making surveys for the Canadian Government's Northwest Territories and Yukon Branch. April, 1929, found him on King William Island. Here he spoke with two old men (he estimates their ages as around sixty) who told him that "when they were both young men, possibly twenty years of age, they were hunting on the ice in the area immediately northeast of Matty Island. When crossing a low flat island came upon a cache of wooden cases carefully piled near the centre of the island and about three hundred feet from the water . . . which contained materials unknown to them, all of which were enclosed in tin containers, some of which were painted red." These Eskimos were interested only in the wood, which they divided. Afterwards "they opened the tin containers but found them to contain materials of which they had no knowledge. In a number they found a white powder . . . which they and their families threw up into the air to watch it blow away." In the light of their later white contacts, the Eskimos concluded that some of the cans contained flour, and others pemmican, but there were still other things which they could not identify. Every can was opened, but nothing was eaten. "They also secured at this time a number of planks . . . approximately ten inches wide and three inches thick and more than fifteen feet long. These they found washed up on the shore of the island upon which they had found the cache and on the shore of a larger island near by." The Eskimos reported that the cache of boxes had been made by white men from a ship which lay on a reef offshore. In 1929 nothing remained of it except the marks of rusty tins.

Burwash's report contains an Appendix C which is an extract from a document "compiled by Mr. George Jamme from the statements of the late Captain Peter Bayne," who had been a member of Hall's expedition and while on it had been out with Eskimo hunting parties. On one of these trips, which lasted thirty days, Bayne reports that the natives talked a great deal about the Franklin party. Crozier seemed to interest them most and they knew of his attempt to travel overland. Bayne tells that they reported: "During the first summer (probably 1847) . . . many of Franklin's men came ashore; that they caught seals like the natives, and shot geese and ducks of which there were a great number; that there was one big tent and some small ones; and many men camped there. . . ."

From a Boothia native Bayne got the same story, and Crozier was identified as Aglooka. He got more than that— the suggestion that Franklin's remains were buried on King William in a cement vault: ". . . that some of the white men were sick in the big tent; and died there, and were buried on the hill back of the camp; that one man died on the ships and was brought ashore and buried on the hill near where the others were buried; that this man was not buried in the ground like the others, but in an opening in the rock, and his body covered over with something that 'after a while was all same stone.'" This Eskimo was not present but was told that at the time "many guns were fired."

Bayne and one of his companions, Coleman, were much excited by this report. They gathered the natives together and had the story repeated, whereupon something else emerged. Another native confirmed the story and said there were several cemented vaults, one large and many small. The natives thought the small ones contained papers, as many were brought ashore of which "some blew away but others were buried."

When Hall rejoined the party, Bayne eagerly gave the information. However, he appeared resentful, "upbraiding them for their presumption." Bayne did not know whether Hall queried the natives, but believed he did. Hall's account in no way mentions Franklin's burial "either in the deep or on the land." Bayne considered that Hall, while a high-type man, withheld the information out of pique. "The great ambition of the old Captain [Bayne] was that he might be able to go, himself, and prove to the world the existence of the Cemented Vaults." He died, however, without realizing his ambition.

We give this story to round out the statement. Most of the comment upon it has been to the effect that it is scarcely credible that Franklin was buried on the island since the Crozier record does not mention it. However, there are so many scarcely credible things connected with the expedition that one more or less doesn't matter. We are inclined to doubt this part of the Bayne version for other reasons—chiefly that it does not crop up in any of the stories which were told the explorers who came after Hall, and particularly that Rasmussen, who understood both the language and the culture of the Eskimos, did not hear it.

In 1931, two Hudson's Bay men, William Skinner and William Gibson, made a brief search of King William for the purpose of burying any remains that they might find. Following the story which the Eskimos told Hall in 1869, they investigated Todd Islets, where they found partial remains of four men. They could not find the grave originally dug and marked by Hall and later remade by Hansen of the

Gjoa expedition. Along Peffer River other bones were found. Gibson concludes that the greater part of the skeletons had been washed into the sea. On an islet in Douglas Bay the nearly complete skeletons of seven men were found. These were buried and marked with a cairn.

In 1936, two more Hudson's Bay Company men, L. A. Learmonth and D. G. Sturrock, assisted by Eskimos, located scattered remains west of Starvation Cove. The only relics found were a silver George IV half-crown dated 1820 and an ivory button. Gibson reports, "It is noteworthy that here, as elsewhere, every scrap of wood and other durable material had vanished"—i.e., had been taken by Eskimos.

From the record and the stories, we gather that in April, 1848, Crozier and the survivors, one hundred and five in all, landed at Victory Point, on the northwest coast of King William Island. By Eskimo report one of the ships had gone down fairly quickly. The other was still in the pack, and from it they had removed many bulky and heavy articles. Some of these were abandoned soon; many useless and heavy things were carried to distances that would be incredible except that the proof is there—"modern explorers" would not have done it, as M'Clintock said in considerate understatement.

The party now started for Back River (Great Fish River), and several died as they marched. Their bones were found along the route. At first these men were buried; but as the strength of the party failed they were left lying where they fell. The explorers believed that King William was connected with Boothia, as their charts showed (Rae later discovered the strait which separates it from the mainland). In other ways, too, their maps were deceptive. James Browne says: "They started to march 220 miles in utter ignorance of the general charcater of the country, for the charts had Point Victory, Cape Herschel and Fish River marked but nothing else. Only one man had knowledge of the country—Blanky who had been ice master of the *Terror* and who with James Ross had discovered it, but as there were nine officers dead it is quite possible he was one of them."

Burwash concludes that somewhere along the road the party divided, some going south with Crozier, while no one knows where the others went. It will be remembered that the Eskimo stories report traces from Boothia Peninsula and from islands near Melville.

In any case, Crozier and about forty men were seen by the Eskimos at Washington Bay, King William Island, July, 1848. Subsequently, at Starvation Point, Adelaide Penninsula, thirty-five to forty skeletons were found. The story of the cache near Matty Island, which lies in James Ross Strait between King William Island and Boothia Peninsula, would tend to confirm the reports that some of the men reached Boothia. However, although skeletons and relics were found on King William all the way down the west and south coasts from Victory Point to Douglas Bay, nothing was found along the east coast, which would have to be traversed before a crossing to Boothia could be made. The map accompanying the Burwash report marks the "possible drift of the *Erebus*" south, east and north to where the cave was found. Gibson discounts this, as the ship's drift would have been almost a circumnavigation of the island. He discounts, too, for lack of traces, the possibility that the *Erebus,* freed from the ice, was sailed in this direction by her crew. In other words, he is not much inclined to believe in the story of the cache near Matty Island; for it was shown to be in the middle of one of the main Eskimo sealing areas and could not have escaped attention for so many years. He considers it significant that the story was not told Rasmussen, and believes it did not exist in 1923.

We have now examined that part of the Franklin evidence which seems pertinent for a decision on our problem: How and why did the men of the Franklin expedition perish?

In a sense we have already told how, for we have given the testimony. To an extent we have told why, for much of the testimony is plain. It remains, then, to fill what gaps there appear to be in the explanation, and particularly to fix responsibility. Who or what was responsible for this greatest of all tragedies in the history of polar exploration?

The commander of an expedition, whether military or

exploratory, gets the lion's share of credit when there is success. He takes corresponding blame when there is failure. A man who has been gone a hunderd years, like Franklin, is scarcely the subject of either praise or blame; but we do want to know the facts—the how, and chiefly the why.

It is really clear, and has seldom been disputed, that the deaths were from a combination of hunger and disease. It has been equally clear to a few, though not so universally admitted, that while there were still large quantities of food on the ships scurvy took so heavy a toll as to require special explanation. Besides the twenty-four who died on ship-board, some at least of the men who left the ship dragged themselves, or were dragged, to shore in a weakened state. Among those who perished on the march there was both disease and hunger.

One of the positions frequently taken is first to admit that the commanders of the expedition did not realize fresh meat was a necessity if scurvy was to be prevented, and then to call it unreasonable to expect people of a hundred years ago to realize this necessity. In trying to determine the caliber of leadership on the Franklin expedition we examine that position.

A complete examination of whether Franklin, Crozier and the rest might have been expected to know that a dependence on European food and on the traditional "antiscorbutics" would bring death to the men and failure to the expedition— a full discussion of this would be a volume in itself. We confine ourselves to showing that Franklin and his officers need not have gone beyond the experience of two then recent expeditions to get a command of the situation.

At any rate it is obvious to us now that when you compare the John Ross expedition of 1829–33 with the George Back expedition of 1836–37 you have the complete answer to how a polar residence should be managed in order to keep men in good health, capable of doing their work. But what is so very easy for us to recognize must have gone unrecognized by the Franklin expedition commanders; else they would not have had the scurvy and the starvation which resulted from the lethargy of that disease. Then why was it that Franklin could not read in the stories of those expeditions what any schoolboy can read today? To arrive at an answer we mean to survey those features of the Ross and Back expeditions which apply.

First, did Franklin have the opportunity we possess to study the evidence from Ross and Back?

Ross had returned to England in 1833, twelve years before Franklin's start upon his tragic third expedition. He may not have paid much attention to the Ross findings because of the Ross quarrel with the now-great Sir Edward Parry which originated in the expedition of 1819. There were many reasons for the unpopularity of Ross, with most of which Franklin no doubt sympathized, and with some of which we can sympathize even today. So Franklin had at least an emotional bias against studying the Ross findings. However, a commander is not of the first rank if he closes his eyes to useful knowledge through prejudice against the source.

It is, however, really academic whether Franklin studied the Ross voyage at his first opportunity. The things necessary to guide him were all printed in the 1835 edition of the Ross narrative. He could have read there a lesson on scurvy in plenty of time, while sailing from England to the first winter quarters at Beechey "Island."

That Franklin had the Ross book we know from a letter which he addressed to Lady Franklin and sent back from Melville Bay. This letter contains the statement that he has not neglected to take with him the narratives of previous explorers, and he specifically mentions taking Ross.

By the Beechey winter, at latest, Franklin will have had opportunity to know how Ross kept scurvy at a minimum and how Ross believed scurvy could be both prevented and cured. We know today that Ross was correct. Presently, as we review the evidence, we shall see whether Franklin or Crozier had cause for disbelieving Ross.

In trying to determine whether Franklin had cause for disbelief, it is most pertinent to remind ourselves that he carried also Back's account of the 1836–37 *Terror* expedition. If the success of Ross had not impressed Franklin when it stood alone, it surely must have impressed him when it was thrown into relief by the glaring failure of Back.

The records do not say specifically that Franklin had with

him the Back narrative; but he must have had it, for Back and he were still good friends, as they had been from their earliest association, now a quarter of a century behind them.

True, Franklin may have resented the invidious comparison between his friend and Ross. If to that extent he was blinded by emotion, we return to our point that a man of caliber is not swayed by friendships or animosities in matters that are crucial to his task.

We arrive, then, at a consideration of the narratives of Ross and Back.

It seems from his book that Ross did not understand the health situation quite so well while on the expedition as he did when writing about it later. That may have been too bad for himself but did not handicap Franklin. He would be taking his knowledge from the published work—except in that he had with him one of Ross's men, Thomas Blanky.

The Ross expedition had spent the four years 1829–33 in the Boothia and King William district, the very region where the Franklin expedition was to meet its doom. We give a few passages from Ross which might have served as beacon lights to the Franklin commanders in a campaign to guard the health of their men:

". . . all experience has shown that the large use of oil and fat meats is the true secret of life in these frozen countries . . . I have little doubt, indeed, that many of the unhappy men who have perished from wintering in these climates, and whose histories are well known, might have been saved if they had been aware of these facts, and had conformed, as is so generally prudent, to the usages and experience of the natives" (pages 201-2).

The Eskimos of the King William and Boothia district were "enjoying the most perfect vigour, the most well-fed health . . . they were as amply furnished with provisions, as with every other thing that could be necessary to their wants" (page 248).

"It was much more interesting to us to find [in an Eskimo snowhouse], that . . . there were some fresh salmon; . . . we were informed that they were abundant . . . " (page 250).

"A summary of the success of the natives in hunting during this month [February, 1830], gives two white bears, three gluttons, a dozen of foxes, and fifty seals: and as we had also, ourselves, killed or taken five foxes, with some hares, ptarmigans, and willow partridges, this [the King William and Boothia region] is a country not so destitute of game, even at this time of the year, as has been generally supposed; while it is thus proved that they do not migrate to the south in winter" (page 288).

We pause for a special lesson from this paragraph which, though easier for us to read than for Franklin, should not have been vague even to him. The first part of the lesson is that while twenty white explorers were securing a few hundred pounds, live weight, of game a corresponding number of Eskimo men of active years were securing perhaps seven thousand pounds. The second part of the lesson is that the great Eskimo success was due to their applying themselves to big game while the explorers followed hares and partrides.

The trapping of foxes by the Englishmen was apparently because they wanted the skins to take back to England. The Eskimos, on their own account, hunted foxes chiefly for food and only incidentally for skins. However, during these particular years they had a special motive for trapping foxes in that they could sell the skins to the Ross expedition.

Paragraphs like our quotation, which are numerous in the literature of exploration, are among the reasons which incline us to believe that Rasmussen secured in King William Island the true information about the Franklin expedition—that their hunting was largely or wholly confined to fowling.

We return to quotations from Ross which show the degree to which he and his party appreciated the necessity of fresh provisions to keep an expedition in good health—fresh provisions in the Arctic necessarily meaning flesh from fish, fowl or mammal.

"As yet [May, 1830] there was no appearance of scurvy; but two or three of the men showed just enough of threatening to make us fear that they would not be long exempt, unless we obtained a more ample supply of fresh provisions . . ." (page 379).

James Ross, in the field with three men, met Eskimos who

gave them fish and seal blubber. "Being now much recruited by a day's rest and all this good living [i.e., the fresh fish], we set out . . . [with] an ample supply of fish; which, in addition to the blubber . . . fully provided us for all the remainder of the journey" (page 430).

"We [says John Ross] had thus more than we could well carry [a ton of salmon, bought from Eskimos]; but as this fresh meat was most needful for the health of the crew, especially for those who were threatened with scurvy, we adopted several contrivances for transporting at least as many as we could" (page 450).

The surgeon of the Ross expedition, Dr. George M'Diarmid, has several pithy passages.

Describing a scurvy outbreak, the doctor says it shows "how poor a defense a vegetable regimen (chiefly farinaceous) is." He fastens responsibility for scurvy on the European food by remarking, "It was during our stay at the *Fury's* stores (where least fresh meat was eaten) that the worst form of the disease appeared." Comparing two illnesses, he says, "Another case . . . promised to be equally severe; but . . . he had all the benefit of the warm season, and of a change of diet, which our shooting parties afforded us in the summer months." One of the doctor's conclusions points to "the failure of lime juice as an antiscorbutic, unless aided by nutritious food." The general context shows that the only "nutritious food" that here availed was fish or game.

However, belief in the virtues of lime and lemon juices and the rest of the antiscorbutics was so dominant a hundred years ago that it was possible to discount everything Ross and his surgeon told regarding the benefits of meat and to claim that the comparative immunity from scurvy which the Ross party enjoyed through four years was due to such rations as he in one place describes for eighteen men for fourteen days. This included for each man 7 ounces of lemon juice, 4½ ounces of cabbage and 4½ ounces of onions per week. However, the argument (that these were the true preventives) ceases to be of value in defending Crozier and Franklin when you turn from the four-year Ross expedition to the one-year expedition of George Back. For, among the things of supposed antiscorbutic value which Back carried to protect his sixty men from scurvy for one year, we find listed:

798 lbs. of lime juice
798 libs. of lemon juice
203 lbs. of vinegar
1320 lbs. preserved vegetables
4480 lbs. of potatoes
10 casks of carrots in sand
100 pots essence of spruce
125 lbs. pickled cabbage
50 lbs. of horse radish
50 lbs. of onions
100 lbs. of cranberries

It is a deduction from many voyage narratives that scurvy is a disease of slow onset and that when dependence is upon food brought from home there is comparatively little scurvy the first year (while the food, including the lime and lemon juice, is reasonably fresh), more the second year and most the third, leading to such appalling figures as three men out of every four dying with scurvy. So the lesson from Back is striking when in one year of the antiscorbutics we have listed, and of the complete absence of fresh meat, he developed a higher percentage of cases of scurvy than Ross did in four, and succeeded in losing three men by this disease where Ross lost one.

With the practice already brought in by the two Rosses that even the commander and the second in command of an expedition might lend a hand fishing and hunting; with the idea expressed by Ross that the Greenland diet (i.e., seal) was the best for the Arctic; with seal-hunting Eskimos living all around the Franklin vessels during the two years near King William Island—with these things admitted, the mere numbers of the crews were not an excuse for letting the Franklin men hang around and sicken at the base camp. Doubly was Franklin without excuse when Back's volume, published three years after Ross's, showed what startling inroads scurvy would make even in one year if "antiscorbutics" brought from home were the sole dependence.

Ten men could have looked after each of the Franklin ships during every month of the winter, leaving a hundred free to scatter in parties of five, ten, fifteen, or twenty various distances in all directions. These parties could have taken with them as much British food as they wanted, for there was an abundance on the ships (this has not been disputed), and men do not have to live exclusively on fresh meat in order to prevent scurvy. All they need is such a percentage as we nowadays call average. The dispersed Franklin parties could have had the interest of goings and comings between camps and vessels, of dealing with the natives, and of exploring the country.

The blood of Englishmen was the same a hunderd years ago as it is today. There is no reason other than mental why those healthy young men of 1845 could not have had as much fun every month of the year as is now the rule when graduates and undergraduates from Cambridge and Oxford go off on their exploring expeditions to Greenland, Spitsbergen, the Antarctic—to many places where the winters are longer and colder than they are in the Franklin region, where the resources of the country are fewer, where the winter "darkness" is longer, where conditions on the whole are much less favorable than around King William Island.

The best defense of Franklin we have been able to devise is that the Watkins school of young explorers are successors of John Rae; the Franklin school were his predecessors. True, the Rosses, uncle and nephew, and their surgeon had explained to Franklin that fresh meat prevents scurvy, and they had applied the idea that it is not beneath the dignity of an officer to share in providing local food. But the Rosses had not demonstrated that whites could be adequately self-supporting. We need not dwell on the pathetic showing by the twenty men of the Ross expedition during one month of the winter of 1829–30—a hundred pounds of meat secured, against several thousand pounds secured by a like number of

Eskimo hunters. The Ross party learned a good deal in the years 1830–33; but they never approached self-support.

We have said that of the three associates of 1821 and after, Back learned nothing, Franklin little, and Richardson a good deal. Yet even Richardson did not fully realize until 1848 such things as that one white man (Rae) could support by one rifle a party of forty.

None of the things which the British expeditions of a hundred years ago relied upon will prevent scurvy. They themselves proved that the lime juices and lemon juices and the "antiscorbutics" which they carried would not do it. They proved also that physical exercise, devotional exercises, fresh air, dramatic clubs, schooling of the illiterate, games and buffoonery would not do it. They tried to fight the gloom of scurvy with merry song and with entertainment. But that plan cannot succeed. The gloom of scurvy is symptom and part of the disease; and the very exertion of standing up to sing the jolly song will increase the disease and thereby the gloom. Exertion, even though mild, is one of the things to be avoided by a man who has scurvy—to that extent the patient's own tired feeling is a correct guide to behavior.

The main cause, then, of the Franklin tragedy was cultural. It derived from the social and mental outlook of the period. A point of view brought scurvy. The scurvy brought death, both as a disease and as a cause of starvation.

That some of the one hundred and five men who struggled ashore on King William Island were far gone with scurvy, we know from descriptions correct for advanced cases of this disease which were given by the Eskimos later. These descriptions are the more convincing in that the Eskimos themselves, constant livers on fresh meat, never have scurvy and therefore could not describe it correctly unless they had observed its symptoms among the white men.

Perhaps all the one hundred and five men were suffering. Scurvy has a slow approach; for it appears that the human body carries ahead from a period of a fresh food diet its own antiscorbutics that will last for several weeks, perhaps up to three months. The first signs of trouble are irritability, gloom, lack of ambition, a reluctance to plan or to do. Then develops the tired feeling, with shortness of breath and a dizziness on sudden movement. No doubt the mental symptoms will appear in less than three months, and perhaps some others, if the diet is completely without fresh elements.

We believe that Franklin organized hunting parties. Even if these were fowling parties and, through hard luck and negligence, there was little other game secured by hunting or purchasing, still there would be some fresh food and scurvy would advance slowly.

We might try here to invent a descrpition of how the Franklin expedition was conducted in relation to his announced plan to organize hunting parties; but it is doubtful whether we should come nearer the truth, though we used all sources, than the picture which we get from the account of the 1836–37 voyage of George Back. However, the Back picture could not be more than approximately true after the first winter spent by the Franklin ships in the King William region. As a result of the first year's procedure, if it was at all like Back's, the members of the party would have been so weakened, and their dispositions so affected by the mental outlook which accompanies scurvy, that the second winter would have seen a lessening of activity and a deepening of pathological gloom.

We shall quote snatches from Back. Those sufficiently interested will turn for the full and more convincing story to the book itself—the previously quoted account of the *Terror* voyage.

During the autumn of 1836, Back tells us, local Eskimos sold the expedition mittens, boots, and similar things, but could not "be prevailed upon to part with bags of oil, or anything of real value without something better in return than the old iron hoop, which was all that I would permit to be offered in exchange." (Page 38.)

"The officers amused themselves with shooting, and picked two or three brace of dovekies. . . . They also endeavoured to kill some seals . . . yet in no instance could they be secured before they sunk." (Pages 47–48.) There is no suggestion, here or later, that there was any thought of seals as food—

killing them was just sport. On September 7, 1836, they secured a lean polar bear. They measured it in every conceivable way but there is no indication that they ate any of it. Back says: "This novelty, trifling as it was, was sufficient to give a turn to our conversation." (Pages 93–95.) September 19 an Arctic fox was shot by Graham Gore, and a raven wheeled around the ship. "What must be the wearisome uniformity of a life in which incidents such as these become memorable!" (Pages 104–5.) They apparently never thought of eating the raven or the fox. By September 22 birds and animals had left, they then believed, except a solitary seal which an officer tried for but failed to get.

October 6 two officers and two men went ashore for an "excursion." "Not a single track of an animal was seen to allure them on or cheer their exertions." (Pages 119–20.) On the 23rd Back himself went ashore—alone because he was the only one who had snowshoes. He discovered no tracks of men or animals. (Pages 131–2.)

October 31, November 1 and November 16 tracks of bears, wolves and foxes were seen. No attempt was made to follow them.

On December 13 Gore secured a deer (caribou). Later the same day a few more deer were seen—so they had not left for the south, after all. A polar hare and two partridges were shot. Lines were set for fish, but none secured. December 26 the officers had the haunch of venison from Gore's deer.

In December "all occupation outside the ship, except for amusement merely, was now abandoned." Scurvy was then first noted. The men were feeling pretty bad by the end of the month, and the officers played football with them for encouragement! January 13 one man died; January 31 another. In January five or six of the officers also became affected, thus showing "incontrovertibly that the evil . . . was at all events not attributable to any difference in food." (Page 194.)

January 20, 1837, some men went out with guns but secured nothing. February 1 they shot a dovekie, and on March 29 two more. They "explored" for seals, but none were found. April 22 a polar bear was shot. There is no sign they ate it. "To us the adventure was a novelty, and gave occasion to some jests." (Page 322.) April 25 the third scurvy case died.

June 1 there was a fowling excursion: "The party altogether shot upwards of thirty loons, which being first skinned, and allowed to seep for two days in salt and water, were then dressed like jugged hare, and with red wine sauce and currant jelly, were esteemed by us as nearly equal in flavour." (Page 349.)

Franklin could not have known, as we do now, that by this handling of the loons on the Back expedition their antiscorbutic value was lessened. It was not destroyed, evidently, for these and other fowls—by our present interpretation— kept the party from having more deaths. There may have been some value, too, in a ration of "antiscorbutics" which was increased by Back after the scurvy first broke out. Remember, all this was on the first year of the Back voyage, so that the lime and lemon juices, and the rest of the "antiscorbutics," may still have retained some of their freshness.

For it is freshness, of course, which matters. The scurvy that is produced by salt (and otherwise preserved) meats, by hams, bacons and sausages, is cured by beefsteak or roast beef, or by any other fresh meat that is not "cooked to death." (In one of our roasts the Vitamin C is probably destroyed, or greatly weakened, only in the outer crusts, perhaps for a quarter or half an inch.) Scurvy can be produced with cereals and "preserved" things like dried apples and desiccated onions and then cured by the same vegetables and fruits in a fresh state.

That the keyword is "fresh" was unknown to the medical profession at the time of the Franklin search, although it was well known to several commanders who were engaged in the search (some of them, true enough, doctors). For instance, Dr. Elisha Kent Kane, the American, who took part during the fifties, speaks frequently in his journals of meat as a preventive and cure for scurvy, and emphasizes again and again that it has to be fresh. However, as said, that truth did not then gain a permanent footing in the disciplines of medicine and physiology—it never did until the first and second decades of the twentieth century.

Reminding ourselves that the Hudson's Bay Company "servants" in the north of Canada, and explorers like John and James Ross, knew that meat secured in the country was antiscorbutic, we return to quotations on Back's experience of 1837.

Back says that in June "the officers amused themselves in endeavouring to kill an immense seal"—vainly. "Numerous parties were tempted by the novelty to try their skill in shooting, and as the cheerfulness which the sport was calculated to excite was valuable at the moment of recovery from indisposition, I encouraged the inclination. There were, however, other substantial advantages; for such was the success of the day, that a sufficient number of loons were killed to allow of the distribution of an extra allowance to each mess in the ship." (Pages 348–50.)

By the end of June three men were dead, four or five were entirely disabled, while "symptoms of disease [were] lingering in many more." The fowling was going pretty well and, as we think, it prevented further deaths. Back considers the scurvy inexplicable because they had the advantage of the best provisions and every comfort which persons in their situation could have.

Clearly an expedition like Back's would have found itself in a vicious circle had it spent a second year. For the fowling, and a stray large beast, would not have been enough for more than a partial recovery from the first year's scurvy. At the beginning of winter the men would have been low in the initiative and mental resourcefulness which lead to success in the hunt. The resulting failure to secure game would have deprived them further of the strength which promotes success. Men who do not hunt in time to prevent scurvy are likely never to try hunting. If they do, they are handicapped by lethargic minds and physical weakness.

Since there is little doubt of the Franklin cannibalism, we have to note that while normal fresh human flesh would prevent scurvy, it is almost certainly true that the flesh of a man who is himself suffering from scurvy will lack the power to prevent or cure the scurvy of others. The cannibalism, therefore, can have had only a negligible effect on the trend of the disease.

Many of the Franklin party no doubt perished without ever tasting human flesh. The ones who did eat were perhaps in an extreme case already, and, as said, the flesh of those who had died from scurvy would have had little therapeutic value. For it is not probable that anyone was killed to be eaten. That phase of cannibalism, usual in melodrama, does occur in real experience; but not often. Usually the course is that men eat the bodies of those who have died and then die in their turn.

We concede again that Franklin had the excuses which many others have used; that medical men told him nothing about meat being a preventive of scurvy, and that they told him instead about lime juice and lemon juice as preventives and curatives. But we return to our point that a man who makes exploration a profession, as Franklin had done, has no business to sacrifice his men to the dogmas of current therapeutics when he can divide the entire literature of his own craft into two chains of events, the expeditions which had a good deal of fresh food and little or no scurvy; and those which had little or no fresh food and much scurvy.

There is, of course, the confusion that both of these classes of expeditions carried lemon and lime juices. But this should have been, to a studious and observant man, but a thin smoke screen—particularly so to Franklin, who had at his command not merely the knowledge which we have been discussing but the more intimate, and in that sense more convincing, knowledge that the traders of the Hudson's Bay Company were living all over the north of Canada without scurvy except in those few posts which were abundantly supplied with European food. Like the northern Indians and the Eskimos with whom these traders dealt, Hudson's Bay men depended on fish, birds and mammals, but chiefly on mammals, for practically all their food.

Our assumption that, in spite of all this, no one on the Franklin expedition understood how to prevent scurvy is based on the testimony of Eskimos who described scurvy symptoms noted among the retreating Franklin men, and on our not having found among the Franklin expedition communications any statement that they expected to prevent scurvy by the use of fresh meat. There are even wanting what might have been indirect proofs that they understood—for instance, references to an intention to have the men learn the Eskimo technique of securing seals. Such a reference would, of itself, show that the commanders knew how to prevent the disease and meant to apply that knowledge. There is no such indication in the Franklin documents. The nearest is a reference to the organization of hunting parties. But, as said, we agree with those commentators who believe that these were usually fowling parties. You cannot secure enough birds to prevent scurvy among a hundred men. That can be accomplished in the Franklin region only by a systematic and proficient hunting of all the big game animals but particularly of the two seals, the "common" and the "bearded."

Franklin died before the ships were abandoned. Crozier was in command of the retreat. He had been with Parry and may have been imbued with Parry ideas. Reading Parry, we gather what it was that Crozier may have learned from him.

On the voyage 1821–23, Parry considered the best means of preserving health and comfort during the winter were: theatrical performances, magic lantern shows, the formation of an orchestra and a school for teaching the crew to read and write. Scurvy was to be prevented or cured by the use of lime juice and by mustard and cress which they home-grew in boxes. Parry did not understand that in a meat country the logical way to prevent and cure scurvy is to hunt the local game and to eat it fresh. His people did secure and eat musk ox and caribou—Parry liked the taste and thought the meat good for the men but did not recognize it as particularly antiscorbutic. When, in 1823, scurvy was a serious problem, Parry followed the surgeon's advice and took the ship back to England.

On the Parry voyage of 1824–25, Crozier may have been impressed, as was a seaman, by Parry's "contempt of fatigue and power of endurance." Schools were started once more.

Imaginations were set at work to create new amusements—one of which was a bal masqué. If Crozier liked and respected Parry he probably noticed, as did others, a change in religious outlook whereby Parry, who had been content "to bow reverently before the footstool of the Creator" was led "to cling confidently yet humbly to the Cross of the Redeemer." (It should in fairness be allowed that the estimate we here quote is from his son, who was a missionary.)

With the traditions of the Royal Navy behind him, and with the Parry training, we have Crozier leading his crews on a long march three years after the Franklin expedition had left England. They were coming from a water district that was good enough for sealing to enable Eskimos to live on it in winter, but where the expedition had not secured meat sufficient to prevent scurvy; they were moving into a region that was good enough for bow-and-arrow Eskimos to support their helpless grandparents and children in summer. They were moving ashore with superior weapons but with minds inhibited by the outlook of their time and service; with strength depleted by malnutrition.

It has been said that the explorers did not know how to hunt. Hall, however, based his Franklin search expedition of years later on a stray remark of Franklin to Captain Martin of the *Enterprise* that shooting parties were to be organized. Guns and plenty of ammunition were found by the bleaching skeletons on King William. In addition, we have Eskimo testimony that the Franklin men did shoot. This has been reported by Hall, Schwatka and Rasmussen. Hall alone says they shot caribou; Bayne alone says they shot seals. Hall, Schwatka and Rasmussen say they shot birds; Schwatka and Rasmussen, that they bought seals. Rasmussen says they shot only birds.

We justify presently the belief that the Rasmussen information is nearest the truth. However, if the Franklin crews did secure a good deal of fresh meat, we can reconcile that fact with their also having scurvy (as no one doubts they did). For whites in the Far North have developed two methods of neutralizing the antiscorbutic value of fresh meat to the point where, in effect, they committed suicide by scurvy on a meat diet.

One thing which removes the antiscorbutic value of meat (we do not know in how many days or weeks) is salting. The Franklin officers, of naval tradition, may well have looked upon it as frugal to permit in the best hunting season only the use of a limited ration of fresh meat, the larger part being salted for uniform distribution through the year.

Now the single unquestioned report which we have concerning Franklin's hunting, and what he did with the meat, is the statement that when they were yet in Melville Bay they killed a large number of birds and salted them against winter use. It is a practical certainty that before they started using these birds in winter quarters the salting and storage had already removed the antiscorbutic value. Since this is our one Franklin record on the handling of fresh meat, we needs must believe he and his successors in command handled fresh meat that way as long as the crews were on shipboard.

The second method of preventing fresh meat from being useful in the cure of scurvy is to cook it to pieces.

It is not improbable that if and when a deer was killed by the Franklin party, a specially large proportion of the fresh meat would have been reserved to the invalids, as a change of diet if nothing else. This, in the correct tradition with invalids, may have been boiled for hours to make the equivalent of beef tea. The patient would then drink the broth and would perhaps eat also the shreds and fragments of that meat which had been used to make the "strong soup."

Neither salted meat, however cooked, nor fresh meat cooked to death is any more valuable against scurvy than the preserved vegetables and ancient, but very sour, lime and lemon juices which the Franklin ships carried.

Strange as it seems to pure modern theory, it is consonant with the record of those British expeditions which antedated Thomas Simpson's, for Englishmen to devote themselves chiefly to fowling, as Rasmussen says they did. This was a recognized sport at home with them, a pastime of nobility and gentry. Many of the birds in the King William Island section were looked upon in England as good food, even as delicacies.

Farther on in the present volume, when discussing Andrée, we bring out what is now commonplace, the folly of carrying shotguns when a mobile party is trying to make a living in the Arctic, whether on sea or on land. Here we just say dogmatically that it is folly, and point out that most of the guns recorded as having been found upon or around King William Island were fowling pieces.

It is more logical, then, to accept the testimony of Rasmussen than that of the other witnesses, for these reasons among others: He was the first man to visit King William Island who thoroughly understood every aspect of the case—the nature of the Arctic, the principles of hunting, the mode of thought of the Eskimos, their language, the degree of reliability of their traditions. He alone among students to 1923 would not ask leading questions, knowing it to be a fundamental of Eskimo culture, an element of high morality with them, to tell the truth only if it is going to please the listener, and to tell him whatever is likely to please him. If an investigator said to a primitive Eskimo that surely the Franklin party must have killed a lot of caribou, the answer—irrespective of fact—would be that they certainly did, that they killed an awful lot.

So the testimony of the Netsilik Eskimos that the Franklin party killed numerous caribou and seals is simply explained by their believing (rightly or wrongly) that the inquirer would be pleased if narrative were forthcoming to that effect.

Since this is fundamental in dealing with Eskimo testimony, we labor the point. Eskimos are about as good judges of weather as the average European sailor. If you ask an Eskimo what he thinks the weather is going to be tomorrow, he will give you as sound an answer as you might expect from a sailor. But if you first refer to the picnic scheduled for tomorrow and then say that you do hope the weather will be good, the Eskimo, if he be still truly of the old school, will look around the sky gravely, think ponderously, and inform you that he is pretty sure the weather is going to be fine.

The same tradition, picked up by Rasmussen at King William Island in 1923, which says that the Franklin party shot only birds, tells that they purchased seals from the Eskimos and that they cooked the lean "with the aid of blubber." This recalls that baffling picture from the Fort Enterprise retreat of 1821, when Franklin's men burnt the food value out of bones and then ate the charcoal. Now we have them burning seal fat to cook the lean of their meat!

We had to believe the story of the charred bones since Franklin himself wrote and published it. Lest we nevertheless dismiss as incredible the Eskimo story of famished men burning food, we should consider that there are similar misunderstandings about food which are well attested even from recent times. For instance, on the Canadian Arctic Expedition of 1913–18 a man on the verge of starvation (who died either of hunger or exposure a day or two later) visited a depot which contained hundreds of pounds of sugar but only negligible quantities of any other food. This man took all the other food but took only a small amount of sugar, indicating that he was going to use it for his tea, as a flavoring. In his mind, evidently, sugar and salt were of equal rank; they were both condiments.

The instances of not eating sugar when you are starving, and of burning fat when you are starving, are unfortunately but special cases of a type numerous in polar exploration where you have to overrule common-sense skepticism in favor of unimpeachable testimony. We give two further samples, both well known from the recent history of Alaska and northern Canada.

The belief that a thing is not frozen unless it is hard, and that kerosene is therefore not frozen as long as it is liquid, has led to such things as the deliberate immersion of a partly frozen foot in a bucket of kerosene that had just been brought from outdoors in weather 40° below zero. The man's foot was frozen solid by the kerosene, and had to be amputated.

While such misuses of kerosene are numerous, they are not as common in the literature as the difficulties and tragedies which have resulted from the general belief that "like cures like," that you can thaw out a frozen part of the human body by applying to it something else that is equally cold or colder. In numerous cases reported in Arctic books snow, of temperatures as low as 40° or 50° below zero, has been applied to a nose or a cheek that was just beginning to freeze and which must have been, therefore, something like 70° warmer than the snow. The results have varied from pathetic to semitragic.

A particularly striking example is that of a doctor of medicine who was in command of a winter traveling party, and who noticed on the face of one man a white spot that indicated the beginning of a frostbite. The doctor ordered camp to be pitched and meantime rubbed the victim's face with snow—protecting his own hand from the snow with a mitten. The doctor remarks in the published account that so intense was the cold of the weather that during the pitching of the camp, which took only a few minutes, the poor man's entire face was frozen!

With such testimony often published by the doers themselves, we are compelled to admit the probable accuracy of the Eskimo tradition that the Franklin men, when on the verge of starvation, used animal fat to make a fire with which to cook their meal.

It is barely possible that the expression recorded by Rasmussen, "cooked the meat with the aid of the blubber," referred to frying the meat. We shall probably never know; for Rasmussen, the only man who could have resolved the question, has died, and the old man who gave him the tradition (which he had received from his eyewitness father) has doubtless also passed away.

In a contention that Franklin's men would know enough to ignore fowling and to depend on big game it may be said that Thomas Simpson's *Narrative of the Discoveries on the North Coast of America*, published in London during 1843, describes his successful reliance on local resources of the Far North in living and traveling, and the role of big game in this success, and that this must have been known to Franklin and his men. They certainly must have heard of it; but it is to be remembered that Thomas Simpson was then under a cloud, and that his giant stature among northern explorers was acquired long after both his own death and that of Franklin. In fact, there seems to be little evidence that British opinion was much impressed by the idea that British expeditions could support themselves by hunting in the Arctic until after the Simpson preliminary success had been reinforced through the even more notable success in this regard of Dr. John Rae. But Rae's success came during the period of the Franklin search and was, therefore, not available to influence the opinions of Franklin, Crozier, or whoever may have controlled the policy during the retreat from the *Erebus* and *Terror*.

Rae's self-training in Arctic technique began in 1846–47 when he commanded a Hudson's Bay Company expedition in the eastern Arctic. This was not a search for Franklin, for few persons were as yet worrying much, but a survey on behalf of the Company.

In the autumn of 1846 Rae found himself in the vicinity of Repulse Bay. Both from his experience and from what we know through other sources, this would seem to be a district worse than average for game in autumn and winter. He had with him eighteen men, some whites and some forest Indians. He told these to busy themselves in scouting around the country and in pulling up small bushes or other things which they thought might be useful for fuel. Rae did the hunting, with some help from one Eskimo. The amount of food the party had with them when they camped (chiefly meat, in the form of pemmican) was negligible considering the wants of eighteen men through a whole winter—certainly less than an eighteen-man party of Franklin's expedition could have possessed after landing from their beset ships.

Rae's preliminary report, as published first in the London *Morning Chronicle* for November 2, 1847, and copied in Littell's *Living Age* for December of that year, shows that by October 16, one hundred and thirty reindeer had been killed, and in November thirty-two more. With these and two hundred partridges and some salmon, he considered his provision storehouse (built of snow) pretty well stocked.

The full book narrative, published later, confirms the advance notice. Rae learned to dwell with fair comfort on the Arctic prairie by adopting—at first in part, and then more fully—the Eskimo way of life. Although James Ross used snowhouses before him, Rae was apparently the first enthusiastic British convert to the view that they are more comfortable than tents; and he actually used snowhouses on his later expeditions, in the fifties.

To judge from the writings of Franklin, Back and Richardson that were published before 1846, the idea that an explorer might fend for himself in the Arctic, live and travel there in health and comfort sustained by the resources of the country, made no progress with Back and a negligible advance with Franklin. There are signs that Richardson was learning small bits of local technique and beginning to consider new methods. At least he was in a frame of mind to appreciate Rae when the story of his work began to reach England. In 1847, when he was asked to take command of an overland expedition in search of Franklin, he saw to it that Rae was detailed to accompany him.

The Richardson party crossed west from the Atlantic to the rivers of the Mackenzie system, descended the streams to the Arctic Sea in the summer of 1848 and proceeded east along the coast. Richardson's book speaks with growing admiration of Rae's success in securing game as the party of about forty-five proceeded toward the Coppermine. Finally he comes to the conclusion that "in this quarter a skilful hunter, like Mr. Rae, could supply the whole party with venison without any loss of time," leaving the other members free to do their own scientific or other work.

The gun with which Rae was doing that hunting cannot have been materially better than the guns which were carried by the Franklin expedition—indeed, it was probably of the same kind as some of them. The section between Capes Lyon and Krusenstern, in which Richardson came to the conclusion that Rae's one gun could feed forty-five men, is probably not as well supplied with game as average for the Arctic coast of North America.

After the Rae success it was taken for granted by many people in England that the Franklin party would subsist by hunting. An anonymous writer in the *Quarterly Review* was among those who put the hope for the survival of Franklin's men in terms of what might be expected from Rae's success. Much attention was given to what Lieutenant John Irving had written to his sister-in-law from Whalefish Island, Greenland, July 10, 1845, when the expedition supply ship was returning to England: "We will eke out our provisions with all the game our guns can procure." Lady Franklin pointed to what Sir John was reported to have said to Captain Martin—the statement we have already given in connection with Hall.

From the *Narrative of the Four Russian Sailors Who Spent Six Years on the Island of Spitzbergen*, three of whom sustained themselves by hunting, Mangles quotes the testimony on their condition after their rescue: "All three on their arrival [at Archangel] were strong and healthy; but having lived so long without bread, they could not reconcile themselves to the use of it, and complained that it filled them with wind."* He concludes: "The hardships and sufferings of

---

* The complaint of the Russians that the eating of bread filled them with wind (as compared with absence of "wind" on an exclusive meat diet) is confirmed from recent experiments. For instance, a group of scientists supervised an experiment by the Russell Sage Institute of Pathology in Bellevue Hospital with two white men, who, in 1928–29, lived for one year in New York City on a diet of meat and water practically identical with that of the Russians of Spitsbergen in 1743. This committee certified that X-ray pictures taken during the experiment show at different times either unusual or else complete absence of gas from the intestinal tract during the meat-eating period. This met agreement from the subjects of the experiment, who noticed this difference in themselves as compared with previous and subsequent periods on a mixed diet, and also by Professor John C. Torrey of the Cornell University Medical College, noted specialist in alimentary bacteriology, whose observations confirmed the X-ray pictures. He found in the alimentary canal of the subjects evidence that on the meat diet those organisms were relatively infrequent which produce

the first and second years [of living on nothing but meat and water] were probably by force of habit, mitigated in the third, and rendered comparatively light during the remainder of their sojourn. The principle is equally applicable to Franklin and his crews."

William Scoresby, famous whaler of Greenland waters, points out in his testimony before the Franklin Search Arctic Committee that Eskimos can live in the Arctic—so why can't Britons?

On the other hand, many persons believed that the Franklin party could not sustain itself by hunting. They did not usually suggest lack of application or skill but dwelt upon probable lack of game. One of these pessimists was that very man upon whom the optimists relied as having shown that you could support considerable parties by hunting in the Franklin region, Dr. John Rae.

It may seem from Rae's direct testimony in the early part of the Franklin Search that his main reason for thinking the crews of the missing ships would be unable to support themselves was lack of game. However, there are later statements which indicate that perhaps he was trying to save the feelings of relatives and friends, and that his real opinion was that these particular crews would not succeed in saving themselves by hunting.

Rae's general attitude toward Arctic self-support on one hand, and toward people of the Franklin type on the other, was such that he would have considered it academic to discuss success for them—in view of his belief that they would never do the fundamental things which were necessary. Among these fundamentals would have been for the men to study during the wintering in the King William seas the local technique for keeping clothing dry and in good order, and

---

what the Russians speak of as wind and what is nowadays referred to as gas.

Being interpreted, this means that modern science and the Russians agree with the contention of Mangles that if the Franklin party had secured meat in quantity they would have had no difficulty in living upon it, whatever the number of years—might even have returned to England with an aversion to bread!

for them to learn snowhouse building, seal hunting, and the general methods of comfortable and economical living when dependent on Arctic resources. Rae would not have believed in their being wise enough to leave inessentials behind and to equip themselves properly for travel, nor would he have pictured them as dividing themselves into five parties, or ten, and scattering so as to get the maximum prospect of successful and safe life and travel.

This boils down to our interpretation that Rae's direct statements on the Franklin prospects during the most emotional time of the Franklin Search were governed by kindness and also perhaps by a reluctance to get himself into further disfavor. He was already in rather bad standing, for having behaved on his expeditions like a menial (having done his own work) and for having lived like a savage (in snowhouses, and so forth). This behavior did not seem cricket to the British public. Success in polar travel by methods of that kind produced in them subconsciously the effect which Conan Doyle later described in his account of Brigadier Gerard's killing a fox with a saber. The prime object of fox hunting is not the killing of the fox but the observance of good form during the pursuit and at the kill. The object of polar explorations is to explore properly and not to evade the hazards of the game through the vulgar subterfuge of going native.

Our summary will have to be, then, that the crews of the *Erebus* and the *Terror* perished as victims of the manners, customs, social outlook and medical views of their time.

Franklin died a year before the main tragedy, possibly of some ailment connected with his advanced years. A few others may have died from illnesses which come in all countries and on all diets. The rest died from scurvy brought on by dependence upon ships' stores, and from hunger brought on by a lack of physical strength and mental initiative, which were in turn due to scurvy. An antecedent cause of the scurvy was that failure to adapt themselves to local conditions which derived from the mental environment of their country, social class and time.

If the stories be true that a few Englishmen were alive

several years after the main tragedy, then they must have been lost eventually in an effort to cross southerly towards a Hudson's Bay Company post. More likely, however, the tales of a few survivors who remained several years in the King William Island region were invented by the Eskimos in response to the persistent inquiries of men who had come to the Franklin region with a firm belief that some whites still survived there. As we have said, it is the morality of primitive Eskimos to give an inquirer as nearly as possible the answers which will please him.

Let us retrace the ground partly and assume that a few specially adaptable men did survive for a number of years. Then, both on the basis of common sense and on that of Eskimo report, we shall have to agree that they had mastered the technique of the country. They would have been in excellent health, since that has been nearly invariable with whites who had lived in the Eskimo way. Under such conditions they would have out-Eskimoed the Eskimos, for in addition to the primitive knowledge recently acquired they would have had the white man's knowledge and equipment— they would have known such things as the principles of angles which make an acclimated white man better than an Eskimo in finding his way about. They would have had compasses, firearms (plenty of ammunition was found later in King William Island) and many other details of superior ability and equipment. Under these conditions they should not have lost their lives upon such a journey as the Eskimo stories say they attempted, from Back River to a Hudson's Bay post.

As crucial for the Eskimo testimony, we repeat that what is required of an Eskimo, in response to the ethics of his people, is merely that he tell an inquirer the most pleasing thing that is also credible. There would have been no sense, from the Eskimo point of view, in saying to Hall that whites were still living in the neighborhood. The best a King William Eskimo could do was to say that they had been in the neighborhood recently, or else that they were living now, but at a great distance—so far away that Hall would not be able to get there or, if he got there, would think that his informants had been honestly mistaken.

We find, in other words, that the Eskimo stories of a few temporary survivors, gathered by Hall and the rest, are in correct response to the morality of that people. For they deal either with a few whites who survived for a while, or else with some who were still surviving but at a distance.

We emphasize in closing what we said before, that Rasmussen was the first man to visit the King William region who was qualified in every way for getting the truth. He had lived with Eskimos so long it was instinctive with him to reveal no bias in his questions, or in his attitude, in order to secure the most nearly accurate replies the people could give him. The replies which he did receive (the essence of which we have quoted) fit in with the things we know and with the probabilities of the case.

It could be that a few of the most adaptable survived, in the manner related to Hall. In that case they were finally lost through some mischance on a journey towards one of the northern Canadian trading posts. This might have been as late as 1853.

It is more probable that the last man died the winter of 1848–49.

There is no doubt that the disciplined officers and sailors of the Franklin expedition met their fate with a high average of resignation and courage.

Chapter 3

The Strange Fate of Thomas Simpson

A HUNDRED YEARS AGO Thomas Simpson was young and brilliant, as surely on the road to fame as any man of his time. Between 1836 and 1839 he had succeeded where great men before him had failed in the exploration of northern North America. In 1840 he was about to complete the discovery of the long-sought water route by which it was believed great streams of European commerce would flow to the Orient.

By 1840 two hundred years of search for the Northwest Passage had not yet dampened ardor of governments or of private adventurers; this long-awaited discovery was still the chief dream of seaborne commerce. Beginning with Henry Hudson, who perished during 1611 in what is now Hudson Bay, Britain had sacrificed on the quest for a northwestern seaway men and ships and treasure continuously.

Before Thomas Simpson began his work, opinion had crystallized on where the Northwest Passage would be found. British seamen, coming from Bering Straits, had surveyed the western reach of the Passage as far northeast as Point Barrow. Franklin had descended the Mackenzie River and surveyed the Alaska coast westward to Return Reef. Two expeditions of Franklin's had also worked east, and the coast had been charted from the Mackenzie Delta to Coronation Gulf and thence still farther eastward to Point Turnagain on Kent Peninsula. Discoverers from the Atlantic, among them Sir Edward Parry and Sir John Ross, had surveyed what was thought to be the eastern mouth of the Passage, around Boothia Felix.

So it was in men's minds that there remained to be discovered two links of the Northwest Passage, a 150-mile stretch between Barrow and Return, and one of 300 miles between Boothia and Turnagain. During 1837 Simpson closed the western gap; on two journeys, in 1838 and 1839, he had nearly succeeded in closing the eastern. In the spring of 1840 he was bound for England to organize an expedition that would round out the discovery. On that journey he killed himself or was murdered.

To arrive at an opinion as to what happened and why, we must, like our predecessors, study the available sources on Thomas Simpson, on the Hudson's Bay Company, and on George Simpson, in so far as they apply to the mystery of how and why Thomas Simpson died.

There are two main sources on Thomas Simpson. For what gives him front rank among polar discoverers, read his own *Narrative of the Discoveries on the North Coast of America; effected by the Officers of the Hudson's Bay Company during the years 1836–39* (London, 1843). That book, however, bears little upon the mystery of how and why he died. For that problem the chief source remains the biography by his brother, Alexander Simpson, *The Life and Travels of Thomas Simpson, the Arctic Discoverer* (London, 1845). That book, however, is by a loving partisan who wrote in bitterness and sorrow.

We see, then, at the outset that our chief source is colored by affection, and thus prejudiced.

In many cases Alexander quotes his brother's letters. Some of these have since been used by others to weaken the murder theory; to prove that Thomas Simpson was the victim of a persecution complex, neurasthenia, almost uncontrolled egoism; that this mental unbalance had been increasing until it culminated in suicide. Some have taken at face value the statements Thomas makes in his letters; others discount them as products of a diseased mind. On that we can merely reason as others have done before us. We need not stop there, however, but can take a line which no one seems yet to have followed to any extent in print—through the use of independent sources we may be able to confirm or contradict what Thomas says and what others have said about him. Perhaps we can, in the light of these sources, offer suggestions for alternative interpretations to some of the statements. This method we shall try.

We discuss first who Thomas Simpson was, and what he did that merits our consideration.

Thomas was born on July 2, 1808, at Dingwall in the highlands of Scotland. His father, the parish schoolmaster and local magistrate, died in 1821, leaving a widow and two sons meagerly provided for. A half-brother, Aemilius, much older than Thomas or Alexander, son of their father's first wife, helped out the establishment with his lieutenant's half-pay.

As a child, Thomas was sickly, timid, unwilling to play any game that might hurt him. As a college youth he was debonair, gregarious, fond of debate, fastidious in his dress, an idealist. On leaving college he became realistic enough to embrace the rough life of the Hudson's Bay Company "servant" in America, which he enjoyed for a time. Later he became dissatisfied but did little about his grievances. Then he became an explorer, fearless, tireless, careful in observation, thorough in his work. He had hit his stride.

When Thomas was at King's College, Aberdeen, George Simpson entered his life. Or it may have been a reentry.

George, the villain of Alexander's book, first cousin of Thomas and Alexander, was the illegitimate son of their mother's eldest brother. He was twenty-one years older than Thomas and twenty-four years older than Alexander. It was their mother, says Alexander, who was responsible for George's education, and who persuaded her brother to take the youth into his business. Once there, his advance was rapid, for he was clever, active, plausible, and full of animal spirits. He attracted the attention of Andrew Colvile, brother-in-law of the Earl of Selkirk, and was sent to America in 1820 to take part in the troubled situation between the Hudson's Bay Company and the North-West Company. Shortly after his arrival the difficulties were settled, and George Simpson was named as resident governor of one of the divisions of the country. In this position "he exhibited so much address and activity . . . (favourable accidents also occurring) that, a few years afterwards, he was appointed governor of the whole of the Company's possessions in America. . . ."

Alexander states these things as fact, but they might

really be no more than a biased opinion—first as to George's personality, second as to how he achieved the governorship. Therefore we quote John McLean, who resigned from the Company in 1841 after a twenty-five-year service. He says that George, at the time of his arrival in America, "combined with the prepossessing manners of a gentleman all the craft and subtlety of an intriguing courtier."

McLean, in turn, could be discounted as a man brooding on real or fancied wrongs from George Simpson. Therefore we use for counterbalance Douglas MacKay, who wrote the most detailed of the numerous popular histories of the Hudson's Bay Company and was still in their employ when he died. Of the rise of George Simpson to power he says: "In September [1821] came the ticklish meeting of council, and that series of convergent circumstances which made Simpson governor of the Northern Department. That was not all. Williams in the Southern Department retained his technical seniority only until 1826 when he returned to England. Then Simpson became governor-in-chief of the Hudson's Bay Company's territories."

It was as resident Governor of the Northern Department of the Hudson's Bay Company's territories in North America that George Simpson returned to Scotland in 1825. Impressed by Thomas, he offered him the post of secretary. Thomas did not accept then, but four years later the offer was repeated and accepted. Writing to Aemilius, Thomas gives as his reasons that a desired medical career was financially out of his reach, and that he was disinclined to enter the church or to become a tutor. The terms offered were especially good, for he entered the Company on the same footing as if he had been in the last two years of his apprenticeship, even to receiving a salary, which was £40 for his first year, and £50 for the second.

Alexander was in the service of the Company at the time, stationed at Lachine, near Montreal; Aemilius, with the Company too, was on the Pacific Coast.

On June 18, 1829, Thomas Simpson joined the Governor at Norway House and commenced his secretarial duties immediately—a tour through the southeastern part of the Company's territories. Toward the end of August the party reached Montreal. Alexander reports that Thomas "arrived in high health and spirits, quite delighted with the journey, which had been performed in a light canoe."

During 1830, while he was still apprentice, Thomas was given the leadership of the first western brigade, a party of almost a hundred, which he brought to the head of Lake Superior with expedition and with relatively few desertions at a time when they were common. Here, by instruction, he handed over the command and joined Governor Simpson at York Factory. He did not care much about York, but his complaints are of mosquitoes in summer and cold in winter. Otherwise he calls his situation "very comfortable—with excellent accommodation and the best of fare."

On February 10, 1831, he was given another command, this time leaving York Factory for Red River on snowshoes, with a party of men and two trains of dogs. The 700-mile journey took twenty-eight days, six of which were spent resting the dogs.

We gather from Alexander's narrative that between 1829 and 1833 Thomas was fairly happy, reasonably satisfied. His letters to Chief Factor Donald Ross confirm this, the only sad note being when, on April 24, 1832, he writes feelingly of the death of the Governor's infant son.

Not until 1833 do the first of those letters appear that were later used against him. During 1833–34 the Governor was in England and Chief Factor Christie was in charge. Thomas writes:

"You would, perhaps, like to know how we have been going on here this season—exceedingly well; far less bustle and as good and rapid work as if the Governor himself were on the ground. . . .

"To myself, in particular, the difference is very great; as, with all the Governor's good will and kind intentions, he has been to me a severe and most repulsive master."

He knows, he says, that this has been a matter of policy, but it is one which would have brought him (Thomas) into contempt. With Christie, "the only man whom I have yet seen in the country, whom I could now respect and esteem, as my immediate superior," he has been able to command respect. Continuing, he says of the Governor:

"I will not conceal from you, that on a nearer view of his character than I before had, I lost much of that internal respect I entertained towards him. His firmness and decision of mind are much impaired: both in great and small matters, he has become wavering, capricious, and changeable . . .

"His general management of the colony I cannot admire: it is faulty and inconsistent in many respects. . . .

"Viewing the service generally, I must candidly confess . . . that its promises of happiness are hollow. . . . But let not this discourage us, my dear boy, . . . for there are, really, so few men of any pretensions to talent in the country, that if common justice is done us we must soon become conspicuous. I speak the words of truth, not of vanity. Indeed, the Governor told me the very evening before starting, 'Whether my head be under or above the sod, your character and abilities will and must *soon* bring you forward.'"

Following his brother's letter about promotion *soon*, Alexander inserts a parenthetical paragraph that jumps three years ahead of his narrative, quoting a letter from Thomas which says: "A word, even of acquiescence, from the Governor would have procured me a commission as Chief Trader this year; but the name of Simpson is a disadvantage; and, notwithstanding the promises made me when I came to the country, and the new and arduous duty to which I have volunteered, I must wait."

On December 31, 1834, Alexander arrived at Red River for a visit with his brother. The colony was in a state of excitement. An altercation between Thomas and a half-breed, over a further advance on the coming season's wages, had flamed into a race war. The Governor's attitude was one of conciliation. "Even the demand made by them, that my brother should expiate his imputed or imagined offence by receiving a public flogging, could not rouse this vacillating plausible man, to a resolution of defiance, which every one knew might, with the utmost safety, have been given." The Governor compromised, by bribing the half-breeds, by making them promises.

Thomas said he would resign. "This," says Alexander, "was an alternative shrunk from," and Thomas did not resign. The incident left him feeling that he was likely to be assassinated.

MacKay's version is: "The half-breed leaders were indignant, and demanded that the governor have his kinsman publicly flogged. The governor temporized, offered the half-breeds a keg of rum and an assurance that Thomas would be sent elsewhere. Thomas, fired with indignation, threatened to resign and the tension was high for several days. But the governor knew the Metis people better than his clerk did, and the affair quieted down."

That the quiet was mainly of a surface variety is at least indicated. Ballantyne, who did not know Thomas but who was in the Red River country during the years 1840–45, reports local opinion when he says that Thomas was very much disliked by the half-breeds. This is confirmed by J. D. Cameron. Writing to James Hargrave on April 25, 1841, he speaks of the half-castes as "firey" and says they had no great love for Thomas Simpson. However, it was only with his later days that the attitude of the Metis became important.

The great issue with Thomas Simpson was to be the search for the Northwest Passage.

Before Thomas came to America, there had been two overland expeditions by Sir John Franklin, one in 1820 and the other in 1825, to search for the Passage. On the first expedition Franklin had talked with Peter Warren Dease, a trader in the North-West Company, and had received much valuable information. On the second expedition he asked for and got permission to take Dease, then with the Hudson's Bay Company, along to manage the procuring of provisions and to supervise the Canadian *voyageurs* and Indians.

In 1829 Sir John Ross began his second voyage for the discovery of the Northwest Passage by sea. Alarm for his safety led to a search expedition in 1833 with Captain George Back in command. The party followed one of the overland routes—Lake Winnipeg, Fort Resolution, Great Slave Lake. On April 25 Back had news that Ross was safe home in England. The need for search was over, but since they were in the field they continued exploratory work through a chain of lakes in central Canada until they finally completed the descent of the Great Fish River, afterward named Back River. Among other things, the results of this expedition were found to cast doubt on Ross's statement that Boothia was a peninsula, for Back reported finding a sea where there should have been none according to Ross.

In 1836 Captain Back with the ship *Terror* attempted to complete the exploration of the northeastern coast of America, and to open fully the eastern mouth of the Northwest Passage; but his ship was frozen in. Next year they succeeded in getting her afloat and in keeping her afloat until they got back to England.

As said a few pages back, there remained at this stage two gaps in the tracing of the northern American coast—that on the west where now we speak of the eastern north coast of Alaska, between the extreme west of Franklin's discoveries and Point Barrow, a distance of 170 miles but requiring to reach it a retrace of Franklin's 340-mile traverse west from the Mackenzie mouth of 1826; and, on the east, the coast between Franklin's eastern extreme, east of the Coppermine River and Prince Regent's Inlet, a distance of more than 300 miles, requiring a traverse of 180 miles of coast traced by Franklin's first expedition.

In this situation, Richard King, who had accompanied Back on the first expedition, projected in 1835–36 plans for a new one. These plans never materialized; but while they were under discussion they were, says Alexander, a bother to the Hudson's Bay Company. He gives two reasons—King had been too outspoken to be popular with the Company; the Company was about to ask for renewal of its grant of the exclusive trade of the region which was to form the field of the expedition's operations. Alexander quotes the *Morning Chronicle* as pointing out that in conducting an expedition the Company would merely be doing the duty under which its charter was originally granted.

MacKay's statement of the same case is: "The Hudson's Bay Company, having supported expeditions with little credit beyond a note of thanks in the inevitable book, felt moved to get into the game. Possibly some sense of the obligation to renew the search for the Passage may have prompted the Committee, but certainly the impending renewal of the exclusive license to trade in the Indian Territories was recognized as a proper time to display some exploratory activity beyond their present fur-trading areas. As the license was to come up for renewal in 1838, some move to win government goodwill as well as public sympathy would be appropriate."

Not this time running strictly parallel, we quote the sarcastic comment of McLean on a previous exploratory journey: "The Company having learned, through a pamphlet published by the Moravian missionaries of Labrador, that the country produced excellent furs, were induced by the laudable desire of 'ameliorating the condition of the natives,' to settle it; and a party was accordingly sent overland from Moose Factory to take possession in the summer of 1831. The Moravians, finding their intention thus anticipated, left both the cure of souls and trade of furs to the Company."

In any case, George Simpson in Canada was instructed by his London superiors to make arrangements for an expedition under Company auspices. He delegated the plan-making to Thomas, who seems to have been under the clear impression that he was to be in command. Alexander calls the final instructions a mere translation of Thomas's plan into official phraseology. But it then appeared that the command was not to be Thomas Simpson's but was instead given to Peter Warren Dease, who, as we have said, had accompanied Franklin's second expedition, before Thomas even reached North America, and who had been given a Chief Factorship by reason of his work on that occasion.

Official reason for the change was internal politics—that jealousy would be felt by older "servants" were a younger man appointed over their heads. Alexander admits that there is ground for the idea that such jealousy "would be sufficient to induce them to throw every impediment and obstruction in the way of the expedition." However, he gives as the real reason the Governor's unwillingness to let Thomas attain the prominence which command of the expedition would have given him.

MacKay's version is: "George Simpson's faith in his cousin was high, for he named his young relative to lead the party. The jealousies of older officers, however, made it necessary to divide the command with the elderly, popular Peter Warren Dease."

Thomas's enthusiasm, and perhaps the fact that the plans of the expedition were his own, would not permit him to withdraw even under this disappointment. He accepted the place of second-in-command and went from Norway House to Red River to brush up on mathematics and to learn some practical astronomy. He then made the journey of over 1,200 miles to Chipewyan and joined Dease on February 1, 1837. Writing to the Governor on May 31, he mentions that it is the eve of their departure, outlines how four months of waiting have been spent, voices disappointment that the command is not his after it has been promised him, expresses the hope that should accident befall him his mother will be taken care of, and jabs at the Company by saying he does not know whether Alexander is still in its service "or has embraced some more promising line of life."

He also takes a poke at Back in acknowledging receipt of the Captain's journal. "It contains, indeed, little thought, with no small portion of French sentimentality and self-admiration; but, altogether, I think he has made the most of his subject, which was not a fertile one." He notes with pleasure that Back's present expedition is not to interfere with his own.

As usual, Thomas is more outspoken in writing to Alexander than to George. "Captain Back's present 'terrific' voyage is not to interfere with ours. . . . His book is a painted bauble, all ornament and conceit, and no substance."

On June 1, 1837, Dease and Simpson left Fort Chipewyan with two small sea boats and a party of hunters and *voya-*

geurs. The names of three of them occur later in our story—James M'Kay, George Sinclair, and George Flett. By July 4 the party had traveled more than a thousand miles and were at Fort Smith, where reports of friction between Eskimos and Indians kept them from hiring an interpreter from among the Indians. By July 23 they had advanced 1,800 miles to Franklin's Return Reef, where their real exploration was to begin.

Traveling northwestward along the coast, they mapped and surveyed until, 150 miles beyond where Franklin had been compelled to turn back in 1826 but 50 miles short of their goal at already discovered Point Barrow, they reached the limit of boat travel—their Boat Extreme.

Because the ice ahead was jammed too tight against the shore for their clumsy and fragile wooden boats, Simpson undertook to complete the work on foot, "Mr. Dease most handsomely volunteering to remain with the boats, and thus secure our retreat." He started afoot with a party of five, but soon borrowed an umiak from the Eskimos—a stronger and lighter type of boat than his, and in every way suited for the conditions. With this they reached Point Barrow on August 3, thus completing the western section of the Northwest Passage. A known seaway now lay open for 2,000 miles from the North Pacific around northwestern and north central North America to Franklin's farthest east at Point Turnagain.

Simpson rejoined Dease, and the entire party traveled back to Fort Norman where the two leaders reported jointly to the Directors of the Hudson's Bay Company. Their entire journey so far had been some 3,500 miles. Through the competence of Simpson, with benefit (no doubt) of some advice from Dease, it was performed without accident and without hardship. This was a new note in overland and coastal Arctic exploration of the period, where incompetence and resulting suffering had been the rule.

On September 8th Thomas wrote personally to the Governor expressing pride in the interest taken by the Directors, inquiring about a pecuniary reward, and recalling that the Governor had said his services as secretary at Red River had earned a Chief Tradership. ". . . now, however, I have the *exclusive* honour of unfurling the Company's flag on Point Barrow, and of thus uniting the Arctic to the Western Ocean —which I humbly think entitles me to the second step [i.e. Chief Factor]. . . . do not reject my just claims, although I am one of your own relatives. I have always confided implicitly in your kind sentiments towards me, and feel that they will be fully displayed on the present occasion."

Whether Thomas Simpson's request for a Chief Factorship was in order we learn by comparing what he had done on this expedition with the work of Dease on the second Franklin expedition. Dease had received a Chief Factorship for tagging along with Franklin and being sometimes useful, sometimes a handicap. Simpson had accomplished, with Dease as little more than supercargo, what Franklin had failed to accomplish.

Thomas wrote further, to the Governor: "Mr. Dease is a good, honourable man. I believe I have acquired his friendship, for in everything, even to the plan of our little Fort Confidence, he has adopted my advice, and has left the direction of the march entirely to me; the result proves that it has not languished under my directions."

At the same time he wrote Alexander: "Fortune and its great Disposer have this season smiled upon my undertakings, and shed the first bright beams upon the dark prospect of a North American life. Yes, my dearest brother, congratulate me, for I, and I *alone,* have the well-earned honour of uniting the Arctic to the great Western Ocean, and of unfurling the British flag on Point Barrow." Conceit? Yes. But we must remember, here and always, that the letters eventually published by Alexander were written by Thomas in strictest confidence to a brother, and without thought that they would ever become public.

The report to the Directors of the Company (dated September 5, 1837), though forwarded from post to post with all the speed possible, did not reach England until April 19, 1838. It aroused great interest. The Company's Governor, Sir John Pelly, submitted it to the Royal Geographical Society, and it was published in that society's *Journal* (Vol.

VIII, 1838). Alexander Simpson quotes the *Morning Chronical* as saying: "The question which has been a geographical problem for upwards of two centuries,—the *northwest passage* around the continent of America,—is at length determined, and we have the satisfaction to lay before our readers . . . an abstract of the Journals of the intrepid discoverers, by whose enterprise the object has been accomplished, and in the progress of which they have evinced intelligence, activity, and hardihood not inferior to any of those daring and enduring men who have preceded them in the arduous path of arctic discovery."

By September 25, 1837, the party was at winter quarters, Fort Confidence, on Great Bear Lake, increased in number by Dease's native wife, niece, and granddaughter.

On January 22 and 23, 1838, they reported to the Company on the state of affairs and on their future plans. On the 29th Simpson wrote to the Governor in more personal vein. He calls Dease a worthy man but "dull and indolent." Simpson's own plans involve a start in March to survey the route to the Coppermine. "The plan of the portage by stages is entirely my own, and I have every hope of effecting this laborious duty successfully."

To Alexander he wrote gloating over a triumph where everybody thought the expedition would fail: "All our letters despond of our last summer's success . . . and the Governor tells us to try the western coast again. Ha! ha! . . . My singular march from Boat Extreme to Cape Barrow put the coping-stone to that job. . . . Dease is a worthy, indolent, illiterate soul, and moves just as I give the impulse." Thomas reminisces nostalgically of their mother and their home life and says, "Why were we born poor and friendless, when many a dolt inherits a fair estate?"

A report signed by Dease and Simpson on April 20, 1838, tells of the winter's work. Simpson had by that time explored the country from Confidence to the Coppermine along three different lines. On the second of these journeys he conducted the "whole disposable force of men and dogs, laden with part of our provisions and baggage, for the ensuing summer," to a spot on Kendall River which he had selected for a depot. Nowhere in the report, which as we have said both men signed, is there mention of a journey of any sort by Dease.

On June 6 the boats were conveyed by ice to the mouth of Dease River. The party reached the portage to Dismal Lakes (discovered by Simpson the previous winter), and on the 19th arrived at Kendall River, where they found their depot and the two men left there, with Hare Indian hunters, successful in the hunt. One of these two men was Flett.

By June 20 the party reached the Coppermine. They descended that stream and worked their way east from its mouth along the north shore of the continent with such energy and skill as had not previously been displayed on these coasts. A comparison of Simpson's description with that of Franklin, who had been before him, and with those of travelers who have been there since, will show that Simpson was dealing with one of the most unfavorable years. Still they were, by August 9, only three miles short of Franklin's ultimate point. But here the boats were stopped and had to remain icebound till the 19th. Seventeen years before, Franklin had reported from the same place worry over thunder squalls and the heavy waves of an ice-free sea. The Franklin kind of season would have taken the Simpson party several hundred miles to the eastward.

With these ten days spent in idleness, the frosts of autumn beginning to appear, and a long journey back to their winter quarters, Simpson decided upon the only thing possible—to take a light canvas canoe for ferrying across rivers and walk ahead with a party of men, a round journey of ten days. Dease would remain behind with the two boats; if the wind changed and drove the ice from the shore he would follow Simpson in one of the boats, leaving the other with most of the supplies under guard for the return.

Every man in the party volunteered to accompany Simpson; he chose seven and started east. Within an hour or two they passed Franklin's Point Turnagain and commenced the new work. During that time they walked a hundred miles, the men carrying heavy packs but Simpson a lighter, for he had to be running to the tops of hills to spy out the country, to map it, and to determine what course should be taken. During this time, Simpson gave the name of "our most gracious sovereign Queen Victoria" to the land north of the strait named after Dease. The first prominent headland he named after his predecessor Captain Franklin, and shortly before turning back another conspicuous headland after his brother Alexander. Aside from this he cultivated his superiors of the Company and others who might be useful to his future advancement by the names he assigned. He called Mount George "after my respected relative, Governor Simpson," and Cape Pelly after the head of the Hudson's Bay Company in London. The farthest islands he could see when he had to turn back "received the name of the first Lord of the Admiralty, the Earl of Minto."

Simpson's farthest was on the east of what is now called the Kent Peninsula. From that eastward-facing coast he saw an open sea which he rightly conjectured would lead to the mouth of Back River. To the sanguine Thomas this would mean a pass to the discovery of the Northwest Passage. Since he could not proceed now for that demonstration, he would return to the attack next year. The fame which he so burningly desired would have to be made secure.

Simpson's journal records an abundance of game. On the way east they saw only the tracks of deer, but there were moulting geese and bands of musk oxen. On the way back they saw caribou herds. "One magnificent buck marched before us, like a doomed victim, for two days, and was shot near our last encampment" before the reunion with Dease.

According to the official report, as given above, there was joint agreement that progress was stopped by insuperable natural difficulties on the 20th, but a letter written by Thomas to the Governor tells a different story. There is triumph as well as complaint:

"All that has been done is the fruit of my own personal exertions, achieved under circumstances of peculiar difficulty. I speak not of the difficulties of the way—these I have never much regarded; but of those of opinion with which I have had to struggle.

"My worthy senior, like Franklin and Back, was alarmed

by the storms, the snow, and frost, in August, . . . and insisted that the 20th of that month, the date fixed for the return of the Government expeditions, should also be that of ours."

Simpson represents himself as having been loath to return, thinking that the clearest sea and some moderate weather would come in September, and says that had he been in command he would have tried to get far enough east to connect his surveys with those of Ross and Back, and that he could have done so. "But," he continues, "my excellent senior is so much engrossed with family affairs, that he is disposed to risk nothing; and is, therefore, the last man in the world for a discoverer. I write not in anger but in sorrow; I esteem Mr. Dease for his upright private character, while I cannot help regarding him and his followers as a dead weight upon the expedition."

On the return journey conditions were as good as they had been bad on the way east, and they reentered the Coppermine in four days. At Bloody Fall there was an argument with Dease, Sinclair, and M'Kay, who said further ascent was impracticable. Thomas writes to the Governor: "I, however, carried my point against them all; and instead of abandoning our boats (and with them next year's voyage) . . . we got them safely up to near the junction of the Kendall River. . . . The opinions I expressed regarding the Coppermine . . . in every particular proved correct: showing that ten years' experience well applied may be more valuable than that of a life-time."

Some writers call Thomas smug; others say that he was arrogant. He may have been either or both. Having forced his will on the others, he did not refrain from pointing out that they and not he had been in error. The triumph, with the preenings on it, cannot have endeared him to Sinclair or M'Kay, and this may have had some bearing on what his letter goes on to report, that since the return he has had trouble in keeping the expedition together. Dease was apparently longing for recall, and "Sinclair and several others" applied for discharge. Thomas says that, "to bring the matter to a point," he offered to continue the explorations with one boat crew of volunteers. The offer did not please. However, while nobody wanted to back out, the indications are that only Simpson was much interested in completing the work.

Thomas wrote to Alexander: "Had I not been, like Sinbad the sailor, hampered with an old man on my back, I should have immediately turned eastward [i.e. August 29] with both boats; but the apprehensions of my useless senior and of the crews overpowered my single voice. . . . For myself, I am still—and I glory in it—but a clerk in their Honours' service, though I have won a distinguished place among Northern Discoverers. I hope it may be as you say, that a wider field will be opened to me; though I confess I apprehend some slippery trick on the part of the concern on which my discoveries throw lustre."

Simpson's disappointment, so plainly shown by his letters, was soothed in December when news from England bore much commendation of his Point Barrow journey. The eastward venture was also widely reported and the Royal Geographical Society awarded him its gold medal—"a convincing proof," says Alexander, "that it esteemed him [and not Dease] the real director of the expedition."

Alexander is here reading into the award more than the Society itself says. The *Geographical Journal* (Vol. IX, 1839) misprints the name as George Simpson, though obviously Thomas is meant. The actual statement in the *Journal* is: ". . . the Council has awarded the Founder's Medal for the year 1838 to Mr. George Simpson, of the Hudson's Bay Company service, who, in conjunction with, and under the immediate orders of, Mr. P. W. Dease, traced the hitherto unexplored coast to the west between Return Reef and Point Barrow, in 1837; and during the past year has discovered 90 miles of coast eastward from Point Turnagain of Franklin, on the northern shore of America."

The winter of 1838–39 was spent at Fort Confidence. No signs of discontent appear, though Sinclair twice narrowly escaped starvation through being sent out with hunters and being joined by more elderly Indians (who heard rumors of their success) than he could provide for. On the first occasion he returned with them "in a reduced state" for the hunters had bolted and the entire party had been living on scraps of skin. On the second occasion he, M'Kay, and a half-breed were gone for thirty-six days and returned on the verge of starvation for the same reason. However, in June, the expedition was ready to start out.

Before leaving, Thomas prepared his last will and testament, in which he counts his goods and prospects: "Five hundred pounds sterling in the hands of the Hudson's Bay Company; my revisionary share as a chief trader in that concern, worth, at the utmost, fifteen hundred pounds sterling; whatever monies the British Government may award me for the acknowledged discovery in the year 1837, of the long-sought North-West passage, or may arise from the publication of my maps and journal; and my half-share of a house and garden in the town of Dingwall, in the highlands of Scotland." Alexander was named coexecutor and residuary legatee.

In 1839 the Simpson party had normal conditions and made good use of them. Descending the Coppermine and working rapidly east they reached Cape Alexander by July 26. They continued ahead beyond the last year's farthest along the continental shore through a body of water which three-quarters of a century later the Canadian maps began to call Queen Maud Gulf, and entered Simpson Strait at its eastern end where the water narrows between the mainland and King William Island. Passing through, they reached a farthest at Castor and Pollux Bay on the mainland, east of King William Island.

The return was equally successful. The party were back at the mouth of the Coppermine in mid-September after a boat journey which is reckoned at 1,408 miles, probably the longest small-boat exploratory voyage ever made in American Arctic seas. They were home at Fort Simpson October 14.

In his diary when near the farthest east Thomas had forecast a continuation of the expedition, he hoped in 1840, which would complete the demonstration that he had discovered the Northwest Passage. This would compel for him that fame which he so burningly desired, which he felt he had already largely earned, and for which he thought himself qualified through native ability and through that competence which he had acquired by years of frontier training.

The desire of Simpson for an enduring fame, and his high estimate of his own qualities and accomplishments, have been thought to indicate a growing and by this time overweening megalomania which, thwarted, finally led him to suicide. It is therefore pertinent to introduce outside testimony on these points.

One of the deepest and most conscientious students of Arctic history was General A. W. Greely, who has more often been criticized for grudging recognition of his fellow explorers than for overpraise. From passages of general praise for Simpson that are unusual in Greely, we select examples that are found between pages 117 and 121 of his *Handbook of Polar Discovery* (fifth edition):

> "In 1836 the Hudson Bay Company decided to send out an expedition 'to endeavor to complete the discovery and survey of the northern shores of the American continent.' . . .
>
> "The undertaking was viewed by many as impracticable; but among the many energetic and capable employees of the Hudson Bay Company were found two men, whose capacities and judgment were deemed equal to the undertaking. These men were P. W. Dease and Thomas Simpson,—Dease the older, the more experienced, but the latter a man of great ambition and singular resolution, to whose personal exertions may be attributed the wonderful results that flowed from this expedition. They may be well called wonderful, for Simpson succeeded in reaching Point Barrow to the west, and the westerly shore of King William Land to the east. Thus by overlapping the discoveries of Beechey in one direction and the later route of Sir John Franklin in the other, Simpson directly established in conjunction with these two the existence of a northwest passage by water. . . ."

After finding that "Simpson's journeys far exceeded Franklin's in length and duration" Greely has an explanation to the effect that Simpson had mastered the ways of the country, while Franklin, Back, and Richardson were outsiders. Along the same line Greely says:

"As only nine years later the Franklin expedition perished from starvation on this very land, it is interesting to note that Simpson reports it in 1839 as 'a country, abounding in reindeer, musk-cattle, and old native encampments.'"

Simpson's determination to complete the Northwest Passage, or to demonstrate its completion, was conveyed to the Directors of the Hudson's Bay Company in the guise of bolstered joint recommendations from the two commanders. Under date of October 16, Dease and Simpson point out that the failure of Back's expedition with the *Terror* leaves a gap in the information about the Passage, and they urge a plan proposed by Simpson "to perfect this interesting service, which . . . he is prepared to follow up whenever the limited means required are placed at his disposal."

Simpson remained at the Fort to write the narrative of the expedition and to draw up maps of the eastern discoveries. He was enthusiastic about plans for further work in 1840. Dease, because of eye trouble and family affairs, would withdraw. The command would devolve upon Thomas who would explore Boothia Felix, determining whether or not it was an island. If Boothia proved to be a peninsula, he had hopes of reaching the Cape Walker of Parry. In one way or another he would determine the eastern mouth of the Northwest Passage as clearly as he had determined the western. He considered himself already the discoverer of the long-sought water route to the Indies, but he desired to round out the job, to tie up the loose ends.

"The expense of finishing what will remain undetermined by the present expedition may, I think, be safely assumed at half *its* cost. No one can have more reason than myself to wish that this year may witness the conclusion of our labours . . . but if, as I have supposed in this letter, another expedition be required, in consequence of Captain Back's failure to the eastward, I again offer myself unreservedly to command it on the scale which I have proposed."

But the Governor ruled that instead of proceeding with his explorations Thomas should repair to the depot and take a winter's leave of absence, during which plans would be matured for completing the service. Was that, as some feel, a beginning of obstructionist tactics by the Governor, and done because he feared that a complete description of the Northwest Passage might lead to its extensive use, to the rapid colonization of the northern half of North America, to the breakdown of the Company's monopoly, to the ruin of its fur business?

On October 25, 1839, Thomas replied, protesting the suggestion that he take a rest. "So far from wishing to avail myself of the leave of absence, which you have so kindly offered unasked, it gives me great uneasiness that a whole year will probably elapse before the final expedition can be set on foot that is destined to accomplish this *North-east*, as my excursion to Point Barrow in 1837 achieved the *North-west*, Passage. . . .

"As for what remains to be done, I am so far from seeking to convert it to my future advantage, that, with my life, I hereby place at your disposal, towards meeting the expenses of the new expedition, should there be any obstacle, the sum of five hundred pounds, being every shilling I am worth at this moment, besides all the future proceeds of my double commission, till the whole charge of the said expedition shall be redeemed.

"Fame I will have, but it must be *alone*. My worthy colleague on the late expedition frankly acknowledges his having been a perfect supernumerary . . ."

It has a bearing on future events that Simpson at this stage desired to have with him again on his coming expedition both M'Kay and Sinclair. He gives as reason that they had been with Back and so knew the Great Fish River (now called Back River).

Thomas remained at Fort Simpson until December 2, when he left for Red River, arriving there February 2, 1840, after an absence of three years and two months.

When no word of acquiescence or encouragement for the

Northwest Passage work could be pried out of the Governor, Thomas addressed the Directors of the Company in England. On June 3, 1840, London accepted his proposal. Thomas never received that news.

From Red River on May 26, 1840, Thomas writes to Alexander of the year's happenings: "Wretchedness is the inevitable portion of all who remain too long in this service. My own situation at present is a very singular one—uncertain till the canoes arrive whether I shall turn my face again to the North Pole, or towards Merry England."

Alexander's narrative says that the Directors, having ratified the proposal, were anxious that Thomas should start on the new expedition immediately. "Unfortunately, the proceedings of their local representative, Sir George Simpson, had been very different . . . and now [he] effectually prevented the immediate organization of a renewed expedition . . . by desiring his [i.e. Thomas's] presence in England."

However, we know from Thomas's letter of May 26 quoted above, that if he received no word about the new expedition he intended to go to England anyway. His letter of May 25 to Chief Factor Donald Ross is explicit on the subject:

"I fear that the contemplated expedition cannot proceed this year, if His Excellency comes not out. In that case it is my intention to proceed direct to England, via St. Peter's [i.e. Minneapolis] and the United States, and to urge the matter at home 'in person.'

"I have little or no doubt of succeeding, both there and in the Gulf of Boothia, and the intermediate jaunt, through the new to the old country, will benefit my health, which I find has suffered more than I suspected during the last four years of toil and anxiety."

No word from London on Thomas Simpson's plans came to Red River by the spring canoes which arrived June 2. On June 6, 1840, he set out for England via the United States.

The next news Alexander had of Thomas was by a New York paper which reached him at the Sandwich Islands in January, 1841, and which carried an article headed "Extraordinary Murder and Suicide!"

We quote from that paper, the New York *American* of August 3, 1840, which in turn is quoting from the St. Louis *Bulletin* of July 24:

Northern Passage: *Lamentable Suicide of one of the Discoverers*

.   .   .   .

It appears that on their return to York Factory—the principal depot of the Hudson's Bay Company—that they both [Dease and Simpson] set out for England, eager to grasp the rich reward which the British Government never fails to lavish upon all her citizens who contribute anything towards extending her widespread domains—or to perpetuating her well earned fame. On the arrival of the two young men at Lake Winnepick, they disagreed about the route which should be pursued, and there separated. Mr. Simpson, accompanied by Mr. Bird, Mr. Legros, and twenty or thirty of the colonists, struck across for St. Peters, intending to push on to New York, via the Lakes, and from thence sail for Liverpool. Dr. Dace [Dease], his compeer, with another party set out for the Canadas.

About the 20th of June, Mr. Simpson and his party had reached Turtle river, where they encamped for the night. He had from the beginning of the journey, exhibited occasional symptoms of mental hallucination, caused as the party supposed, by the dread of being outstripped by his competitor in their long race for London. On the evening above mentioned, he had continued to push on until a late hour at night, and even then his feverish state of excitement deprived him of nourishment or rest.

When they stopped, and while in the act of camping, Mr. Simpson turned suddenly round, and shot Mr. Bird through the heart; and before the astounded party could fly from the presence of the madman, he discharged the other barrel, and mortally wounded Mr. Legros. It appears the party had separated; and when he committed the murder on his companions, there were only two more present—one of them a son of Legros—who immediately fled a short distance. The dying father earnestly implored Simpson to permit his son to return and embrace him before he should die—which he agreed to, and beckoned them back, saying there was nothing to fear.

On their return, Simpson accused Legros of conspiring with Bird, and asked him whether it was not their intention to assassinate him that night? the dying man said it was, but on being interrogated a second time, he denied having any intention or design of such a deed, and shortly after he expired. Simpson then ordered the two men to bridle their horses and prepare to return with him to the settlement, but no sooner were they mounted, than they dashed off in quest of the main body, and overtook them about 18 miles ahead.

They all returned in the morning, and when they had reached within 200 yards of the camp, they got a glimpse of Simpson at the door of his tent, and immediately afterwards heard a report of a gun; supposing that he was determined to carry out the work of destruction which he had begun, they attempted to intimidate him by firing three volleys in the direction of the camp, and then approached it cautiously. When they came up, they found their commander weltering in his blood, and on closer examination found that he had literally blown his head to pieces!

"Far in the wild, unknown to public view" were the three bodies committed to the same grave by their companions, who then pursued their route with feelings more easily conceived than described.

The party arrived at St. Peters about the first of July, in possession of the important papers, and other property belonging to the ill-fated Simpson.

.   .   .   .

There are, of course, obvious flaws in the above story. There was no race between Dease and Simpson, for instance. If Dease had wanted to go to England, he had plenty of time to do so between October 14, 1839, when he left Thomas at Fort Simpson and June 6, 1840, when Thomas left Red River for the United States. The New York *American* of August

13, 1840, quotes the Montreal *Gazette* as considering the whole story a fabrication:

In the first place, it remains to be accounted for, why Messrs. Simpson and Dease should discover such haste in prosecuting a journey to England. In the second place, it is extraordinary that two gentlemen, who had so long and so far travelled together on the best possible terms, should fall out about the best route either to Canada or New York, at Lake Winnepick, where, if we may judge from the map and the information of travellers in that part of the continent, there is but one sure and expeditious route to the great lakes. And in the third place, we believe that recent intelligence has been received in this city from the interior, without any allusion whatever being made to the deplorable catastrophe alluded to in the St. Louis Bulletin.

Confirmation of the deaths was, however, received from Martin McLeod, St. Peter's, July 20, 1840, and was printed in the New York *American* on August 31.

There were two eyewitnesses to the tragedy—James Bruce and Antoine Legros, Jr. From Legros seemingly no deposition was ever taken. The deposition of James Bruce was made at St. Peter's on July 13, 1840, nearly a month after the event. It was sworn to before Henry H. Sibley, "Justice of the Peace, Clayton County, Iowa" (in 1840 the Minnesota area was attached to Iowa for certain governmental purposes). We quote in full:

Be it known, that on the 13th day of July, 1840, personally appeared before Henry H. Sibley, a Justice of the Peace in and for said county, duly commissioned and sworn, James Bruce of the Red River Colony, Prince Rupert's Land, who, being duly sworn upon the Holy Evangelists of Almighty God, touching his knowledge of the events connected with the death of Thomas Simpson, Antoine Legros, and John Bird, deposeth and saith,

That Deponent left said Red River Colony, in company with several individuals; and that, on the ninth day thereafter, said Deponent, with four others, to wit, said Thomas Simpson, Antoine Legros, senior, and John Bird, as also the son of said Legros, Antoine Legros, junior, left the main camp, with a view of travelling with greater expedition than said main body on their way to St. Peter's. That some days after, having thus separated from said main body, said Thomas Simpson complained of being unwell, and expressed a wish to return. On the morning of the 14th of June he again insisted upon returning to said Red River Colony, and offered a considerable sum of money to each of the others composing the party, if they would return with him, (said Simpson,) to said Colony. Said Simpson appeared very restless and uneasy, and Deponent heard said Simpson express a conviction that he would never recover from his illness. Said Simpson complained of no particular ailment, merely stating that he was not well; and when told that he would meet with a physician at 'Lac qui parle,' said Simpson said, in reply, that a physician could do him no good, and that he did not require one. In consequence of the desire expressed by said Simpson to return, on the 14th of June aforesaid, Deponent, with the rest of the party, turned back to join the main camp; and said Simpson was assured, that upon their rejoining said main body, should he, said Simpson still insist upon going back to said Red River Colony, fresh horses should be furnished, and he, said Simpson, be accompanied back to said Colony. On the evening of the said 14th of June Deponent, with his party, encamped about an hour and a half after sun down within a mile of Turtle River; said Simpson was asked if he would have the tent pitched, to which he replied that it was just as the others pleased. While Deponent was engaged with John Bird and Antoine Legros, junior, aforesaid, in raising the tent, Deponent, having his back towards said Simpson, heard the report of a gun; and, on turning round, perceived that said Simpson had shot said Bird through the body. The said Bird groaned and fell dead. Deponent then saw said Simpson turn and shoot said Antoine Legros, senior, with the other barrel of his double-barrelled gun. Said Legros, senior, did not fall immediately, but leaned upon a cart—he fell about two minutes afterwards. Immediately upon the report of the second barrel of said Simpson's gun, Deponent and said Legros, junior, fled a short distance from the cart, when said Simpson called out to Deponent, and asked him, if he, (said Deponent,) was aware of any intention to kill him, (Simpson,) to which Deponent replied, that he had never heard of such intention on the part of any one. Said Simpson then told this Deponent that his life was perfectly safe; and he further told this Deponent that he had shot Bird and Legros because they had intended to murder him, (Simpson,) on that night for his papers; and further, said Simpson told this Deponent that the laws of England would clear him, (Simpson) from all blame in the matter. Said Legros, senior, who was still alive, then asked said Simpson to allow his (Legros') son to go away unharmed, to which said Simpson consented. Said Simpson then offered this Deponent five hundred pounds to take him, said Simpson, back to the Red River Colony, and keep the affair secret. Said Simpson then asked this Deponent if he would know the road back to Red River, to which this Deponent replied 'Yes.' Said Simpson then told this Deponent to harness the horses. This Deponent remained a considerable time standing in the same place; and Legros, senior, aforesaid, called his son to him, bidding him kiss him for the last time. The said Simpson then asked said Legros, senior, whether it was true that he, said Legros and the said Bird intended to kill him (Simpson), to which Legros answered 'No.' Said Simpson remained with his gun in his hand, while Deponent and Legros, junior, went to where the horses had been placed. This Deponent, and said Legros, junior, then each mounted a horse, and made in the direction of the said main camp. Said main camp might be about two hours' ride from the spot where said Simpson, Legros, and Bird had been left; but said Deponent and said Legros, losing the track, did not reach said main camp until the following morning. Immediately after the arrival at said main camp of this Deponent, with said Legros, junior, this Deponent in company with five others, viz. Joseph Gaubin, James Flett, Harry

Sinclair, Robert Logan, and Michel Richotte, returned to the place where said Simpson had been left. Upon approaching, said Simpson was called out to by name by some of this Deponent's party, but no reply was heard. This deponent saw said Simpson lying in bed on the opposite side of the cart from where this Deponent was. The report of a gun was forthwith heard, and the whistling of a ball in the air. A remark was made by one of Deponent's party, that said Simpson must have shot himself. This Deponent, with his party, then made a circle around the cart aforesaid, to ascertain whether he, (Simpson,) could be seen to move. Nothing was seen, however, but a dog lying beneath the cart. Said Deponent, with his party aforesaid, continued to call upon Simpson by name; and receiving no reply, they fired at the said dog, and drove him away. Said Deponent, with his said party, then discharged their guns at the top of the cart, with the intention of alarming said Simpson if still alive. After the lapse of some time, this Deponent asked one of the party to accompany him, this Deponent, to the cart, this Deponent stating at the same time, he was under the impression that said Simpson had shot himself. Upon arriving near the said cart, said Simpson was found by said Deponent to have shot himself through the head. Said Simpson was quite dead, as were also said Legros, senior, and Bird. The bodies of said Simpson, Legros, senior, and Bird, were interred in the same grave; the bodies of the two latter were found covered when this Deponent reached the spot where they had been left. A trunk and carpet-bag with a double-barrelled gun belonging to said Simpson, were brought on to Lac qui parle, and there left in charge of Doctor Williamson of that place. Said Deponent further saith, that at no time had said Simpson manifested symptoms of insanity; but that said Simpson acted through the whole affair like a man in the possession of his senses. And further this Deponent saith not.

his
James X Bruce,
mark.

October 14, 1840, Robert Logan, one of the men who accompanied Bruce and Legros to the Simpson camp, made a deposition at Red River before A. Ross, J.P. He confirms Simpson's first having joined the larger party and afterwards having left it. His story agrees with Bruce's as to what happened after their arrival at the Simpson camp, except that Bruce says he asked one of the party to accompany him and Logan says: "Richotte then mounted his horse, and rode swiftly by the camp, to see if he could observe Mr. Simpson —some others followed. After passing the spot, we all joined again, when Richotte said he saw Mr. Simpson lying as if dead. Henry Sinclair, James Bruce, and myself, then approached the spot; and on seeing all dead, we called out to the others, and they joined us." He agrees with Bruce that the bodies of Legros, Sr., and Bird were covered. He says that: "Mr. Simpson's body was lying stretched out, with one leg across the other, and the butt end of his double barreled gun between his legs, the right hand, with the glove off, directed to the trigger, the left hand, with the glove on, holding the gun, near the muzzle, on his breast."

The testimony of James Flett is dated October 11, 1840, before "John Bunn, Magistrate." He differs from Logan in his account of the discovery of the body. ". . . Michel Richotte galloped on horseback close behind the spot, but still could not see him. We then approached still nearer-by a hollow, but still could not see him. Then James Bruce and Henry Sinclair crawled along the creek, and to within twenty yards, when they called out he was dead." He differs, too, in the position of the body. "We then approached, and saw him lying with his face downwards, near, but not on, a blanket, which was spread alongside of the cart."

Some of the discrepancies in the stories can be explained as tricks of memory. A month had elapsed before Bruce made his deposition; nearly four months had elapsed before there was testimony from Logan and Flett. We agree that Thomas Simpson killed John Bird and Antoine Legros, Sr. Our problems are why Simpson killed them and how and why Simpson died.

We take first the "official" verdict, suicide while of unsound mind. This theory has the advantage of simplicity. A deranged man, after causelessly destroying two other men, puts an end to his own life. MacKay is effective spokesman for this group. He says: "A close reading of young Simpson's personal letters written in the last year of his life gives unmistakable evidence of a rapidly mounting and almost uncontrolled egoism, the culmination of unbounded ambition and the lonely Arctic winters." This would be in considerable part the letters which show that Thomas did not think he was getting a square deal from George.

It has not been usual in books to confront the apologists for the Governor with the judgments of some of those who disagree with them. Let us do just that.

Thomas had a low opinion of George and expressed it in some of his letters. This has been called a sign of mental unbalance. We can make at least the rebuttal that if disapproval of Governor George was proof of unsound mind, then there must have been an epidemic of this mental affliction in the Fur Empire during his reign.

John McLean says of the Governor that he has not even the saving grace to correct his own blunders. "His caprice, his favouritism, his disregard of merit in granting promotion . . . could not have a favourable effect on the Company's interests."

From McLean, employee of twenty-five years, who had resigned smarting with a sense of long-continued mistreatment by the Governor, we turn to a satisfied Company employee of later years who knew not the Governor personally, but who had documents and later events at his disposal. MacKay says: "In physical and mental buoyancy lay [George] Simpson's strength as an administrator, but in 1832 . . . even these qualities temporarily failed. He wrote to Chief Factor J. G. McTavish, 'I myself am become so melancholy and low spirited that I scarcely know what enjoyment is, in fact . . . I feel that my health and strength are falling off rapidly. I am most anxious to get away from this Country of which I am sick & tired but my means do not enable me to shake off the Harness.' "

Thus we have from the Governor himself, quoted by a historian who is on the verge of being his apologist, substantiation that it was not wholly imaginary with Thomas or spiteful with McLean to consider themselves and others to be victims of the Governor's moods and bents.

We note the use of the word "temporarily" in the MacKay statement. It is possible that the Governor recovered quickly, and that Thomas Simpson and John McLean were making capital out of what was really a brief illness.

However, we have some evidence that the difficulty persisted. For in his *Life of Lord Strathcona*, Beckles Willson quotes a letter from John Stuart to Alexander Stewart, written from London on February 15, 1836, which first praises the Governor's kindness of heart and innate goodness and then concludes with the statement, "But he is alike easily influenced by the flattery and prejudice of others, and when once aroused, excitable and without much reflection, will go any lengths."

For still a year later MacKay quotes an uncle's advice to a newcomer: "The only, or at least the chief drawback is that you are dependent upon the goodwill and caprice of one man who is a little too addicted to prejudices, for speedy advancement . . . It is his foible to exact not only strict obedience, but deference to the point of humility. As long as you pay him in that coin you will quickly get on his sunny side and find yourself in a few years a trader at a congenial post, with promotion in sight."

In 1842, thus two years after the death of Thomas, James Evans began to preach to the Indians against working on Sunday. This led the missionary into difficulties with the Governor. Egerton Young, writing the biography of Evans, says that many Company officials secretly assured Evans of their confidence and friendship, "but such was the despotic power of the governor and the dread that all had of his vengeance, that they could not openly avow it without suffering. All their promotions were absolutely in his hands. . . . Years of faithful service were nothing to him. He only promoted those who did his will and with servile obedience carried out all his commands."

Thus, through a period which covers the years of Thomas Simpson's growing dissatisfaction with the Governor, we have from various people testimony that remains constant and similar to that of Thomas. It has not been suggested that any of these, except Thomas, were having delusions when they wrote as they did.

True enough, MacKay says of McLean that his picture is unfair and quotes A. C. Anderson, who had served in the Company with McLean, to the effect that he is sure McLean would wish that much of what he had written in disappointment and anger had not been written.

This may be true. We cannot say that it is not. But we can point out that, had McLean wanted to retract, he had plenty of time to do it. His book was published in 1849 and his death occurred in 1890. *Elora,* by John R. Connon, a book compiled in 1906 and published in 1930, has an account of McLean's later years but does not indicate that he ever retracted a word of his narrative.

However, Thomas Simpson's anger and irritation were not directed against the Governor alone. We have seen how he characterized Dease—worthy but indolent, an old man of the sea. This characterization has been used against Thomas, for others (who had not been in the field with Dease) did not share his opinion. For instance, a charge of selfishness and perhaps arrogance is aimed by McLean at Thomas Simpson, as McLean testifies for "my friend Mr. Dease" with regard to the narrative of the expedition which, appearing after Simpson's death and not edited for the press by him, was nevertheless strictly his in wording, as we know by the testimony of Edward Sabine. McLean says ". . . I cannot help expressing my surprise at the manner Mr. Dease's name is mentioned . . . where he is represented as being employed merely as purveyor. It might have been said with equal propriety that Mr. Simpson was employed merely as astronomer. The fact is, the services of both gentlemen were equally necessary; and to the prudence, judgment, and experience of Mr. Dease, the successful issue of the enterprise may undoubtedly be ascribed, no less than to the astronomical science of Mr. Simpson."

On Dease, as well as on how men earned (or were supposed to earn) promotion, we next quote from *A Canoe Voyage from Hudson's Bay to the Pacific . . . Journal of the late Factor Archibald McDonald*, edited by Malcolm McLeod (Ottawa, 1872). The quotation is from a McLeod note (page 76):

"Mr. Dease was at the head of the Franklin Expedition of 1825–6–7, in conducting it in all its workings, details, commissariat, &c., leaving the higher work of taking observations and making notes by the way free and untrammeled to Sir John Franklin. He did his work well; and according to what has ever been a rule with the company in such case, Mr. Dease was at once promoted from his Chief Tradership to Chief Factorship, which is a 'double share,' and entails no extra work."

From these testimonials for Dease it does appear that Thomas Simpson was unfair and to that extent unbalanced. But it is at least possible that he was justified in his opinions, and then guilty of no more than having expressed them violently. We get light on this by consulting another who knew Dease in the field, Sir John Franklin.

According to Franklin, the judgment of Dease was not quite up to McLean's view of it. Predisposed to favor Dease, and indeed having specifically requested that he accompany the expedition, Franklin appointed him to take charge of "whatever related to the procuring and issuing of provision, and the entire management of the Canadian voyagers and Indians" on his second expedition.

Dease arrived at Fort Franklin on July 27, 1825. Getting off to a wrong start, he chose the site on which the fort was to be built for its "proximity to that part of the lake where the fish had usually been most abundant"—occupying the site of an abandoned fort of the North-West Company where all the wood in the vicinity had long since been used up and where Franklin's party had "to convey the requisite timber in rafts from a considerable distance, which, of course, occasioned trouble and delay."

By February there was anxiety at winter quarters. The nets were not providing enough fish for the party and the provisions which had been set aside for the voyage along the coast had to be used. Franklin wrote Governor Simpson ordering further supplies. The situation continued until an Indian came along and said fish were plentiful elsewhere, at a station (later called McVicar Arm) where there were Dogrib Indians.

Throughout the Franklin *Narrative*, wherever Dease appears there is incompetence, laziness, near starvation. There is as well the implication that Dease was not a man of his word, in consequence of which he could not get results from Indians, whether neighbors or members of his own party. And all this from Franklin—no shining light for competence himself, but kind and the soul of honor.

Thomas Simpson has also been blamed (with an undertone of the mental-unbalance suggestion) for sneering at Captain Back. Was this because he feared Back's success might overshadow his own? Or was he jealous of a success already secure? On this we have independent testimony.

Richard King, as we have said, was with Back on the Great Fish River expedition. His book, *Narrative of a Journey to the Shores of the Arctic Ocean* (London, 1847) is full of illustrations of Back's incompetence—having a base 200 miles from the scene of operations so that boats had to be dragged this distance; using boats too heavy to lift over portages, and the like. King says that, under such leadership, none of the party ever expected to reach the sea at all. He accuses Back of leaving undone work which he ought to have done. We quote sample remarks:

" 'Why not have ascertained the correctness of the Isthmus of Boothia?' has again been asked; 'since, although prevented . . . from proceeding westerly, an open sea was exposed to view in an easterly direction, and the distance not more than one hundred and sixteen miles—one day's sail or two days' labour only.' This, I beg leave to state, is Captain Back's affair: but I may remark, that his orders were contradictory to such a course; and the impropriety of restricting an officer to this or that line of route . . . is made evident by the equipment of an expedition as lately as July last, at an expense of certainly not less than twenty thousand pounds, to ascertain a fact which might have been determined in a few hours, had the commander of the late expedition been in possession of discretionary orders. The blame, however, does not rest altogether with the Government; for in such services the officer undertaking the enterprise generally dictates his own orders;—at least, such was the case with Captain Back."

Eight years after the book we have just quoted, King returns to the attack in his *The Franklin Expedition from First to Last*. He is still convinced of Back's ineptitude and calls in, for support, a letter from Charles Ross, at York Factory, dated November 7, 1836, wherein Ross says: "Both he, [Peter Taylor] as well as your other companions in adventure, are high in your [i.e., King's] praise, while Sir George Back is the theme of their aversion and contempt."

If King is permitted to write thus of Back without being accused of overweening ambition and a progressive mental decay, why not Simpson, whose ideas on the conduct of an expedition were somewhat similar to King's, and who would be annoyed at the same incompetencies?

To accept MacKay's version calls for more than discounting the independent testimony we have quoted. It calls for accepting other things which are hard to fit in. Just when Thomas was writing to Alexander and to the Governor with what MacKay thinks "almost uncontrolled egoism," he was also writing his *Narrative*. Many judges find that book straightforward. The Earl of Ellesmere, for instance, says of it: "For judicious selection of topics and incidents, for clearness and simplicity of description, it is the model of a diary, and, like the masculine and modest character of the man, reflects honour on Mr. Simpson's venerable Alma Mater, King's College, Aberdeen."

If we accept MacKay's view, we must believe that an unbalanced mind, trending toward insanity through an "almost uncontrolled egoism," can write with clearness and simplicity, that it can make judicious selection, and that it can reflect a modest character throughout a whole book.

At this point it may be asked: How do we know Simpson's printed book was not edited and toned down from such a manuscript as would have sustained the MacKay doctrine?

The full answer to that comes later in our story. We merely say here that Colonel Edward Sabine, whose integrity no one has questioned, edited the manuscript and that he reports making only changes so slight that Thomas Simpson's original manuscript could as well have been published verbatim.

The theory "officially" adopted when Thomas Simpson died, and held by several writers to this day, also wants us to believe, among other things, that an insane man kills two of his companions and is immediately thereafter talked out of killing two more. He spends a night with the corpses of those he has killed and then becomes sufficiently lucid to know what the return of the party means to him. He thereupon commits suicide to escape from the consequences.

We have given the contemporary testimony of James Bruce that at no time had Thomas acted otherwise than as a man in full possession of his faculties. This witness did not sway MacKay against evidence of mental decay which he thought he could read from the letters of Thomas Simpson. William Kay Lamb, Librarian and Archivist of the Provincial Library and Archives, Victoria, British Columbia, is custodian of the largest collection of unpublished contemporary documents known to us that bear on our case. These are "Two Hundred and Nine Hitherto Unpublished Private Letters in the Personal Files of Chief Factor Donald Ross of Norway House, Including Correspondence from Sir George Simpson, Sir James Douglas of the Columbia, Earl Cathcart, Thomas Simpson the Explorer, Bishop Anderson of Rupert's Land, Peter Skene Ogden of the Oregon, and Other Chief Officers of the Hudson's Bay Company and Their Contemporaries." Mr. Lamb has written us on the sanity problem under date June 19, 1936:

"It so happens that I met Mr. Douglas MacKay in the East, and that we discussed the Simpson problem together. Mr. MacKay was under the impression that certain letters in our manuscript collection seem to indicate that Simpson was in an abnormal state of mind in the period immediately preceding his death, but a careful reading of the letters themselves has given me no evidence in support of this conclusion. The latest of our series [of letters from Thomas Simpson] is dated June 3rd, 1840, and was therefore written within a fortnight of his death, and it certainly bears no evidence of being the composition of an insane or even unbalanced individual."

Mr. Lamb is here talking about the very letter so often used to prove Thomas Simpson's unbalance. Of it MacKay says: "Three days before setting out for the south, he wrote of the deep depression that was upon him and of his 'destiny' being settled."

Having quoted witnesses on both sides, we now turn over to the reader for his own judgment the full text of the letter itself. It was written to Donald Ross by Thomas Simpson from Fort Garry, June 3, 1840:

"Yesterday evening our anxiety was partly relieved by the arrival of Mr. McDonald with the express canoe, but without the main documents.

"Our excellent governor, I am sorry to find, suffers from sore eyes and his letters are all written by other hands.

"My own destiny is at length decided and I must away across the plains and through the States, to England. John Ritch has been promised a situation for the intervening years, say either at Norway House, the Saskatchewan, or here [i.e. Fort Garry]. As a friend I beg of you not to let Ritch go home, as that would most seriously interfere with my plans; place him anywhere he may be most required for boat building, but within reach at the specified time.

"Ooligbuck's [the Eskimo interpreter's] family, as before settled, are to be sent into Great Slave Lake, and 'my little chaps' also, under the woman's care. I suppose that three pounds would be a fair remuneration to Harper for his trouble. Please to pay him and give the boys only absolute necessaries, as I cannot afford to lay out much money upon them.

"Pray take the necessary steps to add my name to the testimonial to His Excellency, though I have not 'yet' received my commission. I trust that the canoe brought you yours.

"The specimens of plants, birds, etc., that will be sent out by the McKenzie River boats, you will be pleased to forward to England by the ship. There is a box of books at York Factory, sent out by the Company to joint address of Mr. Dease and myself—pray retain it at Norway House and peruse the contents, if worth your notice.

"I am quite ashamed of troubling you with so many commissions, but necessity has no law, and I think I may safely calculate on your friendship, while nothing would afford me greater pleasure than to be able to return your many attentions and kindnesses, in kind.

"With warmest good wishes to Mrs. Ross and your fireside, and referring you to Mr. Ballenden for Red River news, I am ever most faithfully and sincerely yours,

"THOMAS SIMPSON."

The "destiny" may then have been only this: Thomas Simpson had expected word about his new expedition; he did not get it. He therefore had to go to England to press the matter in person. We have already quoted his letter of May 25 to Donald Ross in which he says that such is his intention. And we must not fail to note Thomas Simpson's care in laying upon a personal friend the crucial preparations for the 1841 expedition: The key men for the Boothia venture are to be within reach and free to serve Thomas when he returns from England. These key men are the carpenter Ritch, who is to build the boats for the coming journey, and the Eskimo Ooligbuck, who is to interpret for the travelers when they reach the Arctic coast.

There is no mention of depression in this letter, though one to Alexander dated June 5, 1840, mentions that his spirits are low. We quote that letter also in full:

"My dearest Alexander,

"I am just on the move for England, *via* the United States; a journey which will, I think, be beneficial to me, as my stomach has been out of order, and my spirits low, for a great part of the spring.

"The light canoe arrived on the 2nd, with Mr. Allan Macdonnell; but most of the letters went on to Norway House.

"I, however, received one from Governor Simpson, written by his Lady, inviting me home. God willing, I shall be out again with him next spring.

"I cannot go into detail regarding friends; it would be a work of supererogation, as you will, no doubt, have volumes from them.

"Our young Queen, you will learn, is mated with her cousin Albert of Cobourg, and the Melbourne ministry is still in power. There are rumours of war with the United States; if true, I may perhaps figure as a *détenu*.

"Three Wesleyan missionaries have come in for Lac la Pluie and the Saskatchewan; and furs have fallen 15 to 20 per cent. in price. Ominous signs these, saying plainly, 'Make hay while the sun shines.' My expenses on this visit will be heavy, and my funds are still light. Government, I fear, will give nothing. However, I shall see.

"To-morrow morning I take my departure, with two companions well mounted and armed, as we expect to fall in with the Sioux, and war is said to be raging in the plains; so that I hope to see something of prairie life.

"Farewell, my dearest brother, and while breath remains believe me ever,

"Your most affectionate brother,

"Thomas Simpson."

But for the insanity theory we should have a plain situation. Thomas Simpson, thirty-one years old, full of enthusiasm about his new plan for exploration and ready to fight for it in England, is on his way home. Whether with or without extensive cooperation from Peter Warren Dease, he had completed a magnificent piece of exploratory work. He knew it. His fame was secure, and he knew that, too—knew it from the time he had reached Point Barrow. Does his letter to the Governor saying, "Fame I will have, but it must be *alone*," mean an ambition so intense that he would seek death when he feared the Governor would try to prevent his perfecting what he (Thomas) regarded as practically completed, the discovery of the Northwest Passage? The sentence need, in fact, mean no more than a determination that this time he shall be in full command, with unshared responsibility for failure of plans, undivided credit for success.

Except for the theory of a persecution complex (which no one has supported beyond proving that Thomas's opinion of his cousin was no higher than that of McLean and several others), suicide while of sound mind renders incredible the one thing no one disputes—the killing of John Bird and Antoine Legros. Why, if disappointment broke his heart, take two innocent men with him? We are, as said, further asked to believe that, after cold-blooded murder, he went to sleep beside his victims, for the disappointment which culminated in suicide is not alleged to have been great enough to make him kill himself at once.

In either of the suicide theories there is at least one more thing unexplained—the behavior of Antoine Legros, Jr. By the testimony of James Bruce, Simpson had a double-barreled shotgun with which he killed two men. After a second shot from a double-barreled muzzle-loader, Simpson was unarmed for some time, since there is no mention of his having a second gun. Antoine Legros, Jr., saw his father shot, heard his father profess innocence, saw him die, and then rode off.

Remember the whole party was specially armed, for the Sioux were on the warpath. Remember, too, that we have no direct testimony from this crucial witness, Legros, Jr. Apparently no deposition by him was ever taken.

Suicide was the "official" verdict. The popular view from the start, or soon thereafter, was either that the manner of death was unknown or that Thomas Simpson had been murdered.

Alexander Simpson, in 1843, was convinced that Thomas was murdered. We have admitted that his opinions were somewhat prejudiced; so we ignore him and pass on to what others have to say.

On April 25, 1841, Chief Factor John Dugald Cameron, writing to James Hargrave, says: "But—do we know all the truth? I feel convinced that we do not . . . I am persuaded—

he shot the two men in self defense, was perhaps himself wounded, or at all events was dispatched the next morning by some one of the returning Party."

In 1845 the Bishop of Montreal in his *Journal* calls the death of Thomas "an occurrence shrouded in mystery and uncertainty."

In 1848 Ballantyne, writing of impressions at Red River from 1840 to 1847, says: "I therefore think, with many of Mr. Simpson's friends and former companions, that he did *not* kill himself, and that this was only a false report of his murderers."

In 1858 the Earl of Ellesmere, while admitting that for lack of details the suicide theory must be temporarily accepted, says that eventually a tardy confession on the part of one of the half-breeds "may confirm our own impression that, after killing two of his half-breed companions, in self-defense, he was murdered in revenge."

In 1887, McArthur's *A Prairie Tragedy* makes a consistent and detailed presentation of the murder theory, and argues that the story of suicide is completely untenable.

If Thomas Simpson did not commit suicide, he was murdered. By whom, then, and why?

Ballantyne, summarizing the views held at Red River from 1840 to 1847, considers that Simpson shot Bird and Legros, Sr., in self-defense and was murdered by one of the survivors. Alexander Simpson believed that when Bruce and Legros, Jr., reached the camp with the others they found Thomas wounded and killed him.

Alexander McArthur, who lived at Winnipeg soon enough to talk with men who knew the parties to the case, was also a profound student of the literary sources. He said in 1887: "Of this we may be sure, that neither Bird nor Legros, Sr., were shot without previous words. There must have been serious disagreement between Simpson and these two men. With weapons in their hands is it likely Simpson alone made use of them? Is it further unlikely that young Legros would have seen his father shot without making an effort to protect or revenge him. . . . To me it is clear, too, that in the mêlée Simpson was seriously wounded. One of the two survivors mounted Simpson's horse and rode away with it. Would he have dared to do this if Simpson were capable of preventing him? Only two things could have prevented him: the want of a loaded weapon or physical weakness."

It may be only a coincidence in names (but surely, then, a remarkable coincidence) that two of the men who rushed back with Bruce and Legros, Jr., toward the wounded or insane Thomas Simpson were James Flett and Harry Sinclair, and that two men who had been with Dease and Simpson on their exploratory work were George Flett and George Sinclair. It is not unreasonable to suspect blood ties between Flett and Flett, Sinclair and Sinclair, for not merely was the white and half-caste population of the Fur Country small in those days, but the Fletts and Sinclairs were looked upon as clans. MacKay observes: "The stories of these men . . . could be told throughout the length of many volumes . . . of the clan of Finlayson . . . the generations of Sinclairs, the McFarlanes, the four Hardistys, the McKays, and the Fletts."

There may have been, then, a long-smouldering grudge in the Flett and in the Sinclair families. By the theory for which McArthur speaks, the returning party found Simpson wounded and one of them killed him. Indisputably Harry Sinclair was present at Simpson's death, whether murder or suicide. George Sinclair had, while with Dease and Simpson, nearly starved to death twice. Five years after Simpson's death the bitterness of Sinclair or M'Kay, or both, delayed John Rae in getting together his expedition; so grudges from the Simpson-Dease expedition did smoulder through at least a decade. How much more bitter they must have been when the grievances were fresh, when Thomas Simpson was returning to England—for all they knew, to receive honors!

We are inclined to have these murder speculations rest lightly on the Fletts, for George Flett had no disastrous experiences with the Simpson-Dease expedition, and he was one of those who, in 1845, were willing to start out with Rae.

The theory that Thomas Simpson was murdered for revenge disposes of everything except his (alleged) statement that there was a plot to assassinate him for his papers. If he was sane, what good would he consider his papers to be to anyone but himself? Alexander replies to that with the suggestion that John Bird, half-breed son of a Hudson's Bay trader, believed Thomas was carrying with him the exclusive secret of the Northwest Passage, a secret which could be stolen, and from which one might become rich. This theory is not implausible, not even improbable. There seems to be no way to prove or disprove it.

Then, too, there has been talk that the murder was instigated by George Simpson, through jealousy of the fame that was to be his cousin's, or, more plausibly, to hinder the development of the Northwest Passage as a route of commerce and thus to delay the settlement of the Fur Lands by agriculturists and the loss of the Company's trade monopoly. Against this, there is the fact that nowhere is there sign that the Governor had homicidal tendencies. He had, if McLean's and similar testimony is correct, on occasion a fine disregard for the lives of his traders. There seems to have been nothing personal in it, but much of devoted loyalty to the Company. McLean, recounting his experiences, ascribes the fact that he and his men were placed in danger of starvation to nothing more sinister than stinginess.

If we absolve Sir George completely, we give ourselves another riddle. Thomas Simpson's effects were delivered by the survivors to an American officer at "Lac qui parle." Alexander Simpson says the manuscript of the narrative did not reach England until October, 1841, while his brother's other papers were not turned over to him until the spring of 1844. He further says, in a letter to Sir George, dated December 2, 1844: "When they reached me a great portion of those letters—I especially advert to those from yourself—were wanting . . . . I hesitate not to assert, that the depositories of my brother were rifled of valuable papers." (McArthur states that the diary, which would have told most of the story, was also missing.)

"The abstractors, though they removed (as no doubt they were ordered to remove) all such papers as might afford me legal grounds for proceeding against the Hudson's Bay Company for the fulfilment of pledges given to my brother, fortunately passed unnoticed a small bundle containing original sketches of letters addressed by my brother to you, previous to and during his Arctic expedition. . . ."

Who abstracted the papers? Who had opportunity? The party with Bruce and Legros had the first opportunity. Suppose, as Alexander considers, the plot to assassinate Thomas arose through his being thought to carry in writing the secret of the Northwest Passage. In such event, the manuscript of his journal, and the mentioned rough drafts of letters to the Governor, might be supposed to contain the secret. These documents, however, were in the parcel received by Alexander.

The American officer at Lac qui parle had opportunity but, so far as we can see, no motive.

Sir George Simpson? Sir George received the papers in May, 1841, while he was at Lake Superior. That statement is contained in his own narrative: "A boat from our establishment brought me the journal and other papers of my late lamented relative, Mr. Thomas Simpson." Sir George, then, had opportunity; for these papers did not reach England until October, 1841.

We have, as said, no evidence to support the idea that Sir George, in his long career, ever plotted with anyone to kill anyone. We have no evidence, either, to prove that he did not go that far in a passionate loyalty to the Company which, unless it be murder, seems to have had no other limit.

W. E. I., writing in the Winnipeg *Free Press* for June 11, 1935, on the ninety-fifth anniversary of Simpson's death, subscribes to the insanity view and says the theory of murder has been controverted, adding: "If it is conceivable that Sir George had any hand in the death of Thomas Simpson, it must be on the supposition . . . that he thought Thomas' activities were against the interests of the Hudson's Bay Company."

If we set aside, for lack of evidence, the idea that Sir George was in the plot, would he have any motive for abstracting certain of the Thomas Simpson documents? There is a hint of such motive in every account of George Simpson, whether the author of it approves of him or not. They all represent him as advancing the Company's interests at all times and in every conceivable way. Those who disliked him, McLean for example, give many examples to show he would do almost anything for the Company. His feelings towards them more resembled patriotism than loyalty to an employer —and with some logic, for the Hudson's Bay Company of those days was no mere trading concern. By arrangement with Great Britain it governed the Fur Country so that opposition to it was in effect a crime against the State—treason.

If Thomas Simpson's statements are correct (and we may accept them since other similar statements are supported by outside evidence) George had promised Thomas two promotions, each of which would increase his salary. On May 20, 1844, Alexander wrote to the Hudson's Bay Company, claiming on behalf of Thomas's estate, the share of profit of a Chief Trader from the year 1837 to 1840, the share of profit of a Chief Factor commencing with 1840, deducting the salary of £100 per annum which Thomas had received during those years. On December 2, 1844, Alexander repeated these claims to the Governor. In other words, he was putting in a bill for between £2,000 and £3,000 as owed the estate of Thomas Simpson by the Honourable Company. The letters from George Simpson, which Alexander considers would have supported this claim, are missing. Were they abstracted by George during the several months when the effects of Thomas were in his possession?

MacKay says of George Simpson for the year he received the papers (1841): "Now he writes to Donald Ross at Norway House about the practice that has grown up of officers sending preserved buffalo tongues to their friends in England. If buffalo tongues are so desirable they should be part of the trade. There are smart penalties for making gifts of furs; why not the same for buffalo tongues?" The loss to the Company from gifts of buffalo tongues would, admittedly, be small. It is at least a possibility that he "advanced the Company interest" by withholding documents that would substantiate a claim of £2,000 to £3,000.

McArthur gives the chief reasons why there is an otherwise strange complexity of doubt on so many things connected with the death of Thomas Simpson: "We are met at the outset with this difficulty that all those interested at once accepted all the charges [i.e. murder and suicide] as true, and acted accordingly. No properly constituted authority ever investigated the charges, nor did any court ever decide upon them. It was possible to have made a thorough and exhaustive examination into all the circumstances, but this was never done. . . .

"There were very apparent ways of settling whether Simpson had shot himself, but we are not told that any of these were adopted. One of the most important points we have not a shred of evidence about. What was the condition of the firearms? Simpson used a double-barrelled gun that night, firing two shots from it, and it is implied he used it next morning—firing one shot. Was the gun loaded in one barrel when the returning party found it? It is in evidence that the guns and pistols were lying on the grass, but this I attach little importance to; they were placed there after the party came up, but why did not the magistrate ask whether the other guns and pistols were loaded or unloaded. . . . Again, while we are told that Simpson was shot in the head, no question was asked as to whether he was shot elsewhere."

McArthur asks the further questions: Why were not Gaubin and Richotte examined? Why did none of the party return to Fort Garry to tell of the tragedy? "Three days travel would have taken them back, and they might be sure their trouble would be rewarded."

Like much that has gone before, the rest of our story is far from pleasant. McArthur, McLean, and Alexander Simpson agree that on the strength of Thomas Simpson's work George Simpson received a knighthood. MacKay dissents, saying the principal basis for the knighthood was probably George Simpson's support of the Crown cause in the Papineau Rebellion and his assistance to the Admiralty's series of Arctic expeditions. In any case, the Company had its charter renewed, and George Simpson was knighted.

We quote McArthur: "Notwithstanding all this, he to whom they were indebted for these benefits and honors received the burial of an outcast. His body was allowed to become prey for wild animals, and it was only when this reached the ears of the governor that orders were given to have his bones picked up on the prairie, and brought here [i.e. Winnipeg] for interment. Bigotry added its mite . . . and burial was refused for what the wolves had left of Thomas Simpson. A grave was dug for him away from those of the good people, and no stick or stone marks the spot."

Alexander had placed a marble tablet as a memorial to Thomas in the parish church at Dingwall, Scotland. During an absence of his the tablet was removed, because of Thomas's alleged suicide. It was later placed in the county buildings of Ross-shire.

As we have said, news of his brother's death reached Alexander in January, 1841. He was then in the Sandwich Islands but started immediately for England, which he reached in May. His brother's manuscript narrative of the Northwest Passage explorations, we know, had not then reached England. It was still in the hands of George Simpson. Alexander "felt much anxiety, as its publication was now the only further evidence that could be given of my brother's merits and services." He soon learned that temporary suppression of the manuscript had been arranged and that it was planned to include it in a compilation to be made at some later date. To substantiate this statement, he quotes a letter from Sir George Simpson to Sir J. Henry Pelly, of February 25, 1841: " 'His' (my brother's) 'Journals or Narrative I should, if you have no objection, wish to be reserved for myself, to be embodied in a work which, if I live to return and can command a little leisure time, I have it in contemplation to publish.' "

Alexander's protests won the promise that the narrative would be published in Thomas's own name. Before the manuscript was received—we have seen that it was not sent to England until October—Alexander was forced to return to Polynesia. Colonel Edward Sabine agreed to revise the manuscript. Alexander quotes a letter from Sabine dated July 18, 1843: "In your absence I undertook to examine the manuscript, and make any alterations which might appear to me to be requried. On perusal, I found the work in a state of such complete preparation, that the alterations which I saw any occasion to make were very few indeed . . . it impressed me with an additionally high respect for your brother's memory, that he should have drawn up the narrative of the expedition on the spot, in such a complete manner that it might well have been printed *verbatim*."

Three of our four chief authorities agree that Sir George owed his knighthood to the work of Peter Dease and Thomas Simpson; one authority gives this no consideration. In any case, in 1840, the year in which Thomas died, the Imperial Government announced its intention of awarding both Dease and Simpson annual pensions of £100 each. Thomas knew nothing of this offer and collected no pension. We have from McLeod the statement that a knighthood was offered Dease, but we do not have any intimation of the date of the offer. Dease declined the honor and accepted the pension, which he presumably collected until his death in 1863.

Alexander appealed in vain to the Hudson's Bay Company as such, to Sir George Simpson, and to the Imperial Government for a payment of monies due the estate of Thomas Simpson. He considered that at least one year's pension was already due. In reply, Alexander received from the Government a brief note expressing Sir Robert Peel's regrets that it was not in his power to appropriate to him any portion of the limited fund for the reward of public service. Alexander countered that the officers of two Government expeditions, sent out to determine the existence of a Northwest Passage, had failed in their aims, and yet promotions and honors were given them. Thomas Simpson had succeeded, "and the claims which he thereby established on his country his death did not abrogate." No reply seems to have been received to this letter.

Part of Alexander's correspondence with the Hudson's Bay Company we have already studied. The answer of the Directors in London to the claims for Chief Trader and Chief Factor promotions (i.e. for some £2,000 to £3,000) was that Sir George Simpson was but a commissioned officer with limited powers, that he had no authority to bestow appointments, and that all he could do at any time was to recommend Thomas (with the approbation of a majority of the Council) to the Governor and Committee. "Whatever promise, therefore, Sir George Simpson may have given your brother, must have been perfectly understood by both parties to be such as he had power to fulfil . . . but cannot, by any reasonable construction, be supposed to imply, that your brother, who had then done nothing whatever to distinguish himself, was to be advanced instanter over the heads of officers who had been more than twice as long in the service, and who had much stronger claims on the Company."

However, we have already noted Thomas Simpson's statement that a nod from George would have meant a Chief Tradership. McLean describes the Governor's as "an authority combining the despotism of military rule with the strict surveillance and mean parsimony of the avaricious trader. From Labrador to Nootka Sound the unchecked, uncontrolled will of a single individual gives law to the land. As to the nominal Council which is yearly convoked for form's sake, the few individuals who compose it know better than to offer advice where none would be accepted; they know full well that the Governor has already determined on his own measures before one of them appears in his presence. Their assent is all that is expected of them, and that they never hesitate to give."

McLean has been called biased, smarting under the same treatment from George that Thomas had received, so we turn to MacKay for evidence that George had powers which were not as limited as the London directors asserted when they were trying to refute Alexander's claims. MacKay does not say outright that the Council had no voice; he believes its members had, but he makes two significant statements: "Control over these annual councils of the field partners is the clearest example of Simpson's authority. . . . In council his policies may have been criticized but his decisions were never reversed."

But whether McLean and MacKay or the Honourable Company have the straight of it, the Company informed Alexander that his claims were "totally inadmissible." McArthur says, however, that the Company paid "but the merest pittance as the balance due to Simpson" to his mother.

The letter from Alexander to Sir George did not receive an answer.

There is one more thing about Thomas Simpson that has been in dispute. MacKay makes the point that while Thomas was writing sneeringly of his cousin, the Governor thought well enough of Thomas to characterize him as "A Scotchman 3 years in the Service 24 years of age . . . is handy & active and will in due time if he goes on as he promises be one of the most complete men of business in the country; acts as my secty or confidential clerk during the busy Season and in the capacities of Shopman, accomptant & Trader at Red River Settlement during the winter—perfectly correct in regard to private conduct & character." This passage has been used to prove the imaginary nature of Thomas's grievances. But, until still unpublished documents prove us wrong, we have no evidence that Thomas complained of his cousin in any way that could be called sneering until 1833, a full year after the above was written; and it was considerably later than that, that he ceased thinking and saying that his cousin meant well and was truly fond of him.

The real affection of the Governor for Thomas, and the approximate depth of his sorrow for his death, we gauge through a paragraph from the Governor's book:

"Early next morning I received occupation enough for one day at least. A boat from our establishment brought me the journal and other papers of my late lamented relative, Mr. Thomas Simpson, whose successful exertions in arctic discovery and whose untimely end had excited so much interest in the public mind. By the same conveyance we got a supply of white fish. This fish, which is peculiar to North America, is one of the most delicious of the finny tribe, having the appearance and somewhat the flavour of trout."

Chapter 4

How Did Andrée Die?

THOSE WHO REMEMBER 1897 will remember the disappearance of Andrée, the Swedish airman, as a world sensation.

Nine years later it was the considered opinion of Gunnar Andersson, eminent scientist, speaking through an official publication of the Swedish Society of Anthropology and Geography, that the departure of no exploring expedition up to that time had ever so captivated the attention of both Europe and America.

There were many reasons why so many were profoundly moved by the launching of the Andrée expedition, and by its failure to return. Andersson puts as first of them that the nineties were times of peaceful and orderly development with few startling spectacles, with few world sensations. There was, too, a spreading fever of interest in polar expeditions. Through the Italian Duke of the Abruzzi, the Norwegian scientist Nansen, the American naval engineer Peary, and through many others there was a steadily developing suspense over which man and which flag would be the first to reach the North Pole. For people were beginning to feel that this former impossibility was now possible—that the winner of the greatest sporting event of all time had already been born, that he was perhaps already one of the leading contenders.

Andrée was one of these contenders. He had announced a plan for reaching the North Pole. The polar spotlight was on him.

There was upon Andrée a second spotlight, that of a rapidly growing belief in man's imminent conquest of the air. This impossibility of the ages was at last beginning to appeal to the general imagination as a probability. The world was not yet conscious of the Wright brothers, but it was more than conscious of half a dozen others who, with publicity rather well organized for those early days of advertising, were draw-

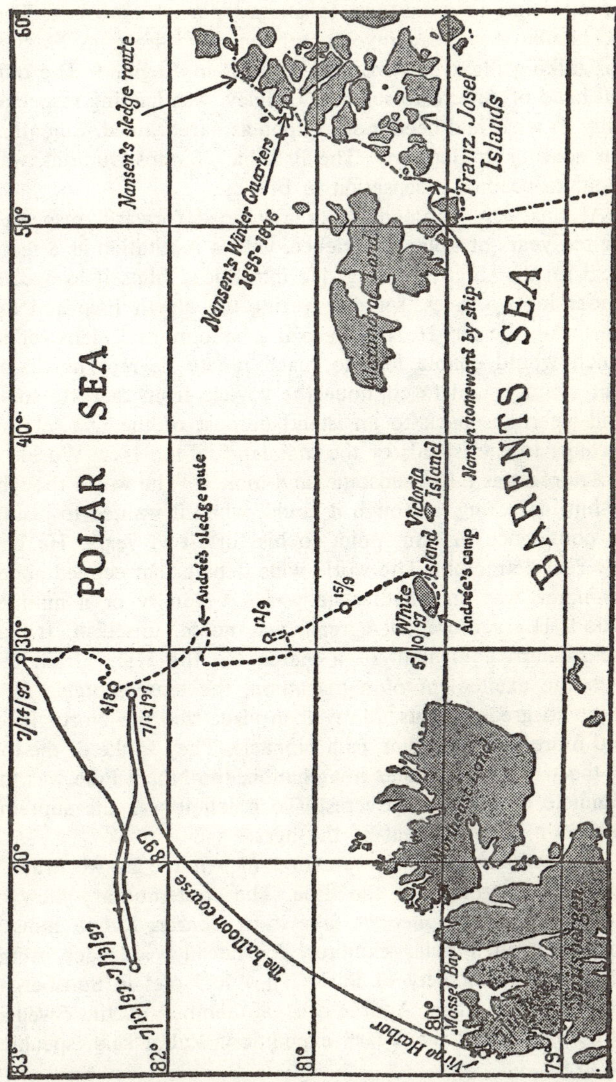

Map showing operations of the Andrée Expedition of 1897 and Nansen's winter quarters, 1895–96. Compiled by Vilhjalmur Stefansson. Base map used by courtesy of H. N. Pallin, from his *Andréegatan,* Uppsala, 1934.

ing attention to plans and to alleged partial successes. The spectacular American inventor of the rapid-fire gun, Maxim, was talking flight and working upon it in England. The official head of American science, Langley, was lending respectability to what had been looked upon as harebrained. Lilienthal was soaring in Germany. The Brazilian, Santos-Dumont, was about to become a sensation in France.

At this tense moment Andrée stepped forward, respected for ten years of polar experience, with a reputation as a technical man of high standing. He introduced himself as a contender in two races, for discovering the North Pole and for mastering the air. He said he had a balloon, and plans for it, which would enable him to reach ninety degrees north, or that vicinity, and to continue the voyage from there to some land—perhaps back to an island outpost of the Old World, perhaps to the islands or the mainland of the New World.

Andrée was tall, handsome, and modest. The world thought of him as young, although it could, when it wanted to justify its confidence in him, point to his forty-two years. He had few real detractors. The world-wide debate that echoed about his name was on whether he was a visionary or a man of vision. His venture, all agreed, was noble, unselfish. It was the modern equivalent of a search for the Holy Grail, but with the excitement of a marathon, the tense struggle of a climb to great heights. Many then visualized the North Pole, and more did thereafter, as a pinnacle. They spoke of the top of the world. In popular imagination, the North Pole was the pinnacle of a greater Everest. To reach it was the supreme mountain climbing feat of the ages.

We have given our impression of Andrée as we draw it from the literature of the time. The contemporary view of a foremost geographer we take from Charles Rabot, himself a distinguished polar explorer, for decades a leader in the Geographical Society of Paris. They had met in Spitsbergen during 1882 when Andrée was a member of the Swedish "International Polar Year" expedition. Rabot said, speaking in 1930:

"Tall, slender, frank, Andrée created sympathy at first sight. I was attracted towards him, at once I felt confidence in him; at our first meeting he gave me the impression of a strong personality.

"Nearly all my day at Cape Thordsen was spent with Andrée. During the afternoon we made a long jaunt in search of fossils. I recall that during our excursion he questioned me on the balloon flights accomplished during the siege of Paris for maintaining postal communication between the besieged capital and the outside world. I told him that in 1870 I was a pupil at the Nantes Lycée and that I recalled having seen descend in the environs of this city a balloon which had left Paris during the preceding night. Everything that I could recollect of these ascensions interested him. Andrée had already applied himself to aeronautics prior to 1882. That evening we parted as old friends.

"The following year, August 29, 1883, . . . I arrived once more in Tromsö. What was my surprise to find there the Swedish meteorologists of Cape Thordsen, returned the day before from Spitsbergen. I passed the evening very happily with my friend Andrée; he gave me a mass of information on their wintering, from which I made up an article for *La Nature*."

Andrée derived much of his inspiration and much of his aeronautical knowledge from the French. That Paris was a center of his interest helped to center the world's interest upon him and upon his enterprise. His men, too, the comrades that later disappeared with him into the mists of the North, had, upon his advice, gone to Paris for their final training.

Nils Strindberg, twenty-three-year-old Bachelor of Arts from Uppsala, was accepted for the expedition by Andrée, and studied ballooning with the French during his twenty-fourth year. At the university he had acquired a knowledge of physics and chemistry, and of other sciences, which made him as admirable in training as in personal qualifications for membership in the Andrée party.

Andrée's second companion, Knut Hjalmar Ferdinand Fraenkel, two years older than Strindberg, was an athlete and adventurer rather than a scholar. He seemed to have a special qualification for the expedition in his physical strength and dexterity.

When the time finally came to start from Spitsbergen, there were in Andrée's balloon three men as well qualified as any in the world—or at least it would have been difficult to find three whose average qualifications were so good. They were two scientists and an athlete, all experienced in ballooning, all believers in the feasibility and comparative safety of their venture, all prepared physically and mentally to take advantage of every resource of the polar atmosphere, of the drifting ice, and of the lands that border the northern sea.

To the newspaper readers of the nineties Andrée seems to have been at first a visionary with a tinge of the dare-devil. But his personal charm gained upon them as the dispatches followed one another across the front pages, and so the belief that such a balloon voyage as he planned would necessarily prove fatal grew slowly into the hope that he would not set out upon it. That hope was strengthened, although the skepticism as to his sincerity was also strengthened, when, after all the preparations and the announcements, the balloon was not released during the first summer in Spitsbergen, 1896. It remained poised for flight week after week but never flew.

Andrée thought he knew the winds in the polar regions, and where they would carry him; he believed that he could from Spitsbergen diagnose with a fair chance of correctness the tendencies of each day. His balloon would not go up except with just the right wind, and during the summer of 1896 the right wind never blew.

Andrée was taking with him sledges and other equipment so that he and his companions should be able to sledge to a suitable land from any point where the balloon might cease to function. They planned to carry on the sledges from their balloon's farthest only a small amount of provisions, say enough for forty-five or sixty days. For the rest they would live by hunting on the way ashore. Perhaps they would live entirely by hunting when they got to shore, for it might be that the only land they could reach would be uninhabited.

They were hoping to get ashore in some land before the dark of the coming winter. This was a reason for not flying too late in the summer. True, you can sledge without daylight in the Arctic winter with the help of a moon that is twice as effective as in the tropics because its useful light is doubled by snow reflection. Indeed, you can travel on a clear night by just the snow-magnified light of the stars, and by the auroras. But these night lights are insufficient for hunting, properly speaking, although by them you can see to kill a bear that walks into camp.

Many of these ideas we believe Andrée had in 1896: we know he had them in 1897. For meantime Nansen and Johansen had completed triumphantly a journey of five hundred and eighty miles by sledge and one hundred and twenty miles by canoe over the polar sea from the *Fram* to the Franz Josef island group. Reaching that uninhabited land, Nansen had built a house of stones and walrus hide, had killed enough game to supply meat for food and blubber for light and heat through the winter of 1895–96. They had lived in Stone Age fashion, without exercise, bathing, or sunlight, coming out in the spring with perfect health.

Scientist, athlete, and sportsman, Andrée had no doubt that he and his two equally competent Swedish companions could do what Nansen and his one Norwegian had accomplished, particularly now that they had Nansen's experience to guide them.

Eagerly devouring the newspaper accounts of Nansen's feats, the world began to think that perhaps Andrée was not so visionary after all. The public now conceded that from where his balloon ceased to carry him he would be able to walk back to shore, Nansen-fashion.

Depots had been placed for Andrée in various northern islands, and there happened to be depots on others, so that, likely enough, the party could reach one of these. Nansen had wintered without a depot and with an equipment mechanically inferior to that which the Swedes would carry.

Had the balloon ascended in 1896, before Nansen returned, to most people a visionary and his deluded followers would have been drifting off into the northern mists. In 1897, with the world's understanding clarified by Nansen, it was a man of vision rather than a visionary who patiently bided his time with an inflated balloon in Spitsbergen, ready to set off with a favorable wind but determined not to go unless the wind were favorable.

For communication with the outside world, Andrée was going to rely upon the only two devices that were then available, buoys and carrier pigeons.

The buoy preparation shows the main trend of Andrée's plan. He carried twelve small messenger buoys and a thirteenth much larger, called the Polar Buoy. This was marked to be dropped out at the North Pole or at the balloon's most northerly turning point. Such a plan means that primarily Andrée hoped for a steady wind that would take him to the vicinity of the mathematical pole and then on, in a similar course, across the polar sea to a land on the other side. Alternatively, he thought that the wind which carried him toward the Pole might turn and waft him back again, probably not on the same track but perhaps at such an angle to it that, starting from Spitsbergen, he might come back nearer to the Franz Josef or to the New Siberian islands. At such a turning point the Polar Buoy would be dropped if the Pole could not be reached.

The smaller buoys would be dropped whenever it seemed appropriate to send a message. Incidentally they served as ballast. Leakage of gas, or a weighting down of the balloon by clinging liquid moisture or hoarfrost, could be compensated for by dropping the buoys. Thus could ballast be used as a vehicle to give news of the expedition.

The buoys were slow messengers. Even the first of them would hardly be picked up on a coast the same year. Their purpose was therefore double. They were to furnish eventually a knowledge of ocean currents, their directions and speeds, through a comparison in latitude and longitude between the places where they were dropped and the places where they were picked up, and a comparison of the times at both ends. Their second purpose was, in the event of tragedy, to supply the story, or at least a chapter of it.

For immediate news the world was to depend on the carrier pigeons. They had been brought up in northern Norway and would carry back to Norway messages in the Norwegian language through the ordinary technique of pigeon post.

July 11, 1897, brought conditions which Andrée believed right for the journey. We quote from the eyewitness account of the balloon's take-off by Alexis Machuron, a member of Andrée's Spitsbergen base party:

"Sunday, July 11th—A decided south wind! Would it last this time, or would it again prove a delusion?

"Andrée and his companions consulted for some time the various instruments from each post of observation. The atmospheric conditions seemed favourable. . . .

". . . Strindberg and Fraenkel wished to start at once, and besides, what were we waiting for? Time was passing, the season was advancing; therefore, the sooner, the better.

"Andrée did not express his opinion; it was not necessary, we guessed it. He was burning to set out for the conquest of the Pole; and he only said, 'The departure is decided upon.'

· · · · · · · · · · · · · · ·

"Andrée is thanking all the members of the expedition for the help they have rendered him in his enterprise. He gives the captain several telegrams written in haste at the last minute; one . . . addressed to the *Aftonbladet*, Stockholm, said:

" 'In accordance with our decision previously arrived at, we commenced on Sunday, at 10.45, the preparations for our ascent, and at this moment, 2.30 P.M., we are ready to start.

" 'We shall probably be driven in a north-north-easterly direction. We hope gradually to reach regions where the winds will be more favourable to us.

" 'In the name of all our comrades, I send our warmest regards to our friends, and to our country!

" 'ANDRÉE.'

"The last farewells are brief and touching; few words are exchanged, but hearty handclasps between those whose hearts are in sympathy say more than words.

"Suddenly Andrée snatches himself away from the embraces of his friends, and takes his place on the wicker bridge of the car, from whence he calls in a firm voice:

" 'Strindberg,—Fraenkel,—let us go!'

"His two companions at once take their places beside him. They are all three armed with a knife for cutting the ropes supporting the groups of ballast bags.

"This being done, Captain Ehrensvärd and Lieutenants Norselius and Celsing give their sailors orders which are at once put into execution.

"The equatorial straps fall at one stroke.

"The balloon, freed from this restraint, moves slightly; it quits the state of torpor in which it seemed to be plunged; it now seems to have come to life, and, notwithstanding its shelter, it rolls greatly on its lower moorings, from which it tries to free itself.

"We wait a few seconds, in order to seize a moment of calm, before the order is given to start.

"Three of the most adroit sailors, armed with knives, hold themselves in readiness, at a given signal, to cut the three cables by which alone the balloon is now held captive.

"The entire crew of the *Svensksund* are present, and also the crews of the three Norwegian whaling vessels anchored in Virgo Bay.

"There is profound silence at this minute; we only hear the whistling of the wind through the woodwork of the shed, and the flapping of the canvas, which hangs over the upper part of the south side.

"Amongst the cordage of the car are seen the three heroes, standing admirably cool and calm.

"Andrée is always calm, cold, and impassible. Not a trace of emotion is visible on his countenance; nothing but an expression of firm resolution and an indomitable will.

"He is just the man for such an enterprise; and he is well seconded by his two companions.

"At length the decisive moment arrives.

" 'One! Two! Cut!' cries Andrée in Swedish.

"The three sailors obey the order simultaneously, and in

one second the aerial ship, free and unfettered, rises majestically into space, saluted with our heartiest cheers.

"We rush to the doors to get out of the shed. I have the chance of getting out first through a secret opening I have made in the woodwork, so as to be able to rush to my photographic apparatus and have time to take a few snapshots at this stupendous moment.

"Being encumbered with the heavy cordage that it takes with it, the balloon does not rise to a height of 300 feet.

"It is dragged by the wind.

"Behind the mountain that is sheltering us stormy winds are raging, and a current of air sweeps down from the summit and attacks the balloon, which for a moment descends rapidly towards the sea. This incident, which we had foreseen before the departure, but the natural cause of which struck few of the spectators at the moment, produces great excitement amongst some of us. The sailors rush to the boats to be ready to lend assistance to the explorers, whom they expect to see engulfed in the waves. Their alarm was of short duration; the descending movement soon becomes slower, and the car just touches the water and ascends again immediately.

"Unfortunately, the lower parts of the guide-ropes, which were made so as to become detached if they should be caught in the ground, have remained on the shore. At the start the ropes were caught in some rocks on the shore, and the screws for separating the parts worked. But Andrée is well provided against this loss, so that this accident is not likely to have serious consequences.

"At the edge of the water, on the beach studded with rocks and large stones, we all stand, breathlessly watching the various phases, rapidly following one upon another, of the commencement of this stirring and unprecedented aerial journey.

"The balloon, which has now righted itself at about 164 feet above the sea, is rapidly speeding away; the guide-ropes glide over the water, making a very perceptible wake, which is visible from its starting point, like the track made by a ship. The state of affairs seems to us on the shore to be the best that could be hoped for. We exchange last signals of farewell with our friends; hats and handkerchiefs are waved frantically.

"Soon we can no longer distinguish the aeronauts; but we can see that they are arranging their sails, as these latter are displayed in succession on their bamboo mast; then we observe a change of direction. The balloon is now travelling straight to the north; it goes along swiftly, notwithstanding the resistance that must be offered by the dragging ropes; we estimate its speed at from 18 to 22 miles an hour. If it keeps up this initial speed and the same direction, it will reach the Pole in less than two days.

"The aerial globe seems now no bigger than an egg. On the horizon an obstacle appears in the route; this is the continuation of a chain of mountains about 300 feet high right in the path of the balloon, which seems very close to the obstacle, and some of the sailors round me, who have never before seen a balloon start on its trip, seem in great terror; they think the balloon will be hopelessly wrecked. I reassure them, telling them that the balloon is still far away from the hills, which will be easily surmounted, without there even being any necessity to throw out ballast.

"The balloon travels on, maintained at the same altitude by the guide-ropes. In the neighbourhood of the hills there is an upward current of air; the balloon will follow this; it would only risk striking against the obstacle if the movement were downwards, which is not the case. Moreover, the guide-ropes first rest upon the rocks and thus lighten the balloon, which gradually rises.

"We see it clear the top of the hill, and stand out clearly for a few minutes against the blue sky, and then slowly disappear from our view behind the hill.

"Scattered along the shore, we stand motionless, with hearts full, and anxious eyes, gazing at the silent horizon.

"For one moment then, between two hills, we perceive a grey speck over the sea, very, very far away, and then it finally disappears.

"The way to the Pole is clear, no more obstacles to encounter; the sea, the ice-field, and the Unknown!

"We look at one another for a moment, stupefied. Instinctively we draw together without saying a word. There is nothing, nothing whatever in the distance to tell us where our friends are; they are now shrouded in mystery.

" 'Farewell! Farewell! Our most fervent prayers go with you. May God help you! Honour and glory to your names!' "

It was July 11, 1897, when the *Eagle* drifted from sight with a few slight mishaps but on the whole with a testimony of success. For the watchers claimed to have seen that the steering wings of the balloon were actually working, and that Andrée had been able, by their use, to change his course from northeasterly to north. Thus the commander had been justified upon one of the debated items of his program. The readers of the newspapers were that much more hopeful.

Through several years before the flight Andrée had been saying, in terms which varied from hope to expectation, that his balloon would be able to keep the air from one to several weeks, and that during this time it would drift, slightly directed by the steering wings, to the vicinity of the North Pole and thence to one or another of the lands which surround the polar Mediterranean.

When the news reached Europe that the *Eagle* had flown, and that the start had seemed promising, the report spread immediately to the northern frontiers of the telegraph in every land and then, more slowly, to the trading, mining, and fishing outposts, to the fur country, and to the more northerly native peoples of Arctic Siberia, Greenland, Canada, and Alaska.

The law of supply and demand may work doubtfully in some fields; it always works when news is wanted badly enough. Reports claiming to be news of Andrée and his expedition soon began to drift in from every northern land and from some not so very northerly—from as far south in North America, in fact, as the southern boundary of Canada, and as far south in the Old World as Sakhalin Island, hard by Japan. If we tried to review these reports in strictly chronological order we should have to go back to July 1, for it appeared on the sifting of evidence that Andrée's balloon had been reported as far away as Winnipeg, Manitoba, as early as that date, which would be ten or eleven days before its departure from Spitsbergen.

Instead of following that strict time scale we begin with a report which was accepted at the time and has never since been doubted. Then we proceed to others, both of earlier and of later date, that passed through vicissitudes of faith and disbelief.

On July 15 the Norwegian sealer *Alken* was at 80° 44′ N., 20° 20′ E., thus a good hundred miles northeast of Andrée's starting point. The ship was a little too far east to have seen Andrée's balloon, and those days were before the radio, so that Captain Ole Hansen had no knowledge that Andrée had yet flown. He was called on deck at two-o'clock in the morning and told that a strange bird had alighted upon the mast. It had come from the south, pursued by two guillemots. It was a dove which, as we now know, had been without food and probably in nearly continuous flight for a day and a half, and was so exhausted that it went to sleep immediately with its head under its wing. The captain mistook if for a ptarmigan, climbed up in the rigging, so near that he could not miss, and shot it with a bullet. The dead body fluttered down before enough of a breeze so that it missed the deck and floated upon the sea.

That day the *Alken* met another sealing ship. It developed from the conversation that this might have been one of Andrée's pigeons. Captain Hansen then took his ship back and launched two boats in search. One of them found the dead bird. It was an Andrée pigeon, and it carried a message.

Andrée's plan had been that each pigeon should carry two messages, written on very thin paper and enclosed in a tiny cylinder that was fastened to one of the tail feathers. One message would be a bulletin written by himself in longhand; the other a news story written by Strindberg in shorthand. The bulletin was to be telegraphed from the nearest post to the *Aftonbladet* of Stockholm. The shorthand message was to be forwarded to that newspaper by the first mail.

Captain Hansen protested later that he could not possibly have lost one of the messages. He had read in his own native Norwegian the directions on the outside of the cylinder which told that there would be two messages within, and which gave instructions as to how the cylinder was to be opened. He had followed directions and found only the bulletin from Andrée. It read:

From Andrée's Polar Expedition to
Aftonbladet, Stockholm

July 13

12.30 midday. Lat. 82° 2′ Long. 15° 5′ E. good speed to E. 10° S. All well on board. This is the third pigeon-post.

Andrée.

Of the thirty-six pigeons, this was the only one which succeeded in delivering its message. In a straight line it had traveled only some ninety miles in a day and a half—which means that it had been bewildered, fluttering about in various directions.

Some messenger buoys succeeded finally in delivering their news, but this did not come into press circulation until two years after the *Eagle's* departure. We turn first, then, to reports from other sources.

At eleven A.M. July 17, the steamer *55 Dordrecht* of Rotterdam, Captain Theodor Lehmann, was at North Lat. 69° 38′, East Long. 35° 34′. He and his pilot saw what they at first took to be a boat floating upside down. Viewing it through hazy weather, unclearly, they estimated the length to be one hundred and fifty feet. They did not then know about Andrée's having flown and did not connect this with him until they got the news of his having disappeared.

Many consider that later determination showed this object to have been a dead whale. But to the newspapers it was Andrée's balloon floating along as a cover for a piece of ice. Strengthening that belief, there appeared in the Danish newspaper *Socialdemokraten* of August 10 a statement signed by Eder Oskar Mortensen:

"I make known hereby that the bark *Ansgar* of Rönne, traveling from Dublin to Onego, Tuesday, July 13, at nine in the morning, a two-day journey east from North Cape [Norway], passed a balloon at a distance of ten fathoms. It was black in color and some of the gas had leaked out. It looked about two fathoms high above water line and was covered with a net. Since there would be no other balloons in these northern districts, and since Andrée had at that time recently taken off, I conclude that it was his balloon which we saw, especially as there had been a strong wind from the north during the previous week."

This testimony was countersigned as accurate by four men, who by inference must have been eyewitnesses, and was believed through having so many earmarks of truth. But a few days later newspapers carried the above quoted Andrée message which the pigeon succeeded in delivering, and which certified that the balloon had been still flying, hundreds of miles to the north, on the day of the sighting of its supposed wreckage.

The discrediting of what had appeared to be a well authenticated and sober report dampened the world's faith in all reports. Still, some of the later myths were so convincingly certified that it was hard to dismiss them.

A Stavanger dispatch, dated August 13, reported observations made by the steamer *Kong Halfdan* between Haugesund and Ryvarden. At 4.50 A.M. a big balloon was sighted. Its elevation seemed to be higher by three hundred meters than the highest of the mountains that lay to the southeast and east. It was at one time so near the ship that its drag ropes were visible. They were estimated sixty meters long.

For years after the *Eagle's* disappearance, the newspapers carried every now and again stories upon which no one thought it worth while to check. The Andrée memorial volume gives as a sample a yarn in *Nya Vexiöbladet* that "an elderly woman of this town, whose truthfulness is beyond question, says that on the evening of July 17 she was about to go to bed, and had gone to her window to pull down the blind, when through the window she noticed something which looked exactly like a balloon with drag ropes and a net. It had a gondola with apparently one man standing in it."

Typical of rumors so impressive that they had to be investigated, was a report which came to Vardö, on the northeastern coast of Norway, late in October. The sealing captain Johan Overli had been with his ship the *Swan* near Dead

Man's Island, Icefjord, Spitsbergen, September 22. The ship's company heard one scream; then three which followed one another closely. A surf was running too heavy for them to send a boat ashore to investigate. Later the wind blew up, the ship had to retreat into the fjord, and finally it was stranded in Advent Bay.

Captain Overli and his people now boarded the *Malygin*, which brought them to Norway. When that ship was passing Dead Man's Island, outward bound, her people heard three screams of the same kind as before. The *Malygin* captain refused to investigate, thinking these were the screeches of birds.

But, it was argued by others, the only birds which might have screamed so would be loons; and there should have been no loons in this locality, or at least not at this season.

Captain Overli's story was considered to have support from Captain Olaus Olsen, who, on the ship *Fiskeren*, eight or ten miles north of Icefjord, had seen on September 23 some wreckage which he was not in a position to investigate, and which only later brought to his mind the possibility that it might have been Andrée's balloon.

The Overli and Olsen reports took such strong hold that the Norwegian government felt itself compelled, although the season was late and difficult for reaching Spitsbergen, to send an exploring expedition. The results were negative.

So far as date of newspaper publication is concerned, the first seemingly important American contribution to the Andrée rumors was sent out over the telegraphs and cables from Philadelphia. As it appeared in Stockholm, September 25, 1897, in special editions of the newspapers, it read: "The bark *Salmia*, loaded with cryolite and on its way from Ivigtut, Greenland, has arrived in Philadelphia and brought the information that the natives of Ivigtut report, as of about three weeks later than Andrée's departure, that they saw a balloon traveling at an elevation of about one thousand feet. They watched it for a while. It disappeared, moving in a northerly direction."

A year later, this Philadelphia report was considered to have been strengthened by information brought by a Danish ship which had been on the east coast of Greenland. Captain Bang reported learning from the natives of Angmagssalik that in late October, or early November, 1897, they had heard a gunshot out on the ice. Since no one from the colony was unaccounted for that night, and since the shot had been heard by many persons who were at the time in several different places, it was considered probable that the shot had been from the Andrée's party. They must have been on the ice drifting southward along the coast.

That men could drift south along the east coast of Greenland, and that reports from their guns would be heard ashore, was not in itself absurd. One of the steadier and more regular of the ocean streams is the East Greenland Current, which at all times of year carries a procession of floes southward along the Greenlandic east coast. Sometimes there is only a narrow belt of them hard up against the land; sometimes the belt is ten, twenty, or thirty miles wide.

Since Andrée's time, there have been two particularly notable drifts in this current. Fresh in our minds now is that of the Papanin group, who, drifting down from the North Pole on a floe where they were encamped, moved south along the northeast coast of Greenland until they were picked up by icebreakers in February, 1938, some five hundred miles short of Angmagssalik.

Less remembered, although preserved in books, is the drift of the ship's company of the *Teddy*, Captain Henning Bistrup commanding, in the summer of 1923. The *Teddy* was caught fast in the ice on August 21 in about 74° N., 16° 40' W., which is northwest from Iceland near the coast of east Greenland. After a southward drift of about three hundred miles, the *Teddy* was so badly damaged by ice pressure that she was abandoned, the party taking up residence on a large ice floe on October 8. The sojourn on the floe lasted from October 8 to November 2, during which time they drifted more than four hundred miles, with a speed of nearly thirty miles on some days.

November 2, the ice floe on which the *Teddy* people were camped was caught fast at the entrance to Sermiligak Fjord, and the drift was finished. They succeeded in making land

and in getting to an Eskimo settlement. Eventually, with the assistance of the Eskimos, they journeyed south to Cape Dan and then to Angmagssalik, where they were picked up by a ship in the summer of 1924.

That drift stopped only about forty miles short of Angmagssalik. But for a chance easterly wind they might well have drifted past that village on a November night in 1923 and they might have fired guns in the hope of attracting notice and being rescued. Thus it seems even more reasonable now than it did at the time of the Andrée search that the Andrée party might have drifted past Angmagssalik on a November night of 1897 and might have used gunshots as signals.

True, gunshots are nearly the worst possible signals when you are in sea ice. The pack makes noises of its own that are just like shots.

The Swedish authorities, who felt duty-bound to do anything possible, were indirectly responsible for a good many of the reports that continued pouring in. For they had taken pains that natives and whites on the extreme frontiers of the northern countries should be informed that Andrée was missing, and instructed to be on the lookout. In order that superstitious fears might not prevent these people from being useful to Andrée, descriptions and pictures of the balloon were conveyed to them as well as much other information through which they might recognize Andrée or remains of his expedition.

Typical of these indirect results, though special in the excitement created, was a story which appeared in *Novaya Vremya* in St. Petersburg as a telegram from Ustyug, a town that lay easterly from the Russian capital halfway to Siberia. The message was signed by an engineer, Sokolf, and by Sidlof, a member of the faculty of the University of Novaya Alexandria:

"The night of September 20 [i.e., October 2, New Style] at half-past two in the morning, the undersigned observed a balloon drifting rapidly southeast over the town of Yakovlevskaya. Its apparent size was about four versyok [seven inches]. The balloon had an electric [phosphorescent?] sheen. It was visible for less than three minutes, disappearing rapidly over the horizon."

The Ustyuk message revived interest in a previously little regarded message from Krasnoyarsk, Siberia, dated September 17:

"In the town of Antsiferova in the district of Yeniseisk on September 14, New Style, at eleven in the afternoon, there was observed through a period of five minutes what is considered to have been Andrée's balloon. It was drifting in a northwesterly direction."

It seemed improbable, even to newspaper fans, that Andrée's balloon could be still aloft after ten weeks. These reports, accordingly, were about to be forgotten when a new interest developed February 10, 1898. This was not through a further report of a balloon seen in flight. It was a definite and inherently more probable statement that fragments of the balloon had been discovered. The impression made by the report was so strong that the Swedish government considered dispatching an expedition. The full Krasnoyarsk dispatch read:

"Mr. Monastirschin, owner of a gold mine, has received a letter which tells that some Tungus natives have sent to their local police magistrate, January 15, the information that on the 7th of January between Komo and Pit, Yenesei Province, 150 verst from Mr. Sawin's gold mine, they have found what would seem to be a balloon. Not far from it they found the corpses of three men, one of them with his skull crushed. Roundabout were numerous instruments, the use of which was unknown to the natives. A police magistrate immediately set out to investigate. There is a discussion of the possibility that these are the remains of the Andrée party."

This message, by itself, was impressive. It was followed by other telegrams which gave further detail, and there was, as often before, a newspaper discussion throughout the world participated in by scientists, travelers, anybody who seemed entitled to an opinion. The Swedish minister in St. Petersburg applied to the Russian government for an investigation.

One of the first things brought out by the investigation was that the reports seemed to be connected with a fur trapper named Lalin. His reputation cannot have been good, for his connection was considered to have rendered the news of little importance. However, nothing was definitely discredited; and the following March, Professor A. E. Nordenskiöld, then at the height of his world-wide fame as a scholar and as the first man to navigate the Northeast Passage, took up with the Russian government once more the need for investigation.

An experienced traveler, F. Martin, was sent. He reported eventually that on March 1 he had found Lalin in Tomsk. He clung to the substance of his story, claiming to have received it from two separate groups of Tungus natives. Lalin gave plausible reasons for not having visited the site of the reported tragedy and refused to guide Martin to it.

Spring was approaching so rapidly that Martin did not consider it feasible to attempt to reach the place. Moreover, he was able to determine pretty definitely that the story was a fabrication. Lalin had given the names of his two alleged informants, and Martin satisfied himself that no men with these names existed in that part of the country.

Later it was determined that the story had grown out of a report heard by somebody that three dead horses had been discovered. From current inability to explain these horses there had developed an interest, a progressive fabrication of stories. Eventually these were connected with the Andrée problem. The three horses were changed into three men; the rest was adapted correspondingly.

At this stage the element of practical joking entered. A gold miner named Jakowleff thought it amusing to victimize his friend Monastirschin by giving him a circumstantial account of how the remains had been found, and how strikingly the report fitted in with what was known about Andrée. Monastirschin, not suspecting a joke, spread the report. At that time the above mentioned Lalin was visiting Krasnoyarsk. When he heard the story he took the trouble to secure some knowledge which he had not previously possessed about the district where the find was supposed to have been made.

The story, provided with additional verisimilitudes, Lalin sat down and wrote to the editor of *Sibirski Vestnik*.

The farthest afield Asiatic report was from Sakhalin where the wife of the governor reported that one afternoon, late in September, she saw a balloon at a moderate height passing over her head moving in the direction of the Siberian mainland. Balloons were at that time uncommon in Sakhalin. She concluded reasonably that this one must be Andrée's.

There proved to be two chief world centers for the balloon reports. In Asia it was the Yenisei valley; in North America it was British Columbia. It is still debated whether there was a "physical" reason, as perhaps the sighting of a meteor, for the development of these foci of rumor, or whether we are to credit simply the native gifts of the inhabitants.

The Dominion government at Ottawa received, August 11, 1897, a telegram from Victoria, B.C. One of its representatives had gathered reliable information that Indians of two different districts remote from each other had seen Andrée's balloon. These districts were in northern British Columbia near the Alaska boundary. The balloon had been moving north.

Consul Word, who represented Sweden and Norway at Victoria, received eventually from the foreign department of the Dominion government an official communication:

"The mentioned balloon passed over Winnipeg July 1 [the report, previously noted, of a balloon observed ten or eleven days before Andrée set out from Spitsbergen]. The Indian agent at Hayleton [Hazelton?] reports under date of July 3 that at 7:30 in the afternoon of July 1 an Indian boy saw an object described to represent a balloon four miles west from that point. He observed it from a height 400 feet high. A strong northwesterly wind was blowing. A number of the Indians at the headwaters of Sibe Skina report that the same afternoon an object resembling a balloon was seen giving out a considerable amount of light and moving from the northwest."

The rumors from British Columbia would not cease. April 5, 1898, a telegram was sent from Victoria:

"A man who used to be a mail carrier in the United States has arrived from Dawson. He reports that Andrée is now in the Klondike district and says he has with him a letter from Andrée.

This man proved unwilling to surrender the Andrée letter to anybody, even when approaches were made through international diplomatic channels.

Professor Andersson in the Swedish memorial volume referred to cities, as typical of the way newspapers handled Andrée dispatches, the following telegram and its amplification.

The telegram which the newspaper had for text was: "A certain Jack Carr has reached Departure Bay from Alaska. He says he carries documents from Professor Andrée but refuses to give further details. Investigations are being made."

Pending the investigations, the newspaper said that the telegram, as it stood, was difficult to understand. "If, however, we venture upon an interpretation we might suggest that perhaps Jack Carr is intended to mean Jack the Carrier—that is, Jack the mail carrier. This fits in with our previously published information. We cannot find on the map a place called Departure Bay. Perhaps the telegram should have read that Jack had departed. The meaning would then be that Jack the Mail Carrier, who is from Alaska, has said so-and-so. This would bring the telegram into correspondence with previous dispatches."

One day in the autumn of 1897 Mr. Newson, an architect, called upon Consul Lund (in San Francisco?) and reported that he had just returned from Caribou, British Columbia, where he heard that a balloon was seen in the neighborhood of Quesnelle. This was investigated. It turned out that on a day between the 4th and 7th of August, 1897, a Mr. Hobson had been told by his wife that a Mrs. Sullivan and her daughter had seen a balloon passing over in a direction from west to east. A round grey object had appeared in the sky to the south. It grew larger and larger and sank lower as it approached. Finally two shapes were discerned, the smaller hanging suspended from the larger. This would be a balloon with its basket. The balloon changed its course suddenly, in the direction of the east arm of Quesnelle Lake, and then it began to ascend.

We translate Gunnar Andersson's statement in the Andrée memorial volume of 1906, on perhaps the most remarkable of all the Andrée reports, certainly the one that differed most from the generality:

"We close this survey with a brief account of that one of the rumors which stirred up the greatest interest partly because it arrived at the psychological moment, partly because it connected the affairs of the expedition with the beliefs of certain people in the possibility of contact with the departed.

"August 2, 1897, there was dispatched from the little town of Germania, Iowa, U.S.A., a telegram:

"OSCAR DICKSON, GOTEBORG
"ANDREE MOVING SOUTHWARD NEAR LONGITUDINALLY WEST TOWARD EDAM LAND.

"OLE BRACKE

"The *Handelstidning* of Göteborg reports that: 'As might be expected such a telegram drew the greatest attention. The rumor spread rapidly; today everybody has been telephoning everybody else in the whole city: "Have you heard about Andrée? Is the story true about Andrée?" There was little else to be heard wherever one listened. In the editorial rooms the telephone bells have been ringing continuously, and it has scarce been possible to get along with one's ordinary work, one has been so occupied in replying to all these questions, not only from within the city but from neighboring towns and even from the Capital.'

"The first problem was to find out where was Edam Land. This was found upon N. Lat. 77° in northeast Greenland.

"The second question was: Who is Ole Bracke?

"Oscar Dickson had died before Andrée set out. At the

instance of the King, the Dickson estate asked for further information. On August 4 came the reply:

"ANDREE MAKES FOR SAFETY, SEEKING WHALERS.

"BRACKE

"When it was found that Bracke was a man who would answer cables the Göteborg newspaper, *Handelstidning,* conducted the following cable correspondence with him:

"OUR READERS YOUR TELEGRAM DICKSON ANXIOUS LEARN HOW YOU KNOW ANDREES ACTUAL POSITION. PLEASE CABLE US EXPLANATION AND WRITE CONFIRMATION. ARE YOU SURE?

"HANDELSTIDNING

"Bracke answered:

"YES. CONSIDER MY FORMER CABLES OSCAR DICKSON INDICATIVE ANDREES SITUATION.

"BRACKE

"*Handelstidning* continued:

"DOES ANDREE REQUIRE ASSISTANCE, OR IS HE IN SAFETY, AND WHERE?

"HANDELSTIDNING

"There arrived as a reply Bracke's last telegram:

"ASSISTANCE WANTED ANDREE. SEARCH COAST EDAM LAND.

"BRACKE

"When these telegrams came to the knowledge of the American press, Ole Bracke was sought out by reporters. The Swedish American newspaper, *Hemlandet,* sent the Rev. Elfström. We make some extracts from his account.

" 'We found Old Bracke's modest house four and a half miles south of the little town Germania. It was on a desolate prairie elevation.

" 'We were warmly received by Mr. Bracke. He and I

have been acquainted these many years. I have always had a high regard for him but have considered him a little peculiar and mystical. . . . He has written a poem about the Andrée expedition which was published in the Minneapolis *Tribune*. He said that three different times he had seen Andrée and his companions, together with their equipment; he reported himself as convinced of the reality of these visions. He had sent the [first] telegram to induce wealthy men to outfit an expedition for the rescue of Andrée. He was very reticent about his visions.'

"Ole Bracke was not the only one who reports that he has been in spiritual contact with Andrée, but it was he who stirred up the greatest interest. . . ."

An expedition was organized to visit the Edam Land section of Greenland, though not upon Bracke's spiritualist suggestion. We come to that a little farther on when we discuss the formal search expeditions.

By inference, we have pictured the search for Andrée as world-wide in that people of varied frontier occupations and of many races were on the constant lookout for him in the northern forests of the new and old worlds, on the mainland prairies which lie north of those forests, on the islands of the polar sea, and on ships that plied northern waters for the purposes of business and of science. There was a more formal search, too; there were expeditions supported by governments, by learned societies, and by popular subscription. These were based on two things mainly: reports which appeared to have a genuine bearing on the problem, and scientific theories according to which Andrée was more likely to be found in one section of the Arctic than in another.

It seemed not unlikely that the *Eagle* might have drifted toward central Arctic Siberia. The Andrée rumors which appeared most convincing, both in their very number and in what were thought to be the earmarks of truth, came from just these north central districts, the lower Yenisei and Lena regions of Siberia. There seemed special need for an expedition; so one was planned by, and eventually commanded by, J. Stadling.

The expedition, which included in its membership Hans

Fraenkel, a brother of the balloonist, left Sweden in April, 1898. They journeyed through the summer across country from Stockholm to the upper Lena at Yakutsk. They descended the Lena and made an examination of the delta. Thence they moved west and southwest, striking the Yenisei well north of the Arctic Circle, and proceeding upstream toward European Russia.

Stadling picked up on this journey a great many reports that allegedly concerned Andrée but none which would bear close scrutiny. Most of them had something to do with pigeons. The expedition made positive contributions to geography and other sciences, but its contributions to the solution of the Andrée problem were wholly negative.

When the Wellman Polar Expedition, American, went to the Franz Josef Islands in the summer of 1898 there were strong hopes that they would find Andrée and his companions. For it was the general opinion of Arctic men that if there had been a safe landing anywhere near this group, it would be comparatively easy for the party to make their way to Cape Flora, where there was an ample stock of provisions left by the Jackson expedition of 1894–97.

Upon arrival at Cape Flora and finding no trace of the missing men, Wellman gave up hope of their ever being found alive, as is shown by the February, 1899, *Century Magazine:* "Poor Andrée! poor, brave, dead Andrée!"

Next in fame among Swedish polar explorers after Baron A. E. Nordenskiöld, discoverer of the Northeast Passage, was A. G. Nathorst. His first visit to Spitsbergen had been in 1870. His second was in 1882, the International Polar Year Expedition, of which he and Andrée were fellow members. When Andrée announced his plans for a balloon voyage, Nathorst was already planning what he thought would be his last northern expedition.

The Nathorst plans were not completed until 1898, so that his expedition of that year became in part a search for Andrée. No traces were found.

By the end of the summer of 1898 expeditions had examined various shores of various islands in the Spitsbergen, Franz Josef and New Siberian groups, so that it was considered proven that the Andrée party had not reached any of these districts. Then for a while hope was placed in northeast Greenland. Nansen had shown that the ice drifts westerly north of the Franz Josef and Spitsbergen groups. Andrée might have reached Greenland by wind drift of a free balloon, by ice drift after a descent, by a sledge journey over the sea ice, or by some combination of these.

In February, 1899, Nathorst started a movement for an expedition to northeast Greenland. It was said that the drifting sea ice was so well supplied with polar bears, and the coast so well supplied with bears, musk oxen, and other game, that Andrée might have reached that coast and might still be living there. Nathorst cautioned that Andrée's having gone toward this section was a mere possibility; but he said that an expedition to it would, in any case, bring back needed scientific information.

The Nathorst expedition to northeastern Greenland was organized on a wave of popular and government sympathy. They planned to visit the coast between Latitudes 73° and 76°. They did visit it between 70° and 75° and did return with much of scientific value. But they found no trace of Andrée.

The last embers of dying hope were fanned by the wings of doves.

The first rumors concerning Andrée usually referred to balloons having been seen, perhaps in the dark of night, perhaps in fog or clouds, drifting over remote districts inhabited by natives and by an occasional trapper. The most persistent rumors were due to Andrée's having taken with him carrier pigeons. Travelers in remote districts saw strange pigeons flying about. Reports came in that natives had killed a bird unknown to them (i.e., a pigeon) that they had eaten the bird and destroyed or lost a message which had been fastened to it.

The excitement about the pigeons spread far and wide. There is no doubt that hundreds if not thousands of just ordinary pigeons were shot down by boys and men on the theory that they might be carriers from Andrée's expedition. In connection with these shootings, there were sometimes deliberate inventions, as forgeries of messages that were alleged to have been recovered from the birds.

The pigeon stories which came in, except the first, were all based either on mistake or on falsification. The opposite was true with Andrée's second means of communication, the casks bearing messages. Practically all reports eventually proved true which said that a cask thought to be from Andrée had been discovered.

Andrée carried, as mentioned, twelve messenger buoys and one far larger, called the Polar Buoy, which was to have been dropped either at the North Pole or at a time when it seemed that the balloon was at its farthest attainable north. Two of the small buoys and the Polar Buoy have been found.

Buoy No. 7 was found in Kollafjord, on the north coast of Iceland, May 14, 1899. It seemed to the finders that it had not lain on the shore long before it was found—six hundred and seventy-two days after it had been thrown from the *Eagle*. The message read:

Buoy Number 7

This buoy is thrown out from the Andrée balloon at 10:55 P.M. G.M.T. July 11, 1897 at about 82° N. Lat. and 25° E. Long.

We are drifting at an elevation of about 600 meters. All well.

(Signed) ANDRÉE, STRINDBERG, FRAENKEL

So the buoy discovered in 1899 carried older news than the pigeon post of 1897—the buoy had been thrown out two days before the dove took flight.

Buoy No. 4 was found at Lögsletten on the coast of Finmark, Norway, on August 27, 1900, by a woman collecting driftwood. She believed it came ashore just before she found it, "so that it had been carried by the waves one thousand one hundred and forty-two days after it had been thrown from the balloon. During the whole of this long period the buoy, with its valuable contents, had not suffered any damage."

This second buoy to be found carried the oldest of the three messages that were received from Adrée, for it read:

Bouy Number 4

The first to be thrown out. July 11, 10 P.M. G.M.T.

Our journey has gone well so far. We are drifting at an elevation of about 250 meters, with a course which at first was N 10 E True but later N 45 E True. Four messenger pigeons were sent out at 5:40 P.M. Greenwich time. They flew westerly. We are now over the ice which is much broken up. The weather is beautiful. We are in the highest spirits.

ANDREE, STRINDBERG, FRAENKEL

We have been over broken ice since 7:45 G.M.T.

A comparison of the messages indicates that the *Eagle* moved in a straight line less than two hundred miles in two days. This was accounted for at the time by there having been a calm on Spitsbergen the day after the balloon started.

No more of the small buoys were found. The Polar Buoy, with no message in it, was picked up in King Charles Land, Spitsbergen, On September 11, 1899.

No messages from Andrée came after 1900.* Rumors continued to float in, and there were some investigations, but gradually interest faded and hope died. In ten years forgetfulness was beginning to gather. But throughout the world there continued, like the memory of a painful dream, the consciousness of the Andrée mystery.

The mystery of Andrée came to be localized at White Island, which is itself mysterious.

White Island, which is northeasterly in the Spitsbergen group, has been called Giles Land, Gillis Land (with several other spelling variants), and even New Iceland. It is not agreed who discovered it. There is really a dispute as to what island it is, in the sense that authorities debate whether

* One of the by-products of the intensive Soviet polar work of the last few years is that two (or more?) of the small Andrée buoys have been found. But this was after the "solution of the Andrée mystery," and their chief contribution has been to throw light on the direction of Arctic currents.

certain visits to an island named as above were to this island or to another more to the east.

A hypothetical routing for Andrée's balloon was plotted on the chart during the search years by Nathorst, from the Andrée messages and from that day's knowledge of currents in the air and in the sea. This was to prove nearly correct, in that the plotted line runs not far from White Island. Yet Nathorst himself, during the very fever of the Andrée search, landed twice on White Island, at its northern and southern ends, and did so without even searching specially for traces of Andrée.

Toward the end of the first book of his two-volume work, *Two Summers in the Northern Polar Sea,* Nathorst tells that on August 18, 1898, his ship the *Antarctic* reached the vicinity of White Island. They were coming from King Charles Land, Spitsbergen, and passed north along the east coast of White Island, noting everywhere cliffs of ice so steep that there appeared no chance for a landing until the northern tip was reached. Here they found ice-free lowland, and a party of scientists went ashore, returning with a natural history report of what they had seen.

Next day the *Antarctic* passed south along the west coast of White Island, once more noting precipices of ice which extended, continuous and forbidding, until the southwest corner was reached. Here was lowland again, and Nathorst went ashore with two companions. We translate from page 289 of the Stockholm, 1900, edition:

"This low point consists of primitive rocks, gneiss and granite; there were old dykes and even here was driftwood to be found. We saw only non-flowering plants, but as the landscape was covered with newly fallen snow it may be that some flowering plants were hidden by it. . . . There were great swarms of guillemots and their bones were everywhere on the ground, some moss-grown. For all our searching we could not find any guillemot chicks; so it may be . . . that they had already migrated.

". . . Unfortunately we were not able to stay long . . . for the ice began to crowd toward land, so that we must hurry back to our ship. We had to go far out of our way in the poor visibility of the snowstorm, and were guided by the *Antarctic's* siren which every now and then gave us a signal. Snow-crusted and chilled, we arrived on board where our people had been worried that the ice would prevent our returning to them."

By Nathorst's own theory, Andrée's balloon should have drifted near White Island. A search for Andrée was on the program of his expedition and, by the index, he discusses Andrée thirty-four times in the narrative; but he does not discuss him in connection with White Island. He ponders White Island matters of botany and ornithology, and worries that the snow hid flowering plants. There is no sign that the lost explorers were near the thoughts of their fellow countrymen as they walked about the small piece of flat land where the bodies, and the remains of the expedition's last camp, lay hidden by a cloak of new-fallen snow.

For the years before his expedition, Nathorst says that no doubt there were on White Island many unrecorded landings from the sealing ships that ply those waters. The sealing ships continued to ply the vicinity for the thirty years which followed Nathorst's missed opportunity. We know about some; we know there must have been others.

At three in the afternoon of July 9, 1930, Captain Theodor Grödahl of Tromsö, left the *Hanseat* and went ashore at the southwest corner of White Island. He was looking for the remains of a balloon expedition, not Andrée's of 1897 but Nobile's of 1928. There were two men with him and they searched for traces of men and for wreckage where Nathorst had searched for geological, botanical, and zoological details thirty-two years before. He must have covered the whole ground, for he says (in practical accord with careful later measurements) that the land, free from glacier, stretches for about three miles along the shore and that its breadth is four hundred or five hundred yards.

Captain Grödahl later reported having examined the whole of this space between the sea and the ice cap. At about one hundred or one hundred and fifty yards from shore they found a sheet-iron box almost completely rusted to pieces, and by the side of it a hand-wrought wooden peg. They noted driftwood lying in such positions that it could not have been piled there by the forces of nature but must have been arranged by men. There was considerable last year's snow still lying over this ground, but here and there were snow-free patches, some with the nests of ivory gulls.

The Grödahl party returned to the ship at 7:30 in the evening, and sent ashore another party. This was mainly to gather eggs, but they were also to look around for signs of the Nobile expedition. The captain said later: "I never thought a minute of Andrée; when he went on his expedition I was quite young. Had I found anything of what has now been discovered, I should certainly have remembered him. After four or five hours my people came on board again, and we were obliged to leave the island in a hurry for there was a lot of pack-ice."

Even just finding those relics of Andrée and misunderstanding them gave Captain Grödahl's name permanence in the history of exploration. Andrée had not been forgotten after thirty-four years, and the nations were still in a mood to receive the solution of the *Eagle* mystery as a world sensation.

Norway, the land of polar explorers and polar exploration, had by 1930 systematized its work under the guidance of the Norwegian Svalbard and Polar Sea Research Institution, which had for its leader Dr. Adolf Hoel of the University of Oslo. They planned for 1930 a combined scientific and commercial expedition to the Franz Josef Islands, and they would visit the Spitsbergen group on the way. The chief of scientific staff aboard the *Bratvaag* was Dr. Gunnar Horn.

The *Bratvaag* expedition left continental Norway at the end of August. They made good speed to the Spitsbergen group and slower speed thereafter, going ashore occasionally for study. August 5 they landed in southwestern White Island, made geological and other scientific observations, and returned to their ship.

Thus once more a party of scientists, conscious of the Andrée problem, had gone ashore in a district which, thirty years before, had been looked upon as a probable retreat of the Andrée party. They had certainly been within a few hundred yards of the Andrée remains; they had possibly walked over some of them, hidden by snowdrifts which still persisted into the summer. They had failed, like the others, to make the close search which would have brought solution.

The discovery of the Andrée remains came through pure accident. Walrus hove in sight, and this was a combined hunting and scientific voyage. The hunters pursued the walrus, got some of them, and proceeded to cut them up. The men perspired at their labor. The weather seemed hot, as it often does to explorers and hunters in the Arctic summer, even where snowdrifts are persisting. This is the heat with which mountain climbers have experience when they get up above snow line on a bright summer day. Two of the men felt particularly thirsty and went in search of a drink. They came to a brook, drank their fill, and crossed over for a walk along the strip of ice-free land. Just on the other side of the brook they found the lid of an aluminum pot. Farther inland something dark was sticking out of a snowdrift. They walked up to it and found a canvas boat half covered by a snowdrift.

Thus Olav Salen, a seventeen-year-old first-tripper, and Karl Tusvik, a veteran of twenty-four, wrote their names not merely into newspaper dispatches that were destined to appear on front pages throughout the world, but into the history of polar exploration. They had found Andrée's last camp.

The walrus hunters now gathered at a signal from the youngsters. Under the guidance of Captain Peder Eliassen, they found many things labeled "Andrée's Polar Expedition 1896." About thirty feet north of the boat they found a "human body which lay leaning against the slightly sloping wall of rock."

The scientists were notified and came ashore for their second visit to the glacier-free lowland strip. Horn summarized his own feelings, and what he believed to be the feeling and attitude of the world:

". . . gradually the whole truth broke upon us, the story of the tragedy that had been enacted here. Our thoughts found their way back to that July day in 1897 when the

Eagle rose from Dane Island in Spitsbergen with three men in the car, and was carried away by the wind on the most daring polar expedition ever undertaken. The men never came back. The last news from them came by the carrier-pigeon which they had released in latitude 82°, and in their communication there were the words: 'All well on board.' That was their last message. Everything that happened afterwards had for a generation been the object of the acutest speculations. Search expeditions had sought for the vanished balloonists of whom no trace could ever be found. Andrée and his comrades kept the secret of their disappearance, and gradually the world satisfied itself with the conclusion that the explorers had been lost on the [sea] ice or had fallen into the sea, leaving no trace behind them. Most people accepted this explanation. Probably no one ever imagined that Andrée would ever be found. And now here we had Andrée's camp before our eyes and the problem of his disappearance was solved."

Horn wrote that the problem of Andrée's disappearance had been solved. He felt (perhaps not on August 6, the day of discovery, but certainly before the official narrative was published the following year) that he and the committee appointed to study the case had arrived at a final solution which gave not merely the time and place of death but also the how and why.

As will appear, there can be no dispute within a few yards as to where Andrée and Fraenkel died. The place of Strindberg's death can not have been more than a few hundred yards away or at most a very few miles.

There is little room for dispute on time. Perhaps Strindberg died October 8 or 9, 1897. Andrée and Fraenkel survived him a few days; at most a few weeks.

There was, at first, a substantial agreement as to how and why the party must have lost their lives. Still, the inadequacy of the solution began to trouble some within a day or two after the appearance of the first dispatches in the newspapers. Serious opposition to the explanation developed upon the publication of the full account—in English called *Andrée's Story*. This book showed, by description and photograph, that the party had kept a voluminous and orderly record of everything throughout the balloon voyage and thereafter until they landed on White Island the first week of October, 1897. A few things were hard to decipher through water-soaking; these were surprisingly few. Photographs taken by the balloonists were developed with success thirty-three years later.

There had been discovered in the White Island camp also brief notes by Andrée, mutilated and only partly decipherable, that covered the first few days on the island. These were published, with conjectural explanations to fill in some of the gaps.

We are concerned here not with the full Andrée story but only with solving what at first seemed plain but later began to form a mystery: How and why did the men die? To pose that question we copy at some length the official explanation as found on pages 217 to 227 of the New York edition of *Andrée's Story:*

". . . the men can hardly have suffered from lack of meat, for there were found in the boat remains of the back and ribs of a polar bear that had been cut up. And out on the campsite there lay two polar-bear skins. . . ."

This is quoted from page 217. Six pages thereafter:

"We have already seen that the party was not in want of food, and that there was ammunition for a considerable period ahead; the men had cooking utensils, matches, and fuel. But they were not equipped to meet the cold of winter on an island almost entirely covered with ice, and affording no better protection against the storms coming from the sea than their tent. This tent, too, was only made of varnished balloon-cloth and, after the long journey on the ice, was probably damaged in many places. The prospects of building themselves a snow-hut were small, the little pieces of stone-brash on the shore being unsuitable for the purpose. The sealer Sörensen of the *Isbjörn* most certainly gave the correct answer to the final riddle of the Andrée Expedition when he declared: 'I think they died in their sleep! The cold finished them. In any case, they didn't die of hunger.'"

To make the position still more clear, the official book traverses this ground once more, three pages farther on:

"Why did they not use the two bear-skins as rugs to lie on in the tent? Why was their sleeping-sack not used? Why did the third sledge stand packed with some of the expedition's most important belongings, as if in preparation for a journey? To all these questions there will never be an answer! The only reply that can be given is in the words of the Norwegian sealer: 'I think they died in their sleep! The cold finished them.'"

Do we agree that "to all these questions there will never be an answer"? Do we agree that "the cold finished them"?

In the foregoing discussion we have said or implied two things which may appear to a degree contradictory. We have said that the official Andrée committee had before them, when they arrived at their verdict, practically the whole story of the Andrée diaries and of the objects that were found in the White Island camp; and we have said also that when this full story, and the listing of the described objects with their position and circumstances, appeared in print, there arose and steadily increased a disagreement with the findings of the official committee.

If we are to arrive at a solution of this contradiction which is worth considering, we must examine the whole body of evidence. The Andrée committee has done that already, as said, in great detail through the book to which we have referred. We shall do it briefly, using both condensation of the parts which we think important and omission of those which we consider beside the point. This method of condensation and omission is fair, because any reader who is sufficiently interested, and who doubts either the honesty or the sufficiency of the abridgment, can turn to the full record. True enough, it is only what was published by the official committee that is available wholly in English. If you want those further discussions which have tended to invalidate the official conclusion, you will have to use several languages, most important of them Swedish.

Among the variables considered by all students of the how

and why of the tragedy there are groupings of human, or psychological, factors such as those which may bear upon the possibility of murder, suicide, or on a fatal incompetence resulting from despondency, panic, or the like. Therefore, it is necessary to make a statement on the character of the men. Then we must scrutinize the record for any sign that favors or counteracts the suggestion of one or another of the possibilities.

Fortunately there is no important disagreement, among the official group or those who oppose them, as to the character of the three men.

Andrée was a veteran both of polar exploration and of ballooning. His northern experience covered fourteen years, and he had among his friends and associates many of the successful explorers of the day, both in his own country and elsewhere. He belonged to a school of thought which considers the dangers of the polar regions to be much overrated by the public; overstated by the usual books. He was of mature but not of advanced years, of good physique, perfect health, an optimistic disposition. He was a skillful workman, resourceful, prepared to adapt himself to whatever condition.

From this angle, that of the possible development of mental unbalance, Strindberg and Fraenkel, though differing from Andrée and from each other, did not differ in the points which here apply. They were both mature but under thirty, therefore at the height of their physical powers. They were even-tempered, inclined to optimism. Strindberg was perhaps the steadier of the two, but Fraenkel made up for that in animal spirits and in optimism. Strindberg was of the scientific type and was a scientist; Fraenkel was the athlete and sportsman.

From the almost miraculously preserved and complete records of the expedition, as found in diaries and photographs at the White Island camp, we know that the disappointment of the balloon voyage was not the sort that leads to despondency. The balloon, although it did not do as well as Andrée had hoped, behaved much better than his critics had forecast. When he came back (and there is no sign anywhere in the record that any of the party ever doubted they would get back to civilization) Andrée could take satisfaction in having, on the whole, made good on his contentions.

The wind had not been as strong as Andrée hoped or as steady as he hoped, and had not trended in the direction he wanted. It had been weak and vacillating, but this had the good point that the balloon voyage was terminated so near land that Andrée and his companions were entitled to say, what they do say or imply in their records, that their task of reaching land and passing the winter was, in view of their equipment and their situation, not difficult or dangerous in comparison with many Arctic situations that had been met successfully before their time.

As we are about to turn to the record of the balloon voyage, reconstructed by the official committee from the written material found on White Island, we note that in our study of the evidence we here change sources.

Up to this point our main reliance has been upon the Andrée memorial volume, published by the Swedish Society of Anthropology and Geography nine years after the disappearance of the *Eagle*.

From now on we use two main sources.

First we take *Andrée's Story,* using the New York edition of 1930. This was "edited by the Swedish Society of Anthropology and Geography" and speaks officially for those who favor a solution of the Andrée problem substantially along the lines arrived at by Dr. Horn, and by the rest of the scientists, the journalists, and others who visited the camp site on White Island in the summer of 1930.

Next we take *Andréegåtan* (*The Andrée Problem*), by H. N. Pallin, using the Swedish (only?) edition, Uppsala, 1934. That volume speaks for most of those who have been dissatisfied with the official solution. We acknowledge indebtedness to it the more easily because Pallin says that his views agree in the main "with those published by Stefansson" in 1930 through newspapers and in 1931 through a magazine article.

We abridge thousands of words, derived from the Andrée records by the official narrative, down to a few hundred which tell the story of the balloon voyage:

The Eagle rose from Dane Island the early afternoon of Sunday July 11, 1897. She behaved well and drifted northeasterly till the early morning of July 12, when a calm stopped her. Presently she moved again, this time westerly.

During her slow westward drift the balloon touched ice for the first time the afternoon of July 12. The *Eagle* had moved freely for twenty-five and one-half hours.

The drift was continued in a generally western direction, with repeated contacts with the ice, until a calm stopped the balloon a little before midnight. The *Eagle* was heavy with accumulated moisture. She did not move again until nearly eleven o'clock in the forenoon of July 13.

That the balloon remained motionless for thirteen hours in spite of a northwesterly wind, which blew up during the morning and increased to eight miles per hour, was because one of the drag lines had caught behind a block of ice when during a practical calm the wind shifted direction by a right angle. During this stoppage all three were evidently still united upon continuing; for, as the official *Andrée's Story* points out, if not anchored, the *Eagle* would have drifted before this wind back to Spitsbergen, and there is no suggestion anybody even considered taking advantage of that circumstance.

As the journey now continued the balloon touched ice frequently. Tuesday evening they tried to get her to fly higher by throwing out sand and other things not very valuable which had a total weight of 73 pounds. Then they threw out not less than 450 pounds of provisions. The balloon did ascend, but just before midnight her gondola again struck the ice. More provisions were evidently thrown out. So arrived Wednesday, July 14.

At 6:20 that morning the balloon took a higher level, no doubt through the discharge of further ballast. But evidently the *Eagle* was soon near the ice again, for at 6:29 both valves were opened to let out gas and to end her movement.

The shortness of the balloon's voyage in miles was due to light, shifting winds, and to calms. Its shortness in time was mainly due to gathering ice and hoarfrost that weighted her down.

The *Eagle* had been in the air 65 hours, 33 minutes. She had traveled about 517 miles. Her landing spot was about 300 miles from Dane Island and 192 miles from North East Land of the Spitsbergen group.

Nansen and Johansen were constantly in the minds of Andrée, Strindberg, and Fraenkel. This would have been, if anything, more true than usual as they transferred their food, gear, and portable boat to the three Nansen-type sledges and began the journey southward over broken, shifting floes which here and there had water between them. So we must also have the Nansen story constantly before us, if we are to fill with reasonableness the gaps that have been left in the preserved written statement of the three balloonists, and if we are to enter sympathetically into their repeatedly expressed and still more consistently implied feeling of confidence and security.

In March, 1895, Nansen and Johansen, with three sledges and numerous dogs, left the *Fram* where she was drifting in the pack some 500 miles north of Siberia and some 400 miles short of the North Pole. They marched north towards the Pole, but the ice on which they traveled drifted in various directions, at times back south but more usually west. By April they were some 250 miles from the Pole. There they turned back. Traveling south and southwest, and usually drifting west, they made a general southwesterly course.

From time to time along the journey they killed dogs and fed them to the other dogs. When their last dog was gone they were still farther north from the Franz Josef Islands than Andrée was north of Spitsbergen when his balloon descended.

Basing most of our statements on diary records or on what Andrée said before the expedition began, but filling occasional gaps in a common-sense way, we derive a picture of how the Andrée party compared themselves with Nansen.

The balloonists had a shorter distance to sledge if they

wished to reach land. The drift of the ice was as favorable to them as it had been to Nansen. They would consider the season more favorable, for they would be in agreement with the principle, emphasized by Peary but deducible from the experience of all sea-ice travelers in comparable latitudes, that as you change seasons from spring to summer you get more difficult and dangerous travel conditions, while as you change from autumn to winter you find easier travel, and safer. Nansen, in late winter, had been facing progressively worse conditions; Andrée in late summer might expect progressively improving conditions of sledge travel.

The Andrée equipment was similar to Nansen's; perhaps it was better in some respects because they had been able to guide themselves by Nansen's experience. They had more food with them than Nansen, of similar kind but of more variety. They had more clothing than Nansen, and it was in better condition, though some of it was not so very suitable. They had more petroleum fuel, and their gear for using it was the same as his. They did not have enough food to last them through the year, but that really had no bearing; for, like Nansen, they expected to live on the animals they killed, using the lean and the fat for food, the extra fat for fuel and light, and the skins to help build their winter dwellings, and if necessary, to piece out their clothing and bedding.

From the point where the balloon descended, which was northeast of the Spitsbergen group and northwest of the Franz Josef Islands, they could reach one or the other of these groups. There were in both islands depots of food and equipment, some made especially for Andrée, some left at known places through the circumstances of previous expeditions. They might reach one of these depots before winter, but if they did not they would still be better off than Nansen, who had reached no depot. Nansen might have worried during his journey ashore in that no one expected him to land in the Franz Josef Islands. Andrée knew that people would look for him next summer both on the Spitsbergen and the Franz Josef Islands.

The Andrée party did not worry seriously over the prospect of living a winter exclusively on the flesh of animals and by the light and heat of animal fat. Neither would they worry about the other terrors of the popular imagination, for Andrée at least was a veteran and uninfluenced by such popular misconceptions as that you cannot be healthy on meat alone; that you get so seriously tired of a "monotonous" diet that it interferes with your health; that you become morose through the absence of daylight; that you need exercise (besides, you can always have all of this you want); or that you require bathing to be healthy. Nansen and Johansen had hibernated during the winter of 1895–96, seldom going more than a hundred yards from the camp. They never had a bath or a proper wash. They had no change of clothing. But they passed the winter in perfect health, in continual amity, without too much boredom. When in spring daylight returned sufficient for traveling they started on their, as it proved, unnecessary journey towards Spitsbergen in health and spirits that could scarce have been better had their winter been spent at the most carefully provisioned expedition base.

The Swedes knew these things about Nansen and Johansen from newspapers and from articles in journals. Andrée knew some of them from having conversed with Nansen. Is it, then, strange that the diaries of the Andrée party are free from worry; that, throughout, they imply confidence? It would have been strange had such men worried over such conditions. Confidence was their only logical frame of mind.

There was, true enough, for Andrée the threat of approaching darkness; but on July 14, when he came down on the ice, there was still perpetual daylight. There would not be less daylight with Andrée than with his friends at home in Sweden until in October. For, as Andrée knew, the light and darkness of the Arctic are not divided fifty-fifty, and the periods of daylight and darkness are not equal at what, following uninformed Mediterraneans, we still call the equinox, September 22, the "time of equal night and day." When you think of the difference between light and darkness, as most of us do, on the basis of whether you can or cannot read ordinary print out of doors, then you would have at Andrée's latitude at least six weeks more of daylight than of darkness per year, half of that time in the fall and useful to Andrée in lengthening the daylight beyond the "equinox."

But although there was neither fear nor despondency, there was with the party an uncertainty as to plan. For motives were mixed. It was not their one concern, nor even their main concern, to get back safe. They were on a scientific expedition, and on a high adventure; they wanted to do well, for they were ambitious men; they wanted to bring back knowledge, for they were scientists. So the question really was, which way they should travel so as to combine safety, to them the minor factor, with what the record shows was their major purpose, that of making a creditable and useful journey.

The nearest place where there were houses, so that they could have lived more or less in European style, was Mossel Bay on northwestern Spitsbergen. That was reasonably near, but the journey back there would have been more or less a confession of failure, an admission that they were ready to sacrifice scientific results and fame for exclusive safety and mere comfort.

Nothing is perfectly clear with regard to the plans, for the records are not complete. It is not so much that records have been lost, though some may have been, as that not everything was written which was in the minds of the party. Generally they seem to have felt that traveling to the Franz Josef Islands would best combine a notable journey, the chances of acquiring knowledge, and the attainment of a desirable wintering place.

It fitted in with this plan that the drift at times seemed trying to carry them in this direction. They would have two means of progress; their own travel over the ice, and the travel of the ice itself towards the warm North Atlantic waters which we connect with the Gulf Stream.

It has been the subject of much comment, and the nearest thing to serious criticism of Andrée, that he seems to have had the feeling that there was nothing much against drifting south between Spitsbergen and the Franz Josef Islands. For his diary mentions, without adverse comment, that if they got down well to the south in the open sea the weather would not be so cold and there might be more game.

These entries are so inconsistent with all we know of Andrée that we practically have to think of what might be called a literary explanation, that he had qualifying and negative ideas in his mind but, for some reason, did not write them down. According to his intellect and knowledge, he should have prefaced his remarks by "While it is true that" and ended them with a decisive negative: to the effect that, even though it would be warmer and game might prove more abundant, a drift southward beyond the island groups was to be avoided at all costs. For nothing is more nearly inevitable than that when you get south into the warm waters derived from the Gulf Stream the ice begins to melt under you. When some of the ice melts the rest is free to spread out, so that waves can break up your floe into small fragments that dissolve the more easily, and that may tip over through wave action and spill your camp into the water some days earlier than they would melt wholly from under you.

However, what we have just said is a mere digression. Between July 22 and August 4 it became clear that the drift was not going to be towards the Franz Josef group sufficiently for the party to get ashore there before the winter darkness. August 4, therefore, the course was changed in the direction of Spitsbergen.

However, conditions did not turn out to favor Spitsbergen consistently, and there was a lot of trouble with open water. The weather was not yet cold enough to form useful new ice, and the movement of the pack was erratic, so that the sledgers were sometimes carried away from land by the motion of the floes. Counteracting this was difficult because of frequent leads of open water. They were traveling with three sledges and a canvas canoe. It was possible to ferry sledges and loads across the leads with the canoe, but that was tedious because the outfit was so big that several ferryings would be needed for each lead.

September 12 or 13 a momentous and, as we know, untenable decision was made. It was for the party to spend the entire winter on a floe, which they now selected. This would have been a prudent decision had they been several hundred miles farther north, with no danger of drifting south beyond the Franz Josef and Spitsbergen groups before the clear weather and hard frosts of February, March, and April made it easy for them to sledge ashore in one of these groups. In fact, the Andrée party had already drifted so far south by September 12 that, to us, it seems obvious their floe was due to be carried into the dangerous "Gulf Stream" waters south of the island groups during that early and awkward part of winter when there is scant daylight and when the temperatures are not yet as low as they are going to be. When you are living on drifting ice, or traveling across it, your two best friends are a northerly latitude and a cold season of year.

As the party were looking forward to a whole winter on the drifting floe, we might consider how they were getting along with their food—how much of it they had, how easy it was to get, how healthy they were on it, and how they liked it. We should keep steadily in mind, as we examine these questions, that one of the theories advanced to explain the eventual tragedy is that of food poisoning. Therefore, we must pay special attention to such things in the diary as may indicate trouble either with the preserved food, which they had brought with them in the balloon, or with the fresh food which they secured from day to day.

Anticipating the finding that the party did have one moderately serious form of illness while they were shifting gradually from the European to the local diet, we use as an interpretative preface a statement of general experience with all-meat diets.

It is widely accepted, and probably correct, that the chief difficulty in shifting from a mixed to a meat diet is psychological—a digestive revulsion based upon the idea that meat is dangerous. For, until recently, it has been a common belief that you cannot be healthy unless you have a varied diet, that meat is injurious if taken in large quantities, and that you become "tired of a monotonous diet." The Andrée party do not seem to have had any such inhibitions. This may have been because they were familiar with the history of human diet and knew that nations and races have lived for centuries and millenniums on a diet mainly or exclusively meat. More likely they expected the desirability and palatability of a meat diet through the recent experience of Nansen and Johansen who, as we have noticed more than once, spent a whole winter (a little farther north than the Andrée party would be spending theirs) on an exclusive meat diet, coming out in the spring with the best of health.

It is a nearly universal experience, when a shift is being made from a mixed to a meat diet under such conditions as those of the Andrée party, that there is little or no prejudice against the lean of the Arctic animals but considerable against the fat. This fat is called blubber, is supposed to be reprehensible, and the very thought of it commonly nauseates the inexperienced.

But it has been found in various parts of the world that a diet of lean meat exclusively will cause diarrhea in from three days to a week. If no fat can be added to the lean, the diarrhea becomes serious and will lead to death. A well known field where such deaths occur is the northern edge of the forest in Canada where Indians are sometimes unable to find any food except rabbits. The expression "rabbit starvation," frequently heard among the Athapasca Indians northwest of Great Bear Lake, means not that people are starving because there are no rabbits but that they are going through the experience of starvation with plenty of rabbit meat. For this animal is so lean that illness and death result from being confined to its flesh.

When a party like Andrée's are making a gradual shift from a mixed to a meat diet, no diarrhea will appear in the early stages; for there is still a considerable percentage of sugars, starches and the accustomed fats, such as butter or bacon. When these elements are materially lowered, and meat begins to play a larger and larger part, you approach the diarrhea stage. The trouble, once begun, will continue until the party overcomes its prejudice against "blubber" and begins to use fat enough to make up for the things (like potatoes, bread, and sugar) which are normally eaten by a man fond of beefsteak who, when he eats his steak, trims the fat away.

With this introduction, we turn to reviewing the food situation as it appears from the Andrée diary.

No suspicious illness was mentioned during the four-day balloon voyage when the food was mainly canned or otherwise preserved. Thus far a clean bill for the tinned provisions.

There is mention of some of the preserved food being in bad condition. The most notable is on July 23, where Strindberg speaks of the Rousseau meat powder as having a bad taste. The diary does not connect this with an illness, nor can we find a connection.

The first bear was killed on July 20. That evening they had fried bear's meat. We infer from what is said later that the frying was in butter, on which they were already economizing. So there was little butter fat used with this lean meat. However, they were still eating a good many kinds of European food, the starches and sugars of which would take the place of fat. Nor is there any reference to diarrhea for a considerable time after the first bear steak.

A week later we find "bear-beef immensely good." Doubtless they were still frying it in butter, economically.

August 1 we read that they are "longing for bears for the meat is finished." Next day they "got a bear. It was an old worn-out male animal with rotten teeth." Andrée does not mention his being skinny, but that sort of animal has to be. They took the fillet, kidneys, tongue and ribs. In a later entry he says that they were particularly fond of the rib meat of bears.

The diary says much in praise of the various meats secured by hunting, and there is only one complaint, which we find on August 3. This is not that bear tastes bad but that the steaks from the last one were "tough as leather galoshes.

[Fraenkel said] he believed it was an escaped menagerie bear."

However, even this bear gets a compliment. On August 6 we read, "The bear meat is very good when it has become old." Probably the temperatures in the sledges at this season of year were similar to those used by the Chicago packers in the chilling of meat which is done partly to make it tender.

By August 9 the food was chiefly meat. Nothing is mentioned for breakfast except steak and coffee. There is no sign yet that any fat was used except the small butter ration. On that date, therefore after several days of a very largely lean meat diet, we have the first trouble. Andrée speaks of Fraenkel as being ill and says that he "gave him opium for the diarrhea."

The next day the party "had a feast with sardines for dinner and a Stauffer cake for supper." We do not know what the Stauffer cake was, but sardines are proverbially greasy. It can have been the opium but, to judge from Stefansson's experience, it may well have been the grease of the sardines which enabled Andrée to say a little later, "Fraenkel's stomach pains are now over."

August 12 they had fried ivory gull and worried because they had "not more than one meal of bear meat left."

August 13 they killed three bears from which they took about ninety pounds, apparently heart, brain, kidneys, tongue, and rib meat, for other parts are not mentioned. As is no doubt common in the carnivores, the tongue of the bear is deficient in fat, as compared with beef or sheep tongue. The only part of the bears taken by Andrée which might have contained clear fat would be the ribs. Since it is several days yet before we find a reference to bear fat being eaten, it is likely enough that, as common with novices, the party were still trimming fat from the meat and eating little or no fat except the small butter ration.

August 15 has Andrée and Strindberg suffering from diarrhea and "eating masses of meat." The 16th they were eating 2.4 pounds of bear meat each and there has been as yet no mention of fat. The 18th they killed a bear and "took out the brain, kidneys, tongue and some pieces along the back." All this would be lean except that there is considerable fat in the brain. But, then, bears have small brains.

August 19 we discover the first reference to the use of native fats when we hear of an "attempt at frying with bear fat."

For August 21 Andrée says: "This evening on my proposal we tasted what raw meat was like. Raw bear with salt tastes like oysters and we hardly wanted to fry it. Raw brain is also very good and the bear's meat was easily eaten raw."

On that same day they made apparently the first experiment with a local vegetable product. They concocted a soup from algae. It was doubtless Strindberg, the biologist, who secured this plant from one of the leads. Andrée says that the soup "gave excellent results" and that Strindberg had made what "should be considered a fairly important discovery for travelers in these tracts."

However, two days later, August 23, we have a two-to-one reversal of opinion, when Fraenkel and Strindberg disagree with Andrée who still likes the soup. This was, apparently, the last experiment with a local vegetable product.

August 22, they found "bear ham several days old exquisite."

August 23, it is noted that the daily bread ration was now less than one ounce, the biscuit ration less than two ounces, and the bear-meat ration just over two pounds. Andrée says, "We thrive very well on the diet."

August 24, we get the first information that the local fat is coming into favor. "We now fry the bear's meat without butter and find it excellent. The butter is eaten now only at dinner. The meat ration per day is now 2.9 lbs. . . . Last night Fraenkel had severe diarrhea."

The 25th, both Fraenkel and Andrée had diarrhea. On the 27th the same men are mentioned as having it. The 28th, Fraenkel is suffering. The general statement shows the percentage of European food in the ration was small and getting smaller. August 30, Andrée had diarrhea. They were on a nearly exclusive lean-meat diet, for they were not yet eating the bear fat—they were just using it as a medium of cooking the lean. And, as we have seen, they were eating some of the lean uncooked. There would be a little grease clinging to the fried lean, but not nearly enough for a balanced ration. There would be no fat with the raw lean.

Although compliments for lean bear meat are frequent before and including September 1, the first complimentary remark about fat, as such, does not come until September 3. Now Andrée says about a bear that "he jogged away and so cheated us both of brains and kidneys, to say nothing of kidney fat and blood pancake."

Hereafter the fat gets more compliments than the lean. On the 4th they had "bear's meat and bear's fat" for breakfast, "fried bear's meat" for dinner, and "bear's meat" for supper. That day they had a considerable amount of European food, specially, for it was Strindberg's birthday.

From the compliments we infer that the party, somewhere between the 1st and 4th of September, began to eat bear fat in appreciable quantity. On the 4th they had fried bread. The kind of fat used in the frying is not specified, but it must have been bear's grease; for the butter had long been scarce, bear's fat was now considered good, and it takes a lot of grease to fry bread, which soaks it up. By the same token, when you eat fried bread you eat a lot of grease.

On September 9, six days after the first complimentary reference to bear's fat, Andrée says that "our attacks of diarrhea seem to have stopped." He proved correct. There are no references to diarrhea from September 9 to the close of the diary October 8. Meantime there are increasingly frequent compliments to the fat. On September 15 the first seal was secured. The record for this day, written on September 17, remarks that "every part of the seal tastes very nice. We are very fond of the meat and the blubber." They now speak of seal meals as feasts.

September 19, Andrée reminisces to the effect that during the first few days both he and Strindberg felt a revulsion to seal meat or blubber. The trend of the entry shows that he is speaking definitely of the past. Today they had excellent blood pancake with seal blood and seal fat.

September 20, they tried strips of raw seal blubber on some bread which they still had left and "it tasted just like bacon and bread and we ate it willingly. . . . The seal meat seems almost to melt away on boiling; after boiling a few minutes it becomes extremely tender and delicate." September 23, Andrée says, "We have now also tried the meat of the great seal and have found that it tastes excellent."

We see, then, the party enjoyed all the native lean meats from the start, except that two of the three, Strindberg and Andrée, had felt revulsion to the "seal meat and blubber" for the first few days. There is nowhere complaint against bear meat as such, but merely against the meat of one particularly aged bear on the score of toughness.

There are references which show that Andrée knew of the belief, doubtless well founded, that some bear livers are "poisonous"; for in one entry he says that "of course" the bear liver was not among the parts used.

The sole illness of record which might be traced to food was diarrhea. Nowhere in the diary can we trace this to the canned food, but the diarrhea of the fresh-meat period can be traced to there being insufficient fat with the lean during the time of rapidly decreasing European rations and rapidly growing quantities of local food. All three men were in perfect health about five or six days after the first entry which shows that they were beginning to like the taste of the local animal fats. They remained in perfect health thereafter.

When they decided upon a winter residence on this floe, and began to construct their "permanent" house of ice blocks, they had on hand provisions for only three weeks at limited rations. Their "patent" fuel was sufficient to cook with for perhaps two months. This means, of course, that they were counting upon the game for fuel as well as food. That was logical, for it runs through the documents of the Andrée party that they believed the pack ice, and the waters beneath, abundantly supplied with blubber-bearing animals; that they believed they could secure these and live on them. By September 12 they had already secured more proofs of the rightness of this view than we have yet mentioned. We give some of them now.

From the balloon, the party saw two seals July 12 and a bear July 13.

July 15, after the balloon's descent, André's diary speaks of "the first bear," which may mean the first killed. On July 20 a bear was killed; July 26, one was killed and two more seen. The last July bear was killed the 27th.

August and September resembled July. From July 15 to September 29 there were killed thirteen bears on ten different days; at last seven others were sighted.

More seals were sighted than bears—too many for bothering to count them, for we have in the notes references to "seals," "seals often in openings," and "many seals." Six are mentioned as killed.

Apparently, then, the party tried to secure most of the bears, but refrained from trying with most of the seals until after the "permanent" camp was made. This was logical. They must have been unable to haul with them more than a small part of the bear meat. Seals would have been an addition to a superfluity throughout the fifty-two sledging days.

Other life was noted, big and small. What was probably a whale was seen on two occasions; a walrus was definitely identified. There were many birds, chiefly guillemots and gulls. There were plants and small animals in the leads. The ice was honeycombed with holes created by the sun when its rays had been changed from light into heat by striking dark plant surfaces.

Our rating of Andrée's judgment drops when we realize what three guns and what ammunition he carried. Two guns were single-barrels, both smooth-bore 20 gauge. The third was double-barreled with a 20-bore shot barrel and a 450-caliber rifle barrel. For these weapons he had 144 cartridges with bullet; 480 with 00 shot; 120 with 4 shot. These were, both the bullets and the shot, for the various 20-gauge smooth-bore barrels. Then he carried 24 solid bullet cartridges for the rifled barrel and 24 with "explosive bullets" (dum-dum?).

One could scarcely think of a hunting equipment less effective for its weight. It is clear that Andrée figured bears and seals would be numerous in the pack; in any case you would surely not expect to find birds where you did not also find bears and seals. Yet nearly all the ammunition carried is designed for birds!

The only defense plea we can think of it that Andrée counted on the balloon carrying him beyond any shore of the Polar Sea, depositing his party on some such land as northern Siberia or Canada. Even there his reasoning would be at fault.

For the basic weakness of trying for birds when you live by hunting is applicable on land as well as at sea—that a shot cartridge, although heavier than a bullet cartridge, will bring you only a few ounces, or at most a few pounds, of bird meat; while the less heavy bullet cartridge will bring a hundred-pound animal if it is a small seal; several hundred pounds if it is a bearded seal or a caribou; 500 pounds, or even more, if it is a polar bear at sea or a grizzly, musk ox or moose on land.

Why carry an ounce cartridge that will only translate into a pound of food when you could carry a half-ounce cartridge that will translate into a hundred pounds of food?

That much for the bad side of the picture. The good side is that this failure in suiting equipment to conditions can have had no bearing on the final tragedy, as will appear in due course.

There are diary entries, however, which show Andrée was troubled by this weakness in his equipment. Samples are two which we quote:

September 8: ". . . Our fresh meat is beginning to run low and we shot two ivory gulls to eke out. We do not like to fire unless we can get at least two gulls to the shot. They taste good but cost us too much ammunition. . . ."

September 22: ". . . Strindberg shot a seal (with small shot) and in addition we got two ivory gulls but we must be careful with our shooting for we miss pretty often as the seals as a rule do not come so near that we can be certain of hitting the head with small shot. . . ."

Adding up the given figures, there were in the balloon 192

bullet cartridges and 600 shot cartridges. Andrée's model, Nansen, had started out on his journey from the *Fram* with only 200 cartridges, 100 bullets and 100 shot. With that ammunition he and Johansen wintered successfully once, and considered that they had left enough ammunition to spend several more winters.

Nansen had secured most of his food and fuel through the bullet ammunition. Strange that Andrée, who knew this, had to learn from his own experience what sort of firearms and ammunition are best.

Later expeditions have confirmed Nansen's confidence in getting much food with a few bullets. For instance, the sledge parties of the various Stefansson expeditions have found that, on the average, they got about 100 pounds of animals, live weight, for each bullet. Those cartridges ran 33 to the pound, so that a pound of ammunition translated itself into 3,000 pounds of live-weight game, or some 2,000 pounds of clear food. But, of course, this high-power ammunition of 1908 to 1918 was, in the ratio of weight to power, greatly superior to the "express" cartridges available to Nansen when outfitting in 1893 or to Andrée in 1897.

September 17, the Andrée party became dramatically aware of their rapid drift. They had known of it from their astronomical observations which, on September 15, showed them to be at N. Lat. 80° 45′. Now they came in sight of land. It was White Island, directly south of them.

One of the reasons for camping and preparing to winter had been most sensible, although by itself not sufficient. This was that if they were sledging when they killed game they could take with them only a little of the meat; but if they were in "permanent" camp they could save every scrap of any animal they killed to use for food and fuel, using the skins for improvised dwellings. They mention these things in their records, but do not mention another favorable point quite as important—that if you remain in camp you develop a source of odors which, though perhaps not very noticeable to humans, can be scented by a polar bear ten or more miles away. It is the nature of bears when they are out in the pack that they investigate whatever they smell. If men stand watch-and-watch at a drifting camp, mainly spying to lee-ward, they will secure nearly every bear that walks into camp.

A further mentioned reason for camping was that Fraenkel had a bad foot which, in Andrée's belief, needed a rest of one or two weeks. This last was perhaps a reason for delay; but not for planning a whole winter's residence on this floe.

Between July 22 and September 11 the party, with a load of some 225 pounds per man, had sledged most of the fifty-two days, working so hard and making so much progress, considering the difficulties of season and the strong currents of the district, that theirs is one of the most creditable jour-neys afoot ever made on the polar sea.

The daily sight of White Island did not apparently stir within the party any thoughts of leaving their drifting home and moving ashore.

September 19, two ordinary seals were secured and a bearded seal. The 20th, they killed a bear; the 22nd, a seal, and the 29th, again a bear. The small seals probably weighed a little over 100 pounds; the bearded seal and the bears weighed several hundred. Andrée computes reasonably that they now had provisions to last them till April. This was both food and fuel. By methods similar to those used by Nansen on land, they would build on their floe a house of ice blocks, chinked with snow and roofed with skins. They would burn seal oil where he had burned walrus, no doubt with equally good results.

September 20, comes a note more ominous to us than to Andrée. He was annoyed that spare parts for his primus stove had been left behind by mistake in Spitsbergen. As we have inferred, that did not seem to him to matter really; he had petroleum for only a few weeks anyway and would be using the blubber of seals for light and cooking most of the winter.

Andrée now mentions some friction between members of the party; but ten days later this difficulty had not recurred, and we get the impression that, with this exception, the three got along without friction.

That, certainly, is the general impression you get from the

Andrée diary. It is, too, the general impression you get if you properly study the records of exploration. But somehow the public is not so convinced of anything about polar work as that two or three men are sure to have a lot of emotional difficulty. In popular belief they inevitably get on each other's nerves, until the strain becomes unbearable.

What appears from the record is that strains of this kind do develop among men who are idle. Idleness on polar expeditions is usually in connection with a fairly large party that is wintering. It is quite clear, for instance, that Nansen and Johansen had no difficulty at all during several months when they saw no one but each other. It has been the experience of Stefansson with perhaps a dozen different journeys made by parties from his various expeditions, of some of which parties he was a member, that two or three men can travel half a year at a time with never a cross word, and that they usually do. There was but one case of friction from all these small-party journeys and that was a squabble which blew over in half an hour, somewhat, apparently, as did the one Andrée mentions. But it was the usual thing that when these small traveling parties of the Stefansson expedition came back to winter quarters they found the men there divided into cliques, with bitterness against each other, against the expedition, and against the world.

Doubtless the key to friction is not the size of a party but the conditions, particularly the activity. When you are drifting on a floe that is in danger of cracking at any time, when you are living by getting every seal and polar bear, when you are traveling in new country, when there are excitements and uncertainties about natural conditions, the rule seems to be, as it was with Andrée, that everybody is cheerful, that most people are optimistic, and that thoughts are directed to issues of common welfare rather than to personal differences.

The latter part of September the party had drifted into the near vicinity of White Island, but still we find no indication that they seriously considered breaking away from the drift camp and moving ashore. They were living in their "permanent" house, built of ice blocks and skins of animals. They expected the floe to continue traveling; but on it they were going to stay put.

We now quote Andrée's record for dates which proved crucial:

September 22: ". . . we were disturbed by hearing the floe break, as we thought, right under the building. We were afraid that we had run aground but our bearings have shown that we are moving although we seem unable to get away from this island. Probably we are lying in some kind of backwater which the current from the north creates at the S. eastern and S. western corners of the island and along its southern side. . . . The patchy black guillemots and ivory gulls are common here, we have also seen several specimens of the before-mentioned 'ivory youngster.' The ordinary fulmar on the other hand is seen remarkably seldom."

A drifting floe is theoretically a better hunting ground than a stationary island. If you are on land, or landfast ice, the game is on one side of you—out on the moving pack. If you are in the pack the game area surrounds you. So far as it goes, this argument is for wintering in the pack. Andrée should not have been swayed by it; for he was finding that the backwater which was holding him by White Island was well supplied with food of a kind which the party considered both wholesome and pleasant. To bring out that point, and several other details, we quote nearly the whole entry for September 23:

"Today all three of us have been working busily on the hut cementing together ice-blocks. We have got on very well and the hut now begins to take form a little. After a couple of more days of such weather and work it should not take long before we are able to move in. We can probably carry our supplies in the day after tomorrow. This is very necessary; as mortar we employ snow mixed with water and of this mass, which Strindberg handles with great skill, he is also making a vaulted roof over the last parts between the walls. We now have a very good arrangement of the day with 8 hours' work, beginning with 2½ hours' work, followed by breakfast ¾ [hour] and afterwards work until 4.45 o'cl. when we dine and take supper in one meal. We

have now also tried the meat of the great seal and have
found that it tastes excellent. One of the very best improve-
ments in the cooking is that of adding blood to the sauce for
the steak. This makes it thick and it tastes as if we had bread.
I cannot believe but that blood contains much carbohydrate,
for our craving for bread is considerably less since we began
to use blood in the food. We all think so. We have also
found everything eatable both as regards bear, great seal, seal
and ivory gull (bear's-liver of course excepted). For want
of time we have not yet been able to cut up and weigh our
animal but I think we now have meat and ham enough to
last on into spring. We must however shoot more so as to be
able to have larger rations and to get more fuel and light."

They now had a particularly good chance for moving
ashore, if not upon the island itself, which looked forbid-
dingly precipitous for climbing, then at least upon the landfast ice. Such ice, which will fringe that kind of shore, has in
winter the residence advantages of an Arctic land, excepting
that land may have driftwood. During their fifty-two days
of active traveling the party had found, as all northern
travelers do in summer and autumn, a chief difficulty with
the open water on and between the floes. Now all the water
on the floes had frozen, and the entry for September 29 tells
that the leads had frozen too; so that there would have been
apparently good sledging all the way to land. We quote in
part:

"We are still lying off the south side of N.I. [White Island].
The ice-sludge has closed and the seals have disappeared.
On the other hand the bears are coming. Yesterday and the
day before we had visits from bears at night and I tried to
hunt a bear in my stocking-feet but did not succeed. This
morning just as we came out Fraenkel saw a bear which
we succeeded in enticing to where we were waiting behind
our hut. Strindberg shot him. . . . The night-bears seem to
be a kind of marauder; the one that visited us last night
dragged away our big seal twice and we should have lost it if
Strindberg had not succeeded in coming so near the bear that
he frightened him and made him drop his booty.

"Our floe is diminished in a somewhat alarming degree

close to our hut. The ice pressure brings the shores closer and closer to us. But we have a large line of old hummocks between the hut and the shore and hope that this will stop the pressure. The sounds are magnificent when there is pressure but otherwise it does not appeal to us.

". . . Yesterday evening the 28th we moved into our hut which was christened 'home.' We slept there last night and found it rather nice. But it will become much better of course. We are obliged to have the meat inside to protect ourselves against the bears."

A turning point in the expedition came October 1. We give that entry in full:

"October 1 was a good day. The evening was as divinely beautiful as one could wish. The water was filled with small animals and a bevy of seven black-and-white 'guillemot youngsters' were swimming there. A couple of seals appeared too. The work with the hut went on well and we thought that we should have the outside ready by the 2nd. But then something else happened. At 5.30 A.M. (local time) [October] 2 we heard a thunderous crash and water streamed into the hut and when . . . rushed out we found that our large beautiful floe had been splintered into a number of little floes and that one fissure had divided the floe just outside the wall of the hut. The floe that remained to us had a diam. of only 24 meters [80 feet] and one wall of the hut might be said rather to hang from the roof than to support it. This was a great reversal in our position and our prospects. The hut and the floe could not give us shelter and still we were obliged to stay there for the present at least. We were frivolous enough to sleep in the hut the following night too. Perhaps it was because the day was rather tiring. Our belongings were scattered among several blocks and these were drifting here and there so that we had to work fast. Two bear carcasses, representing provisions for three or four months, were lying on a separate floe and so on. Luckily the weather was beautiful so that we could work in haste. No one had lost courage; with such comrades one should be able to manage under, I may say, any circumstances."

Not even the diary for October 2, the day on which the floe was split so their belongings drifted in various directions, shows any plan or desire to move ashore. That the cliffs seemed too precipitous to scale would have been a minor consideration had they preferred a stationary to a moving house site, for Andrée had known at least from September 12, when he saw calf bergs, that there was along the cliff landfast ice which would be practically as safe as the land itself for a winter camp. Besides, he would know also that a cliff which looks unscalable from a distance may not prove so on close approach. Still further, they could have planned to sledge around the island to find better access from the far side. There are not even speculations on such things in the (at this stage voluminous) diary.

It is hard to grasp, but true, that the risks of the drifting pack did not produce even talk of a move to White Island or to its landfast sea ice. There have been many theories on what it was that kept them mentally as well as bodily wedded to the drifting ice fragment. The chief suggestions have been that they feared not being able to relay all their meat ashore (the ice might drift off with some of it), that they hated to give up their cozy house (even though one of its walls hung suspended over water!) and that they feared there would be less game on the island than at sea. Each of these reasons has some force; all of them together fail to explain sufficiently why no movement was made towards land between early morning of October 2 and the evening of October 5.

Or shall we say that the explanation is needed only till some time October 4? For on that day we find at last a discussion about going ashore. Some time during that day the floe had drifted in sight of a bit of ice-free lowland. Evidently this kindled a desire to move ashore. Since the mere safety of landfast ice, held there by grounded calf ice, had not been attractive, it may have been partly the charm, the sentimental aspect, of land which now drew them. There were, of course, more practical reasons. You could not expect to find driftwood on landfast ice nor on glacier-covered land; but a low ice-free beach might have driftwood—for fuel, for house rafters, and for other uses.

So, late in the day October 4, they decided to move ashore. This was mainly accomplished during good weather on the 5th, and finished on the 6th. The diary entries show that it was backbreaking work. From this it has been concluded that they did not carry all their food with them—the meat and fat accumulations which Andrée had previously called sufficient to last till spring. Pallin, however, believes they must have taken all the food ashore. He infers this from a portion of the Andrée diary which had not been deciphered when the official account was published in 1930, but which now has been so nearly completed through various technical methods that Pallin can base on it what he feels is a sure inference, that the party still had food with them which they estimated good for many months. This he deduces from the statement that they saw a polar bear, and from the inference that they did not pursue and try to kill it but instead went ahead with their regular labors. That would seem to indicate there was a combination of two ideas—they had a lot of food on hand, and game was so plentiful they felt if they did not get this bear they would later get another.

We agree with Pallin's interpretation and cite further clues which appear to lead in the same direction. The full transcription of the entries from Andrée's small notebook, which we shall give a few pages ahead, will, we think, convince the reader that, although brief, these notes would not fail to mention such a disappointment as it would have been to them had they not been able to carry all the food ashore. Besides, we are told that moving ashore was a heavy labor which occupied a considerable part of two different days. But the camp was near the shore and the ice conditions were fairly good, to judge from the entries. They had three sledges and were accustomed to hauling about 225 pounds on each, even when they were making long trips, so that we might figure they would haul at least that much when they were relaying ashore. They cannot have had material for several three-sledge trips ashore unless they took with them most of the meat. But they became very tired, so that they must have made several trips. So we feel it reasonable to conclude that they took everything with them. They therefore landed on White Island with food which they believed would last them till April.

There is a good deal of relief expressed by the diary after the party came ashore. Andrée speaks of what a blessing it was not to hear the continual crashing, growling and din of the ice. Still, Pallin would seem right that the strictly emotional or sentimental reaction was stronger. He cites as parallel the ecstasy in Nansen's first diary entries when he and Johansen got ashore in the Franz Josef Islands in 1895. He believes Andrée's feelings were similar and thinks that his naming the little piece of flat land Mina Andrée's Place is conclusive of this. For Andrée was extremely fond of his mother, and she had died just as he was setting out upon the expedition. It was affection for the land, rather than gratitude for its safety, that is shown by the diary; and particularly by his naming the beach after his mother.

The party found driftwood as might have been expected, and the bones of whales. The diary says that they planned using these as framework in their house. They at first intended wintering near the landing spot, but later decided to move to another place. Seemingly Strindberg was the controlling spirit here. By temperament and perhaps by training he was a builder. He wanted things as commodious and comfortable as possible. One gets from the diary for the time spent in the "permanent" camp on the floe the feeling that Andrée and Fraenkel were content with a mere shelter. Differences of that kind between travelers usually appear under like circumstances. Some would rather work hard for a good house; others would rather build easily a shelter which they consider good enough.

At no stage does the Andrée party seem to have worried on the score of food. And why should they?

They were near the Spitsbergen group, which has always been a food paradise. The man who first of Englishmen saw it, Henry Hudson, said that he conceived the district would well repay anyone who should adventure it. He had in mind the pursuit of the great mammals, the whale, walrus, and seal. His forecast was proved by experience. For Spitsbergen became, and remained for generations, the light of the world in that so many of these great mammals were killed by ships or from shore stations that Spitsbergen grew to be a chief source of oil from the lamps of Europe. It was the kerosene lamps that finally broke down this great industry.

Andrée knew that in killing the animals that gave all this light through centuries, Europeans had handled, and in the main thrown away, incredible quantities of meat. They ate what they needed as the fresh-meat element of their diet; the rest, it did not pay them to handle.

But such things apply to well found ships and stations. More significant for Andrée was what he knew about Spitsbergen castaways. For instance, he knew Edward Pellham's *Gods Power and Providence* (London, 1631). This little book tells how eight Englishmen were separated from their ship by misadventure and spent the winter in an improvised shelter, even without ammunition. They killed enough bears with their spears and secured enough walrus with their harpoons to be in passably good condition when ships returned to them after nine months.

Most immediate in the consciousness of the Andrée party must have been the mentioned story of Nansen and Johansen, who only two years before had arrived by sledge and canoe from the polar sea, had climbed upon the shore of one of the most northerly of the Franz Josef Islands and had wintered there in good health, deriving food, light, and fuel from animals, and building their shelter of animal skins, stones, and snow.

The ingrained confidence based on knowledge of the past, and on Andrée's own fourteen-year experience of the Spitsbergen vicinity, was reinforced by their constant observations. The diary of seventy-nine days spent on the ice mentions birds so often and in such terms that we gain the impression they must have been almost too common for entries, were seen even more often than they are recorded. Andrée saw seals, often several, on fourteen days and secured six. He saw twenty polar bears on seventeen days and secured thirteen.

There runs through his account how much he was impressed with the richness of the district. Contemplating the wealth of knowledge that there would be in studying this wealth of life in and on the ice, he says, for instance on August 23:

"On the surface of a very large white pressed piece of ice there was made find No. 17, all the parts of which lay near each other. The lighter parts more on the surface. The heavier deeper. After this find I observed that the ice is perforated everywhere and filled with things that are certainly well deserving of a special Polar-expedition on their own account. But then one should be provided with appliances to enable one easily to enlarge the holes and take up the objects. The naturalist would find the interior of the ice to be almost as rich in contents as the earth-crust or the sea. . . ."

Andrée's own diaries contain many observations that were contributions to this study; his party gathered and numbered specimens. The highest numbering of the natural history specimens is nineteen.

Nothing is, then, more natural than what some commentators have thought strange, that optimism and confidence ran throughout the journey, and that they still persisted to the last diary entry, the one of October 8.

Having finished our preliminary survey and analysis of the main points in the written documentary evidence of White Island, we come to the full and approximately literal translation, from the Swedish, of the documents themselves which relate to the stay on White Island.

If Fraenkel wrote anything during the time of moving ashore, or during the stay in White Island, it has all been lost. He kept the meteorological records, and the last we have of them are for October 3.

Any diary or connected notes which Strindberg may have kept during the moving, or on the island, have failed of discovery, but a calendar was found with some notes by him. Although they are few and terse, they are significant. There has never been trouble in deciphering them, nor can there be much debate on their interpretation. We shall use each in connection with Andrée's diary for the same date. It is crucial to note, as will appear later, that, while the entries from October 2 to 7 are in pencil, the one for October 17 is in pen and ink.

The Andrée memorandum book was seriously damaged along its keel, and hard to read. It was so faded and discolored that when the official narrative was published in 1930 only a few words had yet been deciphered along the right-hand margin of page 1, the left-hand margin of page 2, the right-hand margin of page 3, and so on. There were only a few spots where enough words appeared for the Committee to make sense out of them. Later on, however, the mutilated document was photographed in various intensities and kinds of light and from various angles; there were also chemical and physical methods applied. Among the leaders in this study were H. N. Pallin, author of the book on which we so considerably rely, and Sigurd Köhler, a Norwegian engineer, one of those to whom was entrusted the preservation of the Andrée relics.

We now translate the diary as restored, remembering that a few of the words are still conjectural. Wherever the dates fit, we use Strindberg's calendar notes in connection with the Andrée diary. Emendations and suggestions for explanations are in brackets.

October 4: Strindberg note: "Tense situation."

October 4: Andrée's diary: "During October 4, 1897, we have been occupied cutting up the animals killed and also in beginning the construction of a new house to have it ready in case of need, for the farther wall of our snow house is projecting over the edge of our floe. The day passed uneventfully except that we made an important observation. There is a lowland on the island; that is to say, a refuge if we don't drift too far past [before being able to get ashore because of ice movement and open water]. Perhaps this may prove not an insignificant factor in our situation. It turned out that Strindberg was right. Of course, what we need is a landing place that will give us access to the lowland. The problem is to get all our things moved over there. The landing spot we had previously thought possible is impossible to reach. Probably we shall have to hop from floe to floe a good deal for transferring to a large floe so that we can later, by approaching the glacier, investigate how we can climb up from the ice to the island. This afternoon five birds were seen flying towards the island. They were probably eider-ducks or geese."

Tuesday October 5: Strindberg's note: "Moved ashore."

Tuesday October 5: Andrée's diary: "During the morning of the 5th we found ourselves in the neighborhood of the previously mentioned lowland and now we could get a clear idea of the island and were so placed that there was good ice over to it. Also after some search [we determined upon] the best landing place [as I indicated to them] from the shore. It was six hours, Greenwich time, when we reached land and as we traveled along the glacier and then from the glacier upon the land. We did not cease from our hard day's work until well into the night—after the day's labor we did not tent until the middle of the night, and ate our food in darkness as the northern light which flickered outside in the south, neither lighted up nor warmed [our camp]. The cooking apparatus was once more cranky and hard to get along with, so that either boiling or frying was impossible. We did not creep into our bags to sleep until it was already the next day—my mother's birthday. For that reason we named the district where our new camp was Mina Andrée's Place."

Wednesday October 6: Strindberg's note: "Snowstorm; reconnoitering."

Wednesday October 6: Andrée's diary: "When we awoke during the day of the 6th, there was snow, and a strong wind with drift, so that we could not do much. Still, we made a short tour of reconnoitering, then returning to our tent. So it turns out that Swedes have been the first visitors to these icy tracts. What at once interested us was finding high inland, a long way from the sea, logs of driftwood. The whole place consists of granite cliffs, rubble and gravel. Some of the gravel was coarse. The gravel land in part takes the form of extensive flats and of hummocks. . . . Probably the land rises steeply towards the interior. Now it is hard labor as long as there is daylight. During the evening we started in the dark to build a snowhouse and to carry our belongings to its neighborhood. This was heavy work, but it was soon over."

Thursday October 7: Strindberg's note: "Moved." (That is, moved camp.)

Thursday October 7: Andrée's diary: "I wanted to move the camp for I feared, in case of a snowstorm such as we had yesterday, the site we were on would be covered with snow and would be made unsuitable for winter quarters. The glacier, which none of us had yet examined, was now visited to see if it could be utilized, and for getting a view of our surroundings. It turned out that the glacier was very steep and must be higher inland than we had previously believed. During the afternoon a bear was seen coming from the sea, but he avoided us and has not since been heard from. There do not seem to be any foxes. The worst robbers are the gulls, which are around our camp and our meat depot. They fight, scream, and struggle with each other; in their jealousy they no longer give the impression of innocent white doves, but of being outright beasts of prey."

Friday October 8: No notes by Strindberg.

Friday October 8: Andrée's diary: "During the 8th the weather was bad and we had to keep to the tent all day. Still we fetched enough driftwood so that we could lay the beams for the roof of our house. It feels fine to be able to sleep here on fast land as a contrast with the drifting ice out upon the ocean where we constantly heard the cracking, grinding, and din. We shall have to gather driftwood and bones of whales and will have to do some moving around when the weather permits."

Sunday October 17: Strindberg's note: "Home 7:05 A.M."

Thus ends the shore diary, with not even premonition of trouble. So the testimony of what led up to the tragedy, and upon the tragedy itself, will have to be given by the camp site, by the skeletons of the dead, by the remains of their handiwork, by inanimate witnesses generally.

To understand the camp better, we scrutinize what we have that was written about it.

In the night following October 5 the party landed and camped on the first passable spot. The next day they reconnoitered by daylight and selected a place a build a snowhouse for wintering. They even started building, but on account of the weather they did little that day except move their gear to the new site. It seems probable that they did not unload the sledges but just placed them near the new site, and that they themselves for that day remained in the tent down where it was first pitched.

October 7, the tent was moved to the snowhouse location so that they could be near their work and have things more convenient. On this point, however, we possess no direct information, except Strindberg's "Moved."

Andrée's journal for this day tells that he ascended the glacier. Apparently the weather was not clear, for he says nothing about having seen other islands. Two lands should have been visible on a clear day, Spitsbergen and Northeast Land. Surely he would have mentioned these, in connection with the account of his walk, had he seen them.

October 7, Andrée writes, with evident surprise, that they found no tracks of the usually ubiquitous Arctic fox. This entry gives an impression of desolation. Pallin notes, however, that it was on this very day the party saw a polar bear and did not pursue. It is in what you think a land of plenty, rather than a land of desolation, that you do not bother to pursue a thousand pounds of food. To Andrée, as we have it from a previous entry, a bear is "a walking butcher shop" of excellent meat.

For proving White Island a place of desolation you dwell upon the absence of fox tracks. For proving the opposite you cite the gulls and the polar bear.

Still for October 7, Andrée tells that they were greatly annoyed by sea gulls, which swarmed about and were thievish.

Andrée's last discovered entry was October 8. He mentions that they had secured some whale bones and driftwood, no doubt intended for walls and rafters in their house, the driftwood also for fuel. It is this last entry that describes his great satisfaction in being ashore where he does not have to hear the "cracking, grinding, and din" of the milling floes. The party are going to continue their preparation of the camp "when the weather permits."

At the landing the weather had been rather good; during the later days it had been more snowy and blowy.

Pallin emphasizes that in the late entries, and in the last one, there is a continuation of optimism, a complete absence of foreboding. He finds they were "looking with equanimity to the future."

The last *penciled* notation on Strindberg's calendar was October 7, thus the day before Andrée's diary stops. Fraenkel had ceased keeping his meteorological record when they started moving ashore—or else the notes have been lost. Likely enough, he was keeping temporary memoranda somewhere, planning to expand them when the long days of hard work, the short nights of insufficient sleep, were replaced by the converse situation of long rests and small activity, as in the case of their forerunner of two years earlier, Nansen.

Nansen, by the way, tells us that he ceased keeping diary entries in the excitement of getting ashore in the Franz Josef Islands on August 24, 1895, and did not start keeping a diary again until December 6. He must have been making occasional fragmentary notes, however; for when he begins to write up this period from memory he does give us an occsional date upon which so-and-so happened.

The written memoranda of the Andrée party which have been recovered extend a few days into their camp construction period. Had Nansen lost his life, as Andrée did, there would seemingly have been fewer records to discover at his camp than we have found in Andrée's. It will not seem out of the way to anyone familiar with Arctic sledge journeys that several weeks go by, at critical or exhausting periods, with few or no diary records.

As mentioned in his diary and in his remarks before the balloon voyage began, Andrée frequently compared his venture with Nansen's. The comparison is nowhere more significant than on fuel, where Andrée had as much reason for optimism as with the food. The Nansen party were two; the Andrée party three. Nansen came ashore in the Franz

Josef Islands with no petroleum fuel to a land of no drift-wood; Andrée came ashore in Spitsbergen with at least a month's supply of petroleum and he found driftwood. Still, the Nansen case was really the better, for he killed four walrus, each of which must have had more blubber than An-drée's total of one bearded seal, three small seals, and two bears.

As to food: Nansen killed for camp use thirteen bears, against the two bears actually recorded by Andrée—remem-bering that the Swedes may have killed other bears after reaching White Island. That skins of only two bears were found thirty-three years later in the Andrée camp is not con-clusive, for a hungry bear may either devour the skin of a fellow bear or drag it out on the sea ice where, next spring, it would disappear with the thaw or the ice movement.

It has been said by Swedish commentators that driftwood could not have been burned indoors by the Andrée party during the winter, since they had no stove and stovepipe—that they would have had to use it outdoors in campfires. Such comments do not look back to those times in Scan-dinavia itself when wood was burned in about the same type of fireplace that Eskimos use today.

There are, in fact, two primitive ways of burning wood indoors. One is to burn it in the living room, the air for the ventilation and the draft coming in through the door and the smoke going out through a hole in the roof, both door and smoke vent being closed after each time of cooking. The other would be to construct in an alleyway, just in front of the living-room door, a tiny kitchen.

There is a further elementary way of heating houses known to many primitive peoples and surely not unknown to Andrée. When you have wood, you can make a fire out-side and heat stones in it, rolling the hot stones into the house. Stefansson has lived in a house heated in this manner and found it very satisfactory. The custom was to heat stones twice a day with a fire outdoors and then roll them in.

If you cook your food in a fireplace in the center of a room, with the smoke going out through a hole in the roof, you can incidentally heat stones by using a stone fireplace.

Then, when the cooking is over and you close the smoke exit, the warm stones give off heat for hours.

But there is no sign that Andrée used driftwood for fuel or, indeed, that he used blubber for fuel on White Island. The tragedy came too soon for that—it came while he was still using petroleum, burning it in a primus stove.

Enough matches were found on White Island to show that, avoiding waste, the Andrée party were supplied at least for a year. But a practically limitless economy in matches is possible, for you can keep a small seal-oil lamp burning constantly, always lighting fires with a greased stick which you kindle from the lamp. In such housekeeping, for instance, as that of the Mackenzie Eskimos before white influences came in, there was no occasion in a dwelling to strike a light for months at a time because lamps were burning day and night.

We now come to the one line of the record for the White Island period written in pen and ink, and come thereby to one of the most doubtful parts of the evidence.

Strindberg's calendar for October 17 has in ink, "Home 7:05 A.M." On this have been made to hinge, among others, the views that Strindberg was still living October 17; that his comrades, who are known to have survived him, must then have been living at least a day or two later, and that some journey was made. For the journey it has been suggested that an attempt was made to cross from White Island westward to another of the Spitsbergen islands; that a trip was made around White Island to discover a more suitable camp site; that an excursion was made to the top of the island for local investigation and to get a view of the surroundings. It has been suggested, too, that the entry may refer merely to Strindberg's return from a hunting excursion.

Perhaps the main contention has been that an attempt was made to reach the next island westward.

Pallin considers that the evidence, when properly understood, is all against there having been an attempt to leave White Island. His reasons are:

The records express satisfaction with being ashore on White Island. Even though little driftwood was found, there is no complaint at its inadequacy but rather, by inference, rejoicing that some was found.

There is emphasis in the record on how difficult it had been for them to get ashore on White Island (with all their supplies) from the drifting floe, and that was only a few miles, surely less than half a dozen. The distance to Northeast Land would be fifty miles, and at this time of year the ice would be known to Andrée to be still in motion.

Andrée knew that the journey to Northeast Land, though difficult now, would be easy the following spring. On October 16, the presumed time of the attempt, there were if the day was clear only about twelve hours of combined sunlight and bright twilight; during April there would be twenty-four hours of light each day. Now the weather was foggy and snowy, then it would be clear; now there was a good deal of open water, but then there would be little or none. In mid-October the ice was treacherous in that stretches not strong enough to bear a sledge would look safe because of the snow blanketing and because of the bad light, so that accidents and even drowning would be possible. Next spring there would be little weak ice, and what there was could be recognized because of less new snow and better light.

Since the record expresses no worry over food, fuel, or other problems, and no intention to move, Pallin decides that no attempt to move from White Island was made.

Commentators have thought it possible, and even likely, that an attempt was made to leave White Island. This conclusion, seemingly, they based partly on their own "common sense"—if they had been there, they would have wanted to move. But mainly the view has been grounded upon taking Strindberg's entry, "Home 7:05 A.M.," at face value, or at a little more. They interpret this notation as showing that a start had been made toward Northeast Land during daylight on the 16th, that the party had been in serious trouble, had given up the crossing, and had struggled back to shore through the night, not reaching home until the morning hours.

But "Home 7:05 A.M." could just as well mean that Strindberg had returned from a hunt. Possibly, in pursuit of a polar bear, he was separated from White Island by an open lead, which closed toward morning, enabling him to get ashore. The entry can have many other plausible interpretations.

What Pallin considers most significant is that this entry is in ink, while all other entries for near-by dates are in pencil. It was only earlier in the record for the expedition, when they were still out on the ice and the weather was less cold, that ink was used.

You write with a pencil when ink freezes. At this time of year in White Island ink would be constantly frozen unless thawed by the warmth of the body or the heat of a camp. It is difficult in a cold camp to write with ink thawed by body warmth—the surface of the paper you write on is below freezing and the ink congeals quickly. A proper camp had not yet been made on October 8, and both petroleum and blubber fuel needed to be economized. As said, no evidence has been found that driftwood was used for heating.

There are pen entries in the diary which could obviously have been made well ahead, as for October 18 the annotation, "Aée's birthday," which most of the interpreters seem to agree was a memorandum written long before so that Strindberg should not forget about this birthday when the time came. In one way or another, Pallin thinks, the notation "Home 7:05 A.M." had a similar personal meaning and was written perhaps months before the landing on White Island.

Professor Hans Wm. Ahlmann, of Geografiska Institutet, Stockholm, distinguished scholar and polar traveler, no doubt speaks for both majority opinion and the best informed Swedish opinion when he says, in a letter dated October 17, 1938:

"Regarding the notation 'hem kl. 7.5 f.m.' [home 7.05 A.M.] I can state as *settled* that this was written by Strindberg before the expedition left Stockholm, in accord with the following: In Strindberg's almanac No. 2 the dates of the various days are written at the left side margin for easier transfer later into pen and ink writing on the right side where certain astronomical requirements for each day are printed. This advance preparation of the almanac runs from January 1, 1897, to October 18, for which day are written 'Hem' [home] 'Aées föddag' [Andrée's birthday]. There is no doubt that the whole of this was set down before the departure of the expedition, probably at the beginning of the year. 'Home' was later entered in the second almanac with the addition of the exact time of the arrival in Stockholm of a railway train [by which he hoped to return from the expedition]. This situation gives us an intimate view of the young man's optimistic speculations as to the expedition's fortunate conclusion—very likely arrived at by Strindberg as he was talking this over with his financée."

If we accept this interpretation of the pen entry we can no longer hold certain what many have considered basic, that all three of the party were still living October 17.

To support the idea that Strindberg's entry means their coming home to the White Island camp in the morning exhausted from an attempt to cross the ice westward there have been cited material evidences, chief of them that one of the sledges was found loaded and that there were indications a second sledge had been hastily unloaded, as by men who were exhausted and who were preparing a makeshift camp. Pallin explains the same facts by Andrée's statement that it was very hard work to move things from the place where they first landed to the one where they were going to have their permanent camp. This would have been because the beach consisted of stones and gravel and had been swept bare by the wind, so that they had to drag their sledges over the stones or else carry things on their backs.

That the sledges would be left standing loaded from the 6th of October until after the 17th does not seem reasonable. But, as we have seen, the October 17 notation may have been written weeks or months before, and it is not necessary to assume the sledges stood loaded and idle for nearly two weeks. There may have been only a few days between the landing and the final tragedy.

Was a hut built?

The records mention the beginning of the construction of a hut, but no remains of a hut were found. This has been thought particularly strange by those commentators who assume that because stone was now available the walls would have been made in part of stone, snow being used chiefly as mortar. However, the party had built out on the drifting floe a hut, the walls of which had been wholly of ice blocks or of snow that froze after being soaked with sea water. Strindberg had apparently been the chief builder, and seemingly had taken pride in his success. It would appear likely that if a hut was built on land the walls would be again of snow, no matter how many small stones might be available.

The authorities agree that no big stones, suitable for making a wall chiefly of rock, were to be had. If the available small stones were used, the wall must have been a sort of conglomerate of them and the snow. Upon melting next spring these walls would have left ridges of the stone fragments as their representatives. No such ridges were noted. So it would appear that if walls were built they must have been entirely of snow, or of snow and ice.

Andrée mentions bringing to the camp vicinity driftwood and whale bones. The whale bones would have been intended for some use in a building; the driftwood might have been either for rafters or to burn. That neither bones nor driftwood pieces were found in such positions as to suggest that they had actually been used in a building would seem to indicate that, even if the walls of the projected house were partly or wholly built, no roof had been put on. There is the alternative that the house was finished, that the rafters were put on, but that the roofing consisted of the tent folded and laid over the rafters. Then it is possible that, perhaps through a spell of warm weather or for some other reason, the snow walls were melted away by the body heat of the inhabitants or by the warmth of fuel which had been burned. The party might then have concluded that a tent was better, after all, at least until the really cold weather came in November, and they would have removed both tent and rafters.

That a snowhouse could be melted by an October thaw, even when you are far in the Arctic during winter, seemingly strikes most people as unreasonable, except those who have made a special study of northern weather. Stefansson, for instance, reports that during most of his ten Arctic winters there was a thaw, sometimes accompanied by a rain, even in the coldest period (the months between December and March). This was so even in places like Melville Island which have a much lower average winter temperature than the Spitsbergen islands, and which are much farther from any water that has large open stretches in winter.

Our only reason for thinking that the Andrée party built a house is that the late diary entries speak of that intention, and seem to show that the work had actually been started. We have seen that, if any house was built, the walls must have been wholly of material that could melt, since no remains of a house have been found. That the building materials referred to by Andrée, the whale bones and driftwood, were not found in a position indicating their use as part of a house does not really signify anything, for while a snow structure was melting and becoming uninhabitable the men would naturally remove the roof, which would have consisted either of the folded tent or of one or both of the bearskins. In doing this they would remove the rafters that had been supporting the roof and would throw them into just such a pile of driftwood as was found in the camp. However, that pile is also the same kind as would have been made the first time, when the men brought the driftwood into camp.

In other words, the discussion about whether a house was made turns out to be empty and pointless speculation. We indulge in it chiefly because other commentators have done so, though our conclusions are perhaps not identical with any of theirs.

It will appear later that the final camp was almost certainly the tent, whether or not a house had been used previously.

Pallin feels certain, from his analysis of the documents and the rest of the evidence, that the party moved camp from where they had pitched it originally in an unsuitable place just after they landed, to "a lee under the cliffs farther from the beach," and that the camp stood "right up against the foot of the cliff."

Like practically all inexperienced white men, and like some travelers who have had experience, the Andrée party considered that one of the elements in making a camp site suitable was that it should be in a lee, that it should have a shelter from the winds of at least one direction.

As Stefansson has pointed out, in *The Friendly Arctic* and elsewhere, this is directly against the first principle of Eskimo camp pitching. They will never place a winter camp in a lee, for the same obstruction which shelters the camp from the wind will give shelter to drifting snow. This, being interpreted, means that a snowdrift will form in the lee. If the lee is high enough, and the storm lasts long enough, the camp will be completely buried. This may cause death from suffocation or from the caving in of the shelter under the weight of the snow. It may force a hasty scrambling out of camp, perhaps at midnight and in a blizzard.

If the camp you have to scramble out of is a tent, you can do it only by cutting a hole through the fabric and then digging your way up through the snowdrift. Thus you leave behind you your tent and your equipment, emerging only in the clothing you wear, and those clothes pretty well filled with damp snow.

So far, our discussion of the Andrée camp is based primarily on written records, with secondary reference to the camp itself. We will now make objects our primary study, calling on the documents only as supporting witnesses.

Many things about the camp and camp site at White Island were never taken by the theorists as having a bearing on the solution of our mystery; nor do we see their bearing. So we confine our discussion to matters which, to some investigators, have appeared to have some bearing.

Our findings will disagee with those of the official committee, which makes it the more essential to fairness that we shall take from their book, rather than from any other available source, the facts on which we base our dissenting view. We take them chiefly from the chapter "The Camp on White Island and Its Equipment" by Professor Nils Lithberg in *Andrée's Story*, the New York edition.

The most important finds in the camp were the written

records and the photographs. They were (1) Andrée's "large diary" which contained an orderly statement for the period from the balloon's ascension on July 12 to the arrival at White Island October 2; (2) a small diary or pocket note-book for the dates October 4 to October 8 on White Island; (3) an almanac which Strindberg had carried, the memorandum pages containing notes on the flight, July 11-14, and the calendar page with occasional marginal notes for the period July 11 to October 17; (4) Strindberg's logbook from July 15 to September 4; (5) his second logbook, carrying on to October 2 and therewith two narratives written in shorthand; (6) Fraenkel's journal with meteorological observations. Then there were several rolls of exposed photographs. It was possible to develop twelve reasonably good pictures thirty-three years later. These proved to be from the balloon voyage and the sledge journey—none were from White Island.

We think significant a matter to which Lithberg seemingly attaches little significance—that there was a cliff, about thirty feet high, in the lee of which was found the site of a tent. It is agreed than Andrée and Fraenkel died on this tent site and within the tent.

Corollaries, to which Lithberg does not expressly give weight in the solution of the mystery, may be derived from the following sequence:

When Captain Grödahl was at the camp site on July 9, 1930, he saw nothing of the three sledges which were later discovered. The snow in the lee of the cliff was still so deep after, say, a month of thawing, that it hid even big things like sledges. Nearly a month later, August 6, the snow in the lee of the cliff is given by Lithberg as 6½ feet deep at its deepest, the greatest diameter of the drift as 175 feet. By that time the boat on Fraenkel's sledge was partly visible through the drift. September 5, when the Stubbendorff party got there, the drift was estimated at two feet thick in its thickest part, and its greatest diameter had decreased to 100 feet. Now was plainly visible Strindberg's sledge, which the Horn party had not been able to discover a month earlier, despite an intensive search.

For all this melting to take place between July 9 and September 5, the drift must have been some ten or fifteen feet deep when the thaw started in May or June.

Seasons vary a great deal in the Arctic, both as to snowfall in winter and as to thawing of snow in summer. We think it likely that, most winters, there is on White Island enough snow and wind to create in the lee of the cliff—therefore over the site of Andrée's camp—a drift nearly equal to the height of that cliff, sloping away to ground level at some such distance as a hundred feet or even a hundred yards. The date, each summer, at which the Andrée relics begin to appear above the hiding snowdrift would, therefore, vary according to season.

Almost certainly no Andrée relics were visible on August 19, 1898 (the summer after the party died), when, as mentioned, Nathorst went ashore there. True, he mentions a blanket of new-fallen snow, but the impression given is that this was only a few inches deep, so that it would not have hidden any large object—for instance, it would not have concealed the boat on Fraenkel's sledge if this had been exposed by the thaws of the preceding midsummer.

It is believed that sailors were ashore on southwestern White Island on several occasions during the following thirty-two years. The glacier-free area is so small, only a few hundred yards wide by three or four miles long, that surely a number of these visitors must have covered the whole strip. We believe, then, that there was a considerable number of the thirty-three summers in which the thaw was never enough to expose the camp. This goes toward explaining why so many of the relics were found in good condition, particularly the diaries. For no decay or other deterioration can have taken place in the years when the relics did not thaw out.

The Andrée and Fraenkel sledges were discovered standing near the tent site.

Fraenkel's sledge had on it the expedition's canvas boat filled with gear, except that a few things, mentioned by the written documents as being in the boat, had been removed from it to the tent. Articles so removed were specially useful things needed by the occupants of the tent in their cooking or other camp activities.

Andrée's sledge was completely unloaded, as if that were the one which brought up the main equipment, as tent and bedding, so that it had to be unloaded for the mere act of camping.

Strindberg's sledge was by itself farther from the tent. Near it were a tarpaulin, and the contents of this load scattered about. It has been thought that the tarpaulin was originally used as a cover for unloaded gear, and bears are supposed to have torn this covering away, scattering the load. Pallin's interpretation is the reverse. By it the tarpaulin had been on top of the sledge, protecting its load from drifting snow. In a hasty unloading the tarpaulin was jerked off and the rest of the load dumped.

In Pallin's view the belongings of Strindberg's sledge were found helter-skelter in 1930 because they had been removed helter-skelter in 1897—for reasons which we shall state when we give his theory of how the men died.

Andrée's diaries were discovered in a wad of sennegrass (sedge grass) around which a woolen coat had been so wrapped that the whole made a tight bundle which had apparently been lying on the floor of the tent when the men died. A premonition of disaster has been read into this find—it has been said that Andrée was using the sennegrass and the woolen coat to protect his diary in case he himself perished.

The arguments for and against that view cannot be understood without considering the nature and use of sennegrass, the protecting qualities of woolen cloth, and the habits of Arctic travelers.

Sennegrass is a kind of grass found, among other places, in Lapland. The Lapps use it for insoles in their shoes and in place of socks. The Andrée party were equipped with Lapp shoes and sennegrass for winter use.

With cold-weather footgear, the main thing is to keep it dry. All northern travelers, accordingly, take the greatest pains to guard socks and sennegrass against the insidious pulverized drifting snow that sifts during a blizzard into almost anything. Travelers who have woolen blankets or woolen coats will wrap their socks or their sennegrass inside these when they travel. Andrée was using routine northern practice when he wrapped sennegrass in a woolen coat, making a tight bundle.

For the same reason he was using routine practice when he wrapped his diary in the woolen coat. He did not wrap it first in sennegrass and then in a woolen cloth, as has been stated or implied by some of the writers. It merely happened that both the sennegrass and the diary were protected by the same coat.

The great enemies of written records are warmth and moisture. It has, therefore, been standard practice among Arctic travelers for centuries to protect papers intended for deposit, and for recovery in a later year, by wrapping them in the best available waterproof material and then placing the bundle in a metal container. All descriptions of the White Island camp agree that there were lying around it in 1930 pieces of waterproof cloth and numerous metal containers, some of them empty and well suited for the preservation of documents. But they had not been used for this purpose.

Andrée was, of course, using the coat against snow. Like any other traveler, when he was about to break camp, on the last previous occasion, he had wrapped the diary up and carried it out (through the snowstorm which the small Andrée notebook describes) to the sledge where he stuck it well down in the load.

When that sledge was unloaded, after the tent had been pitched, Andrée carried the bundle indoors and undoubtedly placed it on the ground, most likely underneath his bedding. For this, too, is regular northern practice, based on warm air being light and cold air heavy. There is in the chill of the Arctic winter a low temperature near the ground level of a tent, greater warmth higher up. The earth itself below your sleeping gear is frozen hard, so that by slipping under the bedding a garment containing dry snow you can insulate it from contact with the heat of the camp so that everything will remain dry—the ground chill will refrigerate the bundle enough to keep the snow unmelted.

That the diary was found wrapped in a woolen coat shows Andrée died before he had occasion to remove the more or less snow-filled bundle from its dry cold storage. This is one more argument, then, for his having died the very evening of this camp pitching, perhaps within a few hours after he had brought the diary in and placed it on the floor.

According to the records there should have been (disregarding the fresh meat of bears and seals) over five hundred pounds of equipment and supplies in the camp on October 8. There is an extensive list of the equipment in the records, but we do not place it before our readers in detail because no one has suggested that the whole list would be significant.

Most commentators have thought remarkable the quantity and variety of things found in the White Island camp. All agree that considerable food was brought ashore, both European provisions and local game meat. Pallin thinks everything mentioned in the records as having been at the "permanent" ice camp was successfully hauled to the beach. So far as Andrée has been criticized under this head, it is along the line of "Why did he slave to haul along all that junk?"

Some articles, like the boathook, have been called useless. There has been claimed an oversupply of clothes. Pallin lists as recovered from the camp site, in addition to the ample clothing found on the bodies of the three men, nineteen items of coats, shirts, jackets; sixty-three pairs of various garments for legs, hands, and feet; and twenty-eight items of miscellaneous clothes. Surely not many parties sledging over sea ice have ever carried that many extra clothes per man.

Some of these spares were in the tent when the men died; all were near it and accessible.

Commentators have found interesting that on White Island were discovered many things which are not mentioned in the record as having been on the sledges, and that there are missing from White Island things which are said by the diaries to have been in the loads.

The probability is that the men landed on White Island with nearly or quite everything which their records say they had, but with a good many things besides which had escaped their notation; and that there have since been lost a number of the recorded things. These losses were, no doubt, mostly through things being dragged by animals, or blown by a wind, out on the sea ice where, the next summer, they would either sink when the ice melted or else drift away on moving floes.

The tent which everyone agrees must have stood where Andrée and Fraenkel were found, had long ago been dragged away from its site, unquestionably by bears. Some think that pieces of varnished balloon cloth discovered in the camp may have been fragments of the tent. These fragments would then be edges of the tent which were frozen fast when the bear pulled at the tent, ripping it. That bears would do such things is quite in line with their known habits.

At the camp site were found pieces of driftwood and whale bone so located that clearly they had been there to hold down the flaps of the tent. Other driftwood was so placed that we agree it had been part of the flooring of the tent, used to keep the bedding from contact with snow or with frozen ground.

Lithberg says that "Fraenkel's remains were found in about the middle of the tent, and behind them, close to the north-eastern wall, lay a sleeping-sack of reindeer-skin, frozen and wrinkled. It was on the low ridge (ledge) of rock just above the sleeping-sack that the *Bratvaag's* people found Andrée's body. Andrée and Fraenkel had thus expired within the tent, lying about a yard from each other; they had been lying on the floor of the tent, and the sleeping-sack lay close at hand."

Strindberg died first, for he had been buried by his companions in a cleft of rock, the body covered with a layer of small stones a foot deep. There is agreement that he had been wearing when buried a jaeger wool jersey, a jaeger wool shirt, a pair of thin drawers, a pair of thick drawers, trousers, a vest, a pair of thin woolen stockings, a pair of thick stockings, Lapp shoes with sennegrass and puttees. There is agreement that the only garment removed before burial was his outer jacket. This, it seems, might have been either because he was not wearing the jacket when he died or else because his comrades wanted it for possible use later.

Andrée's body was dressed in a jaeger wool jersey, flannel shirt, thin jaeger drawers, a thick pair of brown wool drawers, woolen knee protectors, trousers, vest, jacket of blue cloth, a woolen jersey, and a sweater. On one foot he had two thin socks and a thick one, all woolen; on the other, two thick socks. He was wearing Lapp shoes and puttees. Apparently he was not wearing a cap although there were several caps around.

Fraenkel was wearing a woolen undershirt, a flannel outershirt, a vest of brown cloth, a chamois leather vest, a woolen jersey and a cloth coat with a fur collar. There is doubt as to what the lower part of his body was dressed in, for it seems that bears must have tugged at the body and pulled away the legs. Clearly this would not happen earlier than the next year after death, for an animal powerful enough to tear away a man's leg would naturally bring away the whole body unless it were frozen in ice. But such ice could not form until after there had been a summer thaw followed by a freeze.

Some European food was still in the camp after the thirty-three years. There must have been considerable of it on hand when the men died. Pallin concludes reasonably that although a bear may have been killed on White Island, or two as Lithberg thinks, more likely the two bearskins found were those we know about as secured at the floe camp. He feels it possible that the seal bones found in the camp were brought from the ice, but likelier that one or more seals were secured after landing. All agree that when Andrée died there was still some fresh bear meat on Fraenkel's unloaded sledge; therefore meat brought ashore from the ice camp. We find similar agreement that there was other bear meat on hand, as well as seal meat. Certainly there were shot a good many birds on White Island. There have been found remains of at least ten pairs of wings, mostly guillemots'. Since it is likely that foxes and other animals might have eaten up bones or carried away wings, we would think that ten is only a part, and probably a small part, of the birds shot at the camp.

The wings would surely be from guillemots which had been cooked and eaten by the party; any whole guillemots would have been carried away by foxes. For everybody agrees that Andrée's not finding fox tracks when they landed is of little significance. It is well known that foxes prowl all over the Polar Sea, no matter how far from land. It is equally well known that sometimes in a given spot you will find none for weeks, or even months, while thereafter you may observe great numbers for considerable periods.

All white foxes are land animals in summer, half of them are sea beasts in winter, following the polar bears around and living on the partly eaten seals which they leave behind. How these food-winner bears and parasite foxes come and go, whether at sea or on such a coast as that of White Island, is partly a matter of simple chance; partly it depends on ice drift, which in turn depends on what winds happen to blow. There is dependence, too, on the season.

All three guns of the party were discovered in the camp, with 135 bullet cartridges and 120 shot cartridges. This was more ammunition than Nansen and Johansen carried to support them at least two years; and so the Andrée party had no cause for worry on that score.

There was no cause for worry about fuel, either. Driftwood lay scattered around, and some of it piled up, evidently by the campers. Animal bones which were found indicate that there was available, too, fuel consisting of the blubber of these animals. They still had petroleum, and the primus stove had not merely been in good conditon when the men died— it was in such good condition thirty-three years later that when lighted, and operating on fuel which it contained when found, it "could still make a litre of water boil in six minutes."

The verdict on how Strindberg died we have not found categorically stated in the official narrative, *Andrée's Story*. It can be inferred, however, from a paragraph on page 224:

"The three men had but one sleeping-sack between them. To live for months in continual isolation from the world in one of the most desolate tracts on the globe must, of itself, have gradaully become a serious psychical trial. Being compelled to share the same sleeping-sack night after night, a system that could not but give rise to mutual inconvenience, especially if one of their number were sick, probably rendered the situation even more trying. And, worst of all, perhaps to have been obliged to witness the death-struggles of Strindberg in that one sleeping-sack with them!"

Pallin considers five possibilities of Strindberg's death: an accidental gunshot wound, suicide, murder by one of his companions in a fit of insanity, attack by a bear, and drowning. He thinks it cannot have been by a gunshot, for no indications of this were found either on the clothes in which Strindberg was buried, or in his skeleton. It can hardly have been suicide, for everything shows that the party were getting along amiably together, and that they were optimistic both as to safety and as to being well received by the world when they returned to it next year. He dismisses the possibility of murder for the same reasons. Wounding by a bear seems unlikely—there should then have been tears in the clothing and perhaps injuries on the skeleton, neither of which were found. Apparently there are no cliffs in the vicinity such that falling over one of the would have caused death. Remains the possibility that he was drowned. This would have been when he went out on the sea in pursuit of a bear or a seal.

No poisoning has been suspected that was deliberate, or by accident. But food poisoning has been considered. It has been suggested that in one way or another Strindberg's death was connected with what he ate. For our part, we have really found against this already when we showed that, so far as diary evidence is concerned, no illness was ever traced to the European food; and that the only digestive trouble connected with the seal and bear meat disappeared as soon as the party began to eat the whole of the meat—the fat as well as the lean. Apparently there was plenty of seal and bear fat on White Island; all the factions agree on that. As for the chance of poisoning with bear liver, we have quoted Andrée saying that "of course" they did not use these livers.

After consideration of all theoretical possibilities, we come to the same conclusion as Pallin. It is likeliest that Strindberg died from drowning, perhaps following a bear that ran out on the ice. Certainly this is the most dangerous time of year for breaking through into water, since, as previously noted, thick blankets of new snow will hide weak patches, making them look just like the rest of the ice.

The chief objection to the drowning theory is that all three guns were found at the camp site and that a man who falls into water might be expected to lose his gun before he does his life. Certainly the first instinct of a man sinking through ice will be to divest himself of anything which may weigh him down, but he may throw his gun to a distance where stronger ice keeps it safe.

By this view, then, the comrades either saw Strindberg fall through the weak ice or they heard his cries. They may have arrived too late merely because Strindberg drowned quickly. It is likelier that they got near him in time but were unable to approach close enough to help because the same kind of ice that broke under Strindberg was breaking under them.

In that situation you would do one of two things—you would try to throw a rope to the drowning man; or you would run ashore and get something that would support you on the weak ice through distributing your weight. Such a thing would be an empty sledge.

If the accident took place on October 9 it is likely that all three sledges were standing loaded with the current relay of what was being brought up to the camp site from the beach. Andrée and Fraenkel would rush ashore and hurriedly unload one of the sledges, leaving its load in a more or less indiscriminate pile. Just such a scattering of a load was found when the camp was discovered in 1930.

The probable date of Strindberg's death, if he was drowned, is October 9. If he died from illness, as, for instance, from an appendix which developed into peritonitis, October 9 is the probable date of the onset of this disease. We derive those views, as probabilities, from the records. Strindberg ceased his entry a day before Andrée, perhaps through worry about symptoms of an illness with which he did not yet want to worry his companions. So Andrée would make an entry on the 8th, while his mind was still at ease. He made no entry the 9th, which might show that just after he made his entry the evening of the 8th, or else on the morning of the 9th, Strindberg revealed that he was seriously ill.

From whatever cause Strindberg died, the likeliest time for his burial would be the next day.

Strindberg's resting place was a cleft in the rocks about thirty yards from the tent. They would have buried him farther away according to European ideas, or would have moved the tent away from his grave, except possibly that they had some thought of guarding the body against polar bears.

It would seem that the death of the other two came the evening of the day on which Strindberg was buried, or within a few days, since all investigators have agreed the camp gave no sign of being long occupied.

Under such conditions as we here speculate upon, and generally under conditions of great trouble or even great excitement, travelers do not make entries in their diaries— there are innumerable cases of such omissions in the literature, ranging from one or two days to weeks or months, the diary then being resumed with an explanation of what it was that prevented writing. After October 8 no diary of the Andrée party was ever resumed, for they all died before there came an interval of leisure and peace.

Lithberg thinks that Andrée and Fraenkel froze to death inside a tent, neither of them wearing a cap, neither of them in the sleeping bag, both of them within easy reach of more clothing which they did not put on. Further, he says, "In one of Fraenkel's pockets was found Strindberg's almanac with his marginal notes, and, inside it, a fountain-pen, which was still filled with ink." There were also a mother-of-pearl knife, a whistle of black horn, dark spectacles, a lead pencil and a tube of ointment. He says there were found in Andrée's pockets his small diary, a lead pencil, a pedometer, a chronometer with gold chain, a locket with portraits of his parents, a gold heart, a gold ring with turquoise and two garnets, a chronometer, a handkerchief, a tube of ointment, a pocket-knife, empty cartridge cases, and a matchbox.

So we are asked to picture men who were freezing to death as having all this truck in their pockets and still refraining from putting on caps or any of the extra garments that were lying around—let alone refraining from getting into the sleeping-bag where they could have had both its protection from the outside chill and the interchanged warmth from each other's bodies.

Lithberg says the two men sank into their last slumber side

by side within the tent and, to judge by all appearances, simultaneously.

To justify the verdict of death by freezing the committee, through Lithberg, criticizes Andrée's clothing:

"We have dwelt at such length on the clothing equipment because it seems to have been the weakest point in the preparations made for the expedition. . . . One of the participators in the *Isbjörn* expedition expressed himself as astonished at the unsuitability of the clothing for polar travelling. Among the articles he mentioned as being little suited to the purpose were the knitted gloves, the thin shirts of striped cotton, the thin woolen jerseys, and the short socks marked N.S. The jerseys also seemed to him of little value for polar wear, both as regards material and cut. Another man on board the *Isbjörn* gave it as his opinion that 'the members of the expedition had frozen to death. They did not have enough clothing and were badly equipped. They had nothing but rubbishy clothes and socks!' "

Most students of polar equipment will agree with the Swedish critics of Andrée's clothes that they certainly could have been improved upon. A sweater, for instance, is nearly the poorest garment for its weight that you can wear in a cold wind. But a majority of students will disagree with the Andrée committee where it implies that thin clothes are less suitable than thick. For what keeps you warm is fundamentally the air that is imprisoned within fibers, between fibers, or between layers of clothing. By that reasoning, two thin woolen shirts are considerably warmer than one thick shirt that weighs the same, for there will be a certain amount of air held between the outer and inner shirts. Further advantages of two thin shirts over one thick are that thin garments are more easily dried when they become wet, and that you can more easily adjust your clothes to circumstances, as by removing one of the two thin shirts when you are in camp or when the weather gets warmer.

You will feel, when you read the official narrative carefully, that the Swedish committee would not have criticized Andrée's clothing except that they were forced into doing so as a partial explanation of their verdict that he died by freezing.

The main reason for our discussing the fate of the Andrée party in a book on the unsolved mysteries of the Arctic is that we cannot follow the Andrée Committee when they agree with the Norwegian sailor that Andrée and Fraenkel died from exposure. As a substitute for that view we are advancing, documented, the theory which Stefansson advanced to the London newspapers in the summer of 1930 when interviewed concerning the news which had just come from White Island. This is the same view that Stefansson expressed in a somewhat more considered form in "An Arctic Mystery," a review of *Andrée's Story* in the *Saturday Review of Literature,* January 3, 1931. As said, this view is, in its main arguments and main conclusions, the same as that presented by Pallin in 1934 in his book *The Andrée Mystery.*

Our finding, here set against the official verdict, is that Andrée and Fraenkel died of carbon monoxide poisoning— that they died warm, comfortable. without foreboding, just as people do nowadays when sumptuous cars have their engines running in closed garages.

The view that the men on White Island died of monoxide poisoning is based on what we know of this danger from the history of polar exploration. Indeed, we get one of the most significant cases through what is frequently called the first real polar expedition of modern times.

William Barents, who had discovered Spitsbergen in 1594, was wintering on Novaya Zemlya in 1596. We take the story of what here directly concerns us from pages 129-130 of the Hakluyt Society 1876 edition of the Barents narrative which, however, is, in the part we quote, a reprint of the London 1609 edition, with Elizabethan diction and spelling:

"The 7 of December it was still foule weather, and we had a great storme with a north-east wind, which brought an extreme cold with it; at which time we knew not what to do, and while we sate consulting together what were best for vs to do, one of our companions gaue vs counsell to burne some of the sea-coles that we had brought out of the ship, which would cast a great heat and continue long; and so at euening we made a great fire thereof, which cast a great heat. At which time we were very careful to keep it in, for that the heat being so great a comfort vnto vs, we tooke care how to make it continue long; whereupon we agreed to stop vp all the doores and the chimney, thereby to keepe in the heate, and so went into our cabans to sleepe, well comforted with the heat, and so lay a great while talking together; but at last we were taken with a great swounding and daseling in our heads, yet some more then other some, which we first perceiued by a sick man and therefore the lesse able to beare it, and found our selues to be very ill at ease, so that some of vs that were strongest start out of their cabans, and first opened the chimney and then the doores, but he that opened the doore fell downe in a swound vppon the snow; which I hearing, as lying in my caban next to the doore, start vp, and casting vinegar in his face recouered him againe, and so he rose vp. And when the doores were open, we all recouered our healthes againe by reason of the cold aire; and so the cold, which before had beene so great an enemy vnto vs, was then the onely reliefe that we had, otherwise without doubt we had died in a sodaine swound. . . ."

Thus the discoverer of the Spitsbergen group and his companions came near dying as we think Andrée and Fraenkel may have died in one of the Spitsbergen islands three hundred and one years later.

In April, 1911, four members of the second Stefansson expedition were searching for Eskimos on the ice of Coronation Gulf. In the party, besides Stefansson, were Dr. Rudolph M. Anderson, now (1938) chief biologist of the Dominion Government at Ottawa, and two Eskimos, Natkusiak who was from western Alaska, and Tannaumirk who belonged to the Mackenzie River people.

April 9, the searchers came upon and followed the trail of a migrating group of local people. We want to show from what happened that evening how these four men came near dying within a few minutes of one another while cooking supper. The material will be found on pages 245-247 of *My Life with the Eskimo,* which Stefansson published in 1913, although we quote a somewhat abridged text from pages 270-273 of a reissue of that book printed in 1927:

". . . late that evening we came to a commodious and clean-looking snow house, which had evidently been abandoned by the party we were following not more than two days before. To save ourselves the trouble of building, we camped in this house.

"A new camp is warmer than an old camp, for a new snow house is a snow house, but an old one is partly an ice house. This one had evidently been kept pretty warm by its former occupants, for the walls had been melted into solid, glistening ice. We were all warm from fast travel. In our hurry to get the camp heated up we closed the door tightly. The bed platform was just wide enough for three, and three of us were sitting on the front edge of it, with Natkusiak below us on the floor. My head was a little higher than anybody else's for the cooking was my job that night, and I had set the primus stove on a block of snow and was on my knees cutting up snow into the kettle for water.

"Tannaumirk and Natkusiak were talking and joking as usual. In the midst of one of his funny stories, which he told with a good deal of pantomime, Tannaumirk all at once threw himself backward upon the bed and made a sort of gurgling noise. Anderson was sitting next to him. All three of us thought that these actions and gurglings were a part of the pantomine. Still, I asked Anderson to look and see what Tannaumirk was up to, for he did not get up again as quickly as we expected. When Dr. Anderson turned to look, he fell face forward on top of Tannaumirk. I knew in a moment what the matter was and extinguished the primus stove, for it was clear that we were being poisoned by carbon monoxide, which is so insidious that under ordinary circumstances one does not notice it.

"Natkusiak saw nothing to be alarmed at, and when I told him to hurry and break a hole in the snow wall behind him, he went about it with deliberation. Fortunately, in order to make the hole he had to get up to reach for his knife, which he had stuck into the wall. But when he tried to rise he found himself powerless to do so. That scared him, so that with his last strength he threw himself back against the wall and broke away the loose block of snow by which we had a few minutes before closed up the door. He then crawled outside on all fours, but was too weak to stand up. I followed him out and had strength enough to stand up. But that was only for a moment and I fell down beside Natkusiak.

"It was a calm, starlit night, with the temperature about 45° below zero. The situation was serious, for all of us were lightly clad. My first thought was to try to get back into the house and drag Anderson and Tannaumirk out. But when I crawled to the opening for that purpose, I was so weak that it was evident I could accomplish nothing if I did go in.

"It must have been fifteen minutes that we lay flat outside the snow house before Anderson's face appeared at the hole in the wall. His mind was clear apparently, but he had no realization of what had happened and asked us in a querulous voice what we were doing out there and why we had put out the stove and let the cold air into the house. Before I had time to answer, he realized what had happened, crawled out and started walking about and drawing deep breaths. But he soon found, as I had found a few minutes before, that this was the worst possible thing to do, for it only forced the poison deeper into his lungs. He finally had to stretch himself out flat on the ground like the rest of us.

"It must have been another ten minutes before Tannaumirk also came to his senses and crawled out. By that time I, who had been less affected from the beginning than any of the others, had strength enough to fetch from the house our sleeping bags, into which I helped Anderson and Natkusiak. But Tannaumirk would not crawl into his bag, saying that if he did he would no doubt go to sleep in it and freeze to death. He had been affected much worse than the rest of us, and while we seemed to be able to think clearly his mind was evidently in a fog, as his remark about freezing to death in a sleeping bag showed. After walking round camp in a circle two or three times he started straight off somewhere. He then seemed to realize vaguely that he was getting lost, but had it not been for my loud shouting he would not have found his way back to camp again, for, although the moonlight was bright, he said later that either he was unable to see the camp or else he did not have the sense to recognize it when he did see it.

"After Tannaumirk's return from this excursion I forced him into the sleeping bag, and then went indoors, lit the primus stove again [to warm the house and to heat a drink]. . . .

"An hour later the three of us were feeling comparatively fit again, and the next morning we noticed no ill effects. But Tannaumirk was sick not only that night, but also the next day.

"Of course our trouble had been from closing the house too tightly. Looking back upon our various experiences with primus stoves in the past, I can now see that we must have been near a similar outcome frequently before. We had escaped this time by a narrow margin. Had I gone off my head simultaneously with Tannaumirk and Anderson there would have been no salvation, for the stove would have kept on burning, generating fresh quantities of poison.

"It seemed to us the next day, and it seems so to me still, that this not very romantic adventure was the narrowest escape from death we had on our whole expedition."

The two white men and the two Eskimos later discussed whether there had been any premonitions of trouble. Some had felt nothing; others believed they could recall a slight feeling as of pressure on the temples, a little bit as if from an elastic band or cap. There had been no odor. The lights were burning brightly, for it is carbon dioxide and not carbon monoxide which dims or extinguishes flame and makes it necessary for you to breathe more rapidly.

There is, then, according to the Stefansson testimony, practically no warning for persons who are not on their guard when carbon monoxide poisoning approaches. It is possible that if you were on your guard, and keenly observant, you might detect the pressure feeling on the head and, perhaps, a physical weakening—as in the case of Natkusiak, who found it difficult to stand up.

Many more cases of poisoning from monoxide could be cited from the published literature of exploration, and we were about to quote Admiral Richard E. Byrd from pages 203-4 of *Little America* (New York, 1930) when we had the chance to get an account of the same incident which has not been published and which is in some parts more specific than the Admiral's. We quote a letter dated August 25, 1938, from Lieutenant Malcolm P. Hanson, who was Chief Radio Engineer with the first Byrd Antarctic expedition:

"Relative to our talk the other evening, . . . the facts, to my best recollection, are as follows: It was Davies' turn to be night watchman, keep record of aurora, etc. Fires were out in all buildings except the photo laboratory annex to the bunkhouse, consisting of two rooms heated by a pressure kerosene strove of the built-in room type, with flue pipe carrying vapors off through roof.

"Two men . . . returned after midnight from a walk on the Barrier, and stopped in Photo Lab to see how two sick pups (kept in a box on the floor) were getting along; found pups very ill, cause not immediately apparent. While Doctor was sent for, and pups were being worked over in the bunkhouse, someone found Davies unconscious on the floor, in the back room of the Photo Lab. It was not till then that 'stuffiness' in the room was noticed, and the flue pipe was found to be stopped up by snow from a blizzard. The stove had not gone out. Fuel, ordinary kerosene, I believe.

"Davies later stated he had been in Lab to keep warm and noticed nothing wrong with the air before passing out. He was, of course, weak and sick for some days after the experience."

What happened on the Byrd expedition in 1930 was basically the same as happened to Barents in 1596 and to Stefansson in 1911. Barents was using coal, Byrd and Stefansson were using kerosene; but in the three cases there was imperfect combustion so that one molecule of carbon was combined with one molecule of oxygen to produce the poisonous monoxide.

We now present as a solution of the Andrée problem a reconstructed narrative of White Island from October 2, 1897.

Some paragraphs of the story as we give it may tell of what never happened; but in their place you would then have to imagine corresponding incidents of like effect. Some parts of our statement are things which we know must have happened; some are things which we know happened. The story as a whole is consistent with the evidence. It explains all the material facts; it brings in nothing which is not supported by the evidence, or at least consistent with it.

The Andrée party were driven from their "permanent" camp on the drifting floe when it cracked in several pieces, threatening the safety of their equipment, even the safety of their lives. The three men kept only a fragmentary record during the next few days because they were slaving every hour of the daylight and spent in camp only the briefest part of the night. Perhaps the camp was badly lighted, to explain still further how few were the entries made.

The first camp was near the beach; a "better" site later selected was two hundred yards from the sea and up against a ledge of rock, steep though not precipitous, thirty feet high.

Strindberg made the last notation on his calendar October 7; Andrée made his October 8. If Strindberg died of a sudden illness, such as appendicitis developing into peritonitis, it may be that he stopped writing one day sooner than Andrée because he was distressed by symptoms with which he did not want to trouble his comrades.

The authorities agree that the camp was occupied only a very brief time. The official committee feels that Strindberg died immediately after the 17th of October, the other two soon afterward. We agree with Ahlmann and Pallin that the entry for October 17 was probably not of a diary nature but rather an advance memorandum. Our limiting date is, therefore, not the 17th but the 8th.

On or about the 9th, then, Strindberg was desperately ill and about to die; or else he was drowned that day, or soon after it, when pursuing a bear which they had seen from camp. Perhaps he was pursuing a bear wounded in the camp that had fled out upon the ice.

We prefer the theory of drowning to that of sudden illness chiefly because one of the sledges apparently was hastily unloaded, as for use in an attempt to rescue a drowning man, or to bring his body home.

That Strindberg's body was found lacking the outermost coat might have been because the coat had been removed after the drowning. More likely the coat was not worn at the time of death—Strindberg, as hunters commonly do, discarded it to lighten himself as he pursued the bear. Or he may have been working without the coat when he saw the bear, for the clothes in which he was buried were quite enough for wearing, even on a cold Arctic day, when working out of doors.

Strindberg would have been buried the day after he was drowned. Death may have come to the others that same evening.

We visualize a suppertime in an Arctic camp that stood sheltered by a thirty-foot cliff. It was a tent which Lithberg says was sewed into one piece like a bag; the floor of balloon silk varnished three times, the rest balloon silk with but one coat of varnish. By that statement the whole was airproof, unless there were rents in the fabric, about which we have no information, and except for what ventilation there could be through the door. Pallin notes that the door was not of the bag type, used by Nansen and others, which can be closed airtight with a string, like the mouth of a duffel bag. However, the door may easily have been nearly airtight—it may have had few and small gaps.

The time was October, a snowy season; the weather not yet very cold, and the snow, therefore, likely to be heavy and sticky. The camp was sheltered, in a pocket of nearly stagnant air; the flakes would, therefore, stay where they landed on the outside of the tent.

Autumn snowstorms in the Arctic usually start with falls of snow in a calm, the wind increasing gradually thereafter. We know from the evidence that a great snowdrift typically accumulated in winter in the shelter of the White Island cliff, perhaps to a depth of nearly the full thirty-foot height of the lee.

The beginnings of this great drift were gathering around the tent that fateful evening as the meal was being cooked on a primus stove—a stove the same in name and principle as the one used by Stefansson in 1911.

When the tent was first pitched, there may have been small openings beneath the flaps which helped, through accident or plan, toward good ventilation. There may have been considerable ventilation through the door. But now the soft snow on the ground outside was rising steadily and the vents under the flaps had already been closed. There was less and less air coming through the door as more and more of its lower gaps were being closed October 9 or 10, 1897.

There had been many men in the Barents camp in December, 1596. They were at various levels according to the bunks they slept in, and in various parts of a large house, so that when some collapsed from the monoxide there were others, who had been less exposed, to open the doors and let the fresh air in. At the Byrd camp in 1930 the door was opened and Davies was carried out into the fresh air.

The Stefansson case of 1911 is probably likest to the situation on White Island. One of the Stefansson men was sitting high, two were at a middle level, and the fourth was lower down. The two on middle level collapsed perhaps a minute apart. The second of these, who had the extra minute, was a keen scientist, well aware of the dangers of monoxide, yet he did not realize during his spare minute that his insensible companion was being poisoned.

With the collapse of the second man Stefansson, familiar with the theory of monoxide, knew immediately what had happened, took the air pressure off the primus so that it was extinguished, and directed the man who was low down near the door to open it. Even so, neither of the two still conscious was strong enough to help the others, or to do more than just crawl outdoors and then lie flat.

There were only two men in the tent on White Island and they apparently were on the same level, so that they may have lost consciousness within a minute of each other, like Tannaumirk and Anderson.

In the three cases of Andrée, Byrd and Stefansson, monoxide was generated by a stove of the primus type. The Andrée stove may have produced the monoxide because it was not functioning well mechanically—the written record complains about the stove working badly on previous occasions.

But the Andrée primus could be mechanically perfect and still produce monoxide, just because there was not enough ventilation in the tent.

Seemingly, the two in the White Island tent did not pass out quite as close together as Tannaumirk and Anderson. For if they had, the second man to faint would not have removed the pressure from the stove, which would then burn itself out. This did not happen, for the stove was found still three-quarters full of kerosene in 1930; and, as we have said, in working condition.

We think it was Andrée who was cooking, with the stove on a ledge by his side, where Horn was to find it. Likely the reason why Stefansson suffered less than the other three from the monoxide was that he, being cook that night, was right by the stove where its heat created circulation, bringing a stream of comparatively fresh air in to the vicinity. Andrée, then, still conscious and feeling no symptoms, saw Fraenkel collapse on the middle of the floor. Perhaps he noticed because Fraenkel had been standing. Andrée now did what Stefansson did: he gave the vent screw a half-turn and the primus ceased burning. Stefansson did this because he feared monoxide; Andrée may have done it for that reason, or simply because he wanted to leave the cooking and be free to help Fraenkel.

Anderson and Tannaumirk eventually came to within the Stefansson camp because Natkusiak had opened the door. Fraenkel and Andrée never came to because there was no third man to open their door.

A slight modification of our reconstructed narrative is possible if we assume that the pump on Andrée's primus was not working perfectly. There have been cases in exploration where a party has traveled for weeks, even months, using a primus with a defective pump; for this only means that whenever the pressure grows insufficient and the fire drops low you have to take another spell at pumping. In such a case, a nearly full primus may have continued burning for only a half-hour, after both Andrée and Fraenkel became unconscious—assuming that (like Tannaumirk and Anderson) they collapsed practically at the same time and both without previous grasp of what was happening.

In 1930 when the bodies were discovered on White Island it may not have been too late for a technical determination of whether monoxide was the cause of death. Conceivably it is not too late even now.

Professor Yandell Henderson of Yale University, a foremost authority upon carbon monoxide, has studied the evidence as presented by *Andrée's Story* and feels convinced that Andrée and Fraenkel died of monoxide poisoning. The long winters and snows of White Island almost certainly preserved enough of the body tissues so that a laboratory test for monoxide could have been made. Can it be that enough still remain under the conditions of the burial in Sweden for a test that would yield a verdict?

Professor Henderson writes under date of November 5, 1938:

> I believe . . . Andrée and Fraenkel died of carbon monoxide asphyxia, or else were frozen while in a state of carbon monoxide coma: the difference is immaterial. It is possible that the spectrum of carbon monoxide hemoglobin might have been found in some drop of blood in the fragments the bears left. Was it ever looked for? It should be even now—particularly in the bone marrow where it would never have been exposed to the air.

There is a bare possibility that the death of Strindberg may have occured in the same way. It could be that he was alone within the tent cooking while the others were off, perhaps exploring the island. Coming home they may have found Strindberg dead. On that hypothesis we would assume that when they opened the tent door they let in so much fresh air that they themselves did not suffer on that occasion.

In order to make this view of Strindberg's death tenable we should have to assume that Andrée and Fraenkel were both unfamiliar with how monoxide kills; and that, finding Strindberg dead, they imagined that he had died from some such thing as heart failure. Otherwise, with his death fresh in mind, the others surely would not have permitted themselves to fall victim to the same cause within a day or two of burying Strindberg.

Because it is difficult to imagine that monoxide and its dangers were quite unknown to Andrée and Fraenkel, we think it likelier that Strindberg died by drowning or through some quick illness.

With Strindberg in his grave, and the others dead in their tent, the winter of 1897–98 progressed. Each storm that blew from north, northeast, or east would pile more snow over the tent that stood in the lee of the cliff, until finally it collapsed upon the bodies from the weight of the drift.

The thirty-foot lee was enough for the drift to extend beyond the tent to cover the three sledges so that they were not seen by the Nathorst party when they visied the neighborhood in the summer of 1898. During later summers it would have depended on the season whether the drift melted away completely toward autumn, as it had done by the middle of September, 1930. Some years, no doubt, the thaw revealed part of the evidence, as, for instance, the farthest projecting end of the Fraenkel boat.

Because the documents remained so well preserved through a third of a century, because the camp was not seen during that time by the occasional sealing visitors, we think that most years the snowdrift in the lee of the cliff hid throughout the entire season every sign of the tragedy.

Postscript

This chapter was already in type when there arrived an important letter from a man well placed for having a sound opinion on the problem of how Andrée and Fraenkel died.

Dr. Harald Ulrik Sverdrup studied both at the University of Oslo and the University of Leipzig, and is Ph.D. from Oslo. He has been research assistant at the Carnegie Institution of Washington and professor of dynamic meteorology at the Geophysics Institute of Bergen, with several other posts of scientific distinction, among them his present directorship of the Scripps Institution of Oceanography, La Jolla, California. He was second-in-command and chief of scientific staff for Amundsen's *Maud* expedition while it was in the field and was in charge of its scientific publications, thus occupying the years 1917–25. He was in charge of scientific work for the *Nautilus* expedition of Wilkins in 1931, about which he has published in Norwegian a first-rate book, unfortunately not yet translated into English. By scientific training and field experience Sverdrup is, then, about as well placed as anyone could be for an opinion on what happened that tragic night of October, 1897, upon one of the Spitsbergen islands.

On a recent visit to New York, Sverdrup spoke of the narrow escape which Amundsen had from carbon monoxide poisoning, as related on pages 112-113 of Amundsen's book, *Nordostpassagen,* Oslo, 1921. When Sverdrup learned that the Explorers Club, of which he is a member, was concerned with the publication of a book that deals in part with the Andrée mystery, he wrote a letter which we are permitted to use in full:

University of California
The Scripps Institution of Oceanography
La Jolla, California
November 25, 1938

Vilhjalmur Stefansson, *President*
The Explorers Club
10 West 72nd Street
New York City

Dear Stefansson:

I wish to repeat in writing what I told you about my opinion as to the cause of the death of Andrée and Fraenkel, knowing that this opinion coincides with yours.

It occurred to me in September, 1930, that the two might have died because they had left their primus stove burning in the tent which might have become covered with snow and thus made practically air-tight. If they had died when the primus stove was burning one should expect to find the stove with the air-valve closed, but if they had turned it off and had died from exposure the air-valve would have been open. In the report by Dr. Gunnar Horn who found the camp it was mentioned that the primus stove was found half filled with kerosene. I wrote Dr. Horn asking if he could remember whether or not the air-valve was closed. He replied that he remembered distinctly that the valve was closed. In my opinion, this fact in connection with the fact that the primus stove was found standing between the bodies and still half filled with kerosene strongly supports the view that the two had died of carbon monoxide poisoning.

Although I have not available my correspondence with Dr. Horn, I remember that on receipt of his letter I wrote a note to one of the leading newspapers in Oslo, but the note was never published because the paper considered further discussion of the cause of death unnecessary.

In view of your own experience and in view of Amundsen's experience about which I told you, it seems to me that the above explanation of Andrée's and Fraenkel's death is a logical one and that it represents the explanation which fits best when all known factors are considered.

Very sincerely yours,
(Signed) H. U. SVERDRUP
Director

Chapter 5

The Missing Soviet Flyers

IN JUNE, 1937, Americans were as much startled as thrilled by the arrival in Oregon of a Soviet plane that had flown nonstop from Moscow by way of the North Pole. They were puzzled, too, when Chkalov, Baidukov, and Beliakov found the conditions worse in the Oregon mountains than they had been while crossing the Arctic sea by way of the North Pole, and when they turned back and landed in Vancouver, Washington.

In July, the world had scarcely grasped the achievements of the ANT-25 when Gromov, Yumashev, and Danilin in the ANT-25-1 flew by the same route from Moscow to northwestern Mexico. Gromov turned around, not for weather but because they wanted to land in the United States, and flew back to southwestern California. Even San Jacinto, where they came down, was so distant from Moscow that the plane was found to have broken the long-distance record by 658 miles. The flight, not counting the loop into Mexico, was certified by the National Aeronautic Association of the United States at 6,295 miles.

Both Chkalov and Gromov had flown light planes with a single motor. But the object was scheduled passenger flying between the Soviet Union and the United States by the short routes that cross the Arctic sea. Therefore, on August 12, a four-engined craft of passenger type left Moscow, bound for Fairbanks, Alaska. The H-209 had a crew of six: Sigismund Levanevsky, commander; Victor Levchenko, navigator; Nikolai Kastanayev, copilot; Nikolai Galkovsky, radio operator; Gregory Pobezhimov and Nikolai Godovikov, mechanics. Their plans were well conceived, the men chosen for experience and ability. Three of the six were Arctic veterans.

Levanevsky was among the most beloved of Soviet flyers. Born in 1902, the son of a blacksmith, he was in 1914 compelled to leave school to help his widowed mother with the support of the family. The October Revolution found him an unskilled factory laborer. With others of his factory he joined the Red Guard, serving on both eastern and western fronts. At the age of seventeen he was in command of a battalion; then assistant commander of a rifle regiment.

Levanevsky appears to have enjoyed life only when he was physically active. Sedentary work bored him. So, in 1922, when he was with the air-fleet administration in charge of balloons, he managed now and then to fly one. Not particularly interested in ballooning, he asked time and again to be transferred; and in 1923 he was sent to the Military Hydroplane Institute. After graduation he was with an air detachment, as junior flyer, then as senior, and finally as instructor. Victor Levchenko was one of his pupils.

Levanevsky first became known to the American public in 1933 through picking up Jimmie Mattern, around-the-world flyer, when he cracked up in Siberia. Levanevsky and Levchenko flew the disabled American from Anadir to Alaska. In 1934 Americans again heard of him, for he was in the United States purchasing a plane for use in the relief of the Chelyuskin party which was drifting on an ice floe in the Chukotsk Sea, to the north of eastern Siberia. For his part in the rescue operations he was awarded the decoration Hero of the Soviet Union.

From that point on, Levanevsky directed ship traffic from the air on the eastern part of the northern sea route until he began devoting himself to the problems of transpolar flying and a Moscow to Los Angeles flight scheduled for 1935. In August of that year, he and Levchenko started from Moscow; but an oil leak forced their return after some nine hundred miles.

In 1936, he, with Levchenko, made a flight from Los Angeles to Moscow (by way of Seattle, Juneau, Fairbanks, Nome, Wellen, Yakutsk, and Krasnoyarsk)—11,800 miles.

So Victor Levchenko was linked by his career to Sigismund Levanevsky—first in a teacher-pupil relationship and later, in many flights, as pilot-navigator. Levchenko was born in 1906, the son of a mechanic. The death of his father threw him on his own when he was fourteen, and he joined a ship's crew on the Sea of Azov. Later he became a cobbler's apprentice. In 1925 the Comsomol (Soviet youth organization) sent him to the Naval Academy where, after his graduation in 1928, he finished the naval aviation course the next year. He began his Arctic flying in 1932, directing ships en route from Vladivostok to Kolyma. Since 1933, he had been associated with Levanevsky.

The careers of pilot and navigator, then, are Soviet versions of the old-fashioned American success story—poor-boy-makes-good. It was so with all of the crew of the H-209.

Gregory Pobezhimov began to fly in 1917 as a naval aviator. His Arctic flights started in 1927 and earned for him in that year the Order of the Red Banner. Beginning with 1930, he flew in the western Arctic, organizing new air lines. In 1936 he was pilot-mechanic with Molokov on an 18,600-mile all-Arctic flight. In 1937 he had more than three thousand hours to his credit, had transported hundreds of passengers, visited scores of wintering parties and guided dozens of ships through the ice. His enthusiasm for the flight led him to apply for membership in the H-209 crew as mechanic; he knew planes inside out, and from the earliest models.

The rest had no Arctic experience; but apart from that they were experienced each in his own specialty.

The H-209, with its loved, distinguished and skilled crew, left Moscow on August 12, 1937, to fly nonstop to Fairbanks. They were flying at the most dangerous time of year, as we shall see later—best time of year so long as you are strong and light enough to keep above the clouds, for you have perpetual daylight; but worst if you are in the clouds, or if you have to come through them to make a descent upon the sea. Levanevsky knew this, as we see from Moscow dispatches printed in America—besides, we know that he would have known, for the H-209 had behind it the gathered knowledge of a body of Soviet Arctic flying that is far greater in hours and miles than the combined Arctic and Antarctic flying of all other nations.

Everything went as expected for the first two thousand miles, the clouds being found where they belonged and dealt with in routine fashion. Of course the plane had to fly through clouds at first, because it was too heavy for climbing high; but that was all right since there were no icing temperatures in the low clouds while they were passing over continental land or over the Gulf Stream waters just to the north of Russia. Several hundred miles before reaching the North Pole, they were able to rise above the clouds in time to avoid ice on their wings. Only one difficulty was greater than expected—the wind was stronger than the forecasts had led them to believe, and more adverse to them in direction.

When Levanevsky got to the Pole the wind near the 20,000-foot level was about sixty-two miles an hour and was cutting almost that many miles from their speed because it was nearly straight against them.

Everything continued well for nearly two hours after crossing the Pole and they were moving steadily down upon Alaska along the Fairbanks meridian. Then came the only distress message that, for certain, was from their plane.

The radiogram said that the H-209 had been forced to descend from its altitude of nearly 20,000 feet (where it had been flying in a bright sun and dry air above the clouds) to a 13,000-foot level because one of the four motors had gone dead through damage to an oil line. They were now flying in unbroken cloud, and ice was forming. The last words heard were: "Do you hear me?" As picked up by two or three other stations the message contained a few additional words, "We are landing in . . ." and thereafter some unintelligible signals, or at least ones that were not caught in a readable form.

At first it was hoped that the difficulty was merely one of radio transmission—that Levanevsky's three remaining engines would continue to function and would bring him in, with a somewhat decreased speed, to Fairbanks, or at least to some place in Alaska.

When, by the slower rating, the plane was one hour overdue at Fairbanks, the Soviet Embassy in Washington placed a telephone call for the Explorers Club of New York, an organization that exists to help explorers and exploration. There were special reasons for this call. Professor Otto Yulievich

Schmidt, head of the Chief Administration of the Northern Sea Route, was in general charge of all Soviet Arctic flying and therefore of the Levanevsky flight. In recognition of his individual work as an explorer and in recognition of the work of his department, he had been elected by the Club to an honorary membership which had been vacated by the death of General Adolphus W. Greely. On the same occasion, Levanevsky had been elected to life membership. With the supreme commander in Moscow and the flight commander both members, it was natural to address the Club.

Before going into the details of the search as organized and conducted, we discuss why the Explorers Club thought there was at least a fair prospect a search would be successful. For your verdict upon the Levanevsky case will depend on what you believe the Arctic to be like, in comparison with other seas, as to flying conditions and living conditions.

Comparative Safeties of the Seas

Levanevsky was assumed to have made a forced landing on the polar sea. Therefore we consider the various oceans, how they compare for the safety of forced landings.

Most flyers who have come down on liquid seas far from land and beyond sight of a vessel have been lost. All have been lost who made forced descents beyond sight of rescuers in a gale.

Before the Levanevsky flight there had been perhaps a dozen forced landings on the frozen sea. Some were in good weather, some in falling snow, some in blizzards, and one in a combination of gale and the darkness of night. All these had been safe descents—no lives had been lost and there had been only minor injuries to planes. The flyers were always saved in one of three ways; they made repairs and flew again; they were rescued, by plane or ship; or they abandoned their plane and walked ashore.

Take specifically for the North Atlantic the entire period from its first crossing by the United States Navy airplanes in 1919 to the beginning of survey flights by Pan American Airways and Imperial Airways in 1937. During this period at least nineteen ocean descents were made in all weathers from calm to gale. Nine planes were lost. The people saved were mostly those who had specially good luck, as coming down in fairly good weather either within sight of a ship or after being able to communicate to a near-by ship through radio the approximate position of their descent.

During the same period more than 90,000 miles were flown over the polar sea. There were at least fifty-six voluntary and forced descents in all weathers from calm to gale (not all Soviet figures are available). No lives were lost from any of these descents.

The safety of the polar sea, as compared with the deadliness of the North Atlantic, is the result of frost. If water is liquid, the best you can hope for is to swim awhile before sinking. When water is solid you behave upon it as if it were land. You are warmer on the ice at —50° than you are in the water at 50°, for water gets to your skin but cold air is held at bay by your clothing. In a fifty-mile storm on a liquid sea the waves break over your plane and toss it about until it sinks. In a fifty-mile wind on the pack ice you can lash down your plane as if it were on land. Then you construct a windbreak of snow blocks and tent behind it. You can build a dwelling of snow in which, by Eskimo technique, you can have a warmth of 50° when the thermometer outside reads —50°. If your airplane is beyond repair your radio may not be, and you have time and comfort for getting it into shape.

We focus the broad contrasts through special cases of the liquid and then of the frozen sea.

Captain Charles Kingsford-Smith, Australian, was first to make the east-west and west-east crossings of the Pacific. Then he took off from England on November 6, 1935, accompanied by Thomas Pethybridge, attempting to set a new speed record to Australia. They were last seen on November 8, fighting a monsoon off Siam. A search was immediately undertaken by four Royal Air Force flying boats and mail planes, but no trace of the missing flyers was found.

On July 2, 1937, Amelia Earhart, heroine of American aviation, and her assistant, the competent and experienced navigator Fred Noonan, came down in the tropical Pacific.

While not exactly a calm, there was no high sea running. No ship was right by, and the exact position was not known. The search, begun at once by private vessels, by the United States Coast Guard, and by the United States Navy, was abandoned after ten days. The only hope remaining was that, perhaps far out of reckoning, the plane might have come down near a tropical island. We do not often say it, but we all know it—life is not possible for any length of time in the ocean of the tropics except upon such lands as you may reach.

Swinging from tropics to Arctic, we take the first descent, or rather the first three descents, of a plane upon ice far from shore in the polar sea. On March 29, 1927, Hubert Wilkins and Ben Eielson flew with skis northwest from Point Barrow, Alaska, with the thermometer at take-off around —40°. They planned to fly northwestward for about six hours, to the vicinity of Lat. 80° N., Long. 180° W., where they would descend and take soundings. They would then fly south for two or three hours, and thence return to Barrow on a southeasterly course.

A hundred miles from shore the plane was already beyond the previously known region, for they had crossed the track of the *Karluk*, a ship with which Wilkins had once been connected temporarily. They continued for four hundred miles beyond the *Karluk* exploration, when they had engine trouble, which necessitated not only a forced descent but also the first ski or wheel descent ever attempted on the pack far from shore.

Wilkins selected a landing spot he thought favorable, depending, as he has said, on the experience he had gained when traveling over pack ice afoot during the years 1913-16 when he was a member of the Canadian Arctic Expedition of 1913-18. Eielson, schooled by North Dakotan and Alaskan winters, brought the plane down to a perfect landing. This was in clear and nearly calm weather five hundred miles from shore. A sounding, which Wilkins took while Eielson was repairing the engine, gave more than 16,000 feet, so that they were above the deepest place yet found in the polar sea. During the repairs, the sky had clouded over and snow was beginning to fall.

After a take-off from pack that was made difficult by the softness and depth of new-fallen snow, they flew eastward a little way, had engine trouble again, and made their second descent in a snowstorm. They were still approximately five hundred miles from land.

We must pause here to remind those readers who are not specialists in geography and climate that the frozen sea is not stormy in comparison with any ocean that is wholly liquid. This point was first emphasized by the American explorer George W. DeLong (1879-81) and fully established (1893-96) by Fridtjof Nansen, and by subsequent observers. A forty-mile-an-hour wind is as rare fifty miles from shore in the Arctic as a sixty-mile wind is on the North Atlantic steamer lane between New York and Southampton. But sixty-mile winds do blow on the North Atlantic, and a forty-mile wind was blowing from the south before Eielson and Wilkins had completed repairs.

Upon the second take-off the plane headed back toward Alaska and fought this wind through the afternoon. Planes were not so fast in 1927 as they are now, and speed was cut to something like fifty or sixty miles. They continued through the daylight of the late afternoon. In this latitude at this time of year, and with clouds in the sky, it is practically dark at seven o'clock. At nine o'clock, flying a mile high, the plane's engine stopped for the third time, now for want of gas.

The only thing to do was to keep straight against the wind and to bring the plane down as gradually as possible.

Here was a supreme test of a theory in practice. During a previous expedition Wilkins had arrived at the belief that you seldom have to go more than five miles on the northern sea in winter before you find a patch of ice level enough and large enough for an airplane descent and take-off. These patches, then, are scattered; certainly 80 per cent of the ice is too rough for a plane, perhaps 95 per cent. Even in the coldest weather there is open water here and there; for the ice is continually breaking under the stress of the currents. The chances were, then, at least ten to one that in the darkness and blinding storm the plane would be injured; perhaps one chance in twenty that it would come down in open water.

What happened, however, was that it descended on a fairly level patch. There was not even a severe jolt. Only the fabric of one wing was slightly injured, torn by a snag of ice. This last, however, was immaterial; for the plane, lacking gas, would have to be abandoned. (There were not in 1927 such facilities as now for rescue operations from the shores of the polar sea.)

In the blizzard and darkness, Wilkins and Eielson, able to get only a limited idea of where they were and how situated, went to sleep in the cabin of the plane and had a fairly good night. Morning found them drifting on a medium-size floe, surrounded by leads and patches of open water. The weather was still cloudy and there was not much frost, so that new ice did not form rapidly upon the open water and the floes were comparatively free to move in a drift which appeared to be southeastward, parallel to the north coast of Alaska. An astronomical observation later showed that they were about seventy-five miles northwest of Point Barrow.

In seven days the floe, with the camp on it, drifted about two hundred miles in an easterly direction. Then the skies cleared and the weather became cold so that new ice formed, binding the floes together. Wilkins and Eielson now took their bedding, camp gear, rifles, and ammunition on their backs and started walking toward shore. They averaged ten miles a day and made it in ten days.

In the Wilkins story everything went according to plan—they had counted on the possibility of forced landing, on perhaps having to leave their plane, and they had figured the chance that they might have to walk as much as five hundred miles to shore. Since it is not possible for men to carry on their backs food enough for a five-hundred-mile journey over drifting ice, Wilkins had provisions only for about twenty days—in other words, emergency rations. The main plan for subsistence was through hunting equipment which would provide food and fuel in the manner to which Wilkins had become accustomed between 1913 and 1916 on the above-mentioned expedition.

We supplement the Wilkins story of the expected with Nobile's story of the unexpected.

Umberto Nobile had built the airship with which Amundsen and Ellsworth crossed the Arctic in 1926, and had been its navigator. In 1928 he was in the Arctic again, with the dirigible *Italia,* operating from a hangar at King's Bay, Spitsbergen. He had already made a good exploratory voyage to the east when, on May 24, he flew from Spitsbergen westerly to the northeast corner of Greenland, crossing an unexplored part of the sea. Then he continued from Greenland to the North Pole by a route unexplored because it was far more easterly than the Peary journeys.

From the Pole, Nobile was returning to Spitsbergen, and was a little to the northeast of that island group, when, on May 25, he was overtaken by a cataclysm that has many explanations, each conflicting with one or more of the others, and none conclusive. All we can state beyond argument is that suddenly the airship was found to be dropping rapidly.

It seems that by a quick change of rudders, or in some other way, Nobile had tilted the ship upward before she struck the ice, so that her tail dragged. Two of the three gondolas were torn away. Ten men, with goods and wreckage, were dumped on the ice. Freed of their weight and that of the gondolas and cargo, the dirigible rose swiftly and drifted off before the wind. Men who had not been stunned by the shock got to their feet and watched it soar away. They are in reasonable agreement that when the *Italia* was something like five miles off she exploded. The six men aboard her in the forward gondola must have died, either burnt by the hydrogen or crushed as their bodies struck the ice.

One of the marooned men, Pomella, was killed as the gondola was being torn loose from the airship; two had broken hips and legs, Nobile and Cecioni; Malmgren suffered a fractured shoulder and, as it proved later, his kidneys had been torn loose so that he eventually died from this cause.

If there had been no radio, the Nobile party would have started moving toward shore. Such a twenty- or thirty-mile walk would have been a mere commonplace in the history of exploration—in fact, several exploring parties have walked ashore on this and near-by groups of islands during the last few centuries, some of them covering several hundred miles. Even with the cripples, the Nobile party could have double-tripped ashore, probably in a week or two.

But, since they had a radio, Nobile was correct in staying where he was. It took them some days to get the radio in proper working order and it was not until after nine days (June 3) that an amateur operator in Archangel got and properly interpreted their signals. Days more elapsed before, on June 7, they were in contact with their base ship, the *Città di Milano*. Ten days later they saw the first two planes, Norwegian, piloted by Riiser-Larsen and Lützow Holm, which turned back because of engine trouble shortly before reaching the party. In succeeding days an Italian plane circled near them, and the Norwegians twice approached and then disappeared from view, each time without sighting the Nobile camp.

Finally, on June 20, an Italian plane, working from the base ship, sighted the party, but did not land. It dropped equipment, much of which was broken in the fall. Two days later Italian planes dropped provisions and further supplies. June 22 two Swedish planes flew over, dropping provisions and a note with instructions for marking out a landing place on the ice.

The next day, June 23, almost a month after the disaster, Lieutenant Einar Paal Lundborg descended with his Swedish plane on the pack about five hundred feet from the camp. Hopping from cake to cake, he and his mechanic arrived at the camp to find Nobile demanding, in the best grand-opera tradition, that all others should be saved first and he himself be removed last. Lundborg replied (personal communication; see also his book narrative) that this was no grand opera; that he was in command, and that the rescue would be conducted as seemed best to him and his associates.

Nobile was skin and bones from worry, and he is small-boned to begin with. Cecioni, the other cripple, was always large and had put on an extra fifty pounds lying there in the tent, eating much and worrying little since the accident. Lundborg, glancing at the two men, decided that the plane could not carry Cecioni in addition to himself and his mechanic, but that it would carry Nobile. So, taking Nobile under one arm, he and the mechanic hopped from cake to cake again, returned to the plane and flew to the Swedish base on Foyne Island. A few hours later another Swedish plane delivered Nobile to the *Città di Milano*.

Meantime, leaving the mechanic behind at the Swedish base so as to be able to carry the big and fat Cecioni, Lundborg returned alone. Engine failure compelled him to glide for a landing. He fell short by a yard or two, so that his skis, instead of planting themselves on the floe, stubbed their toes against the edge of it and the plane turned on its back, without, however, injuring the pilot. So the fat man had to remain to get still fatter until the Soviet steamer *Krassin* arrived to pick up the entire party of seven on July 12, a month and a half after their descent. (Lundborg had been taken off the floe a few days earlier by a small Swedish plane.)

We have discussed what we believe about Amelia Earhart and Kingsford-Smith in the tropics, and what we know of Wilkins and Nobile in the Arctic. An even more striking contrast is from Roald Amundsen. For Amundsen had two forced landings, the first on the icy polar sea to the north of the Franz Josef Islands, the second in the never-frozen Gulf Stream just north of Norway.

Amundsen and Ellsworth, with four companions, flew north in two airplanes, pontoon-equipped. They started from Spitsbergen May 21, 1925, and were within one hundred miles of the North Pole when engine trouble forced both planes down within three miles of each other. Pontoons can in an emergency serve as skis upon snow or upon level earth, but the Amundsen planes found open water and descended into leads. These leads soon closed through ice movement, but the party saved one of the planes from being crushed between the floes by hauling it up on the ice.

The ice surface was rough, as it usually is in the vicinity of leads, and the men had to work for days to smooth out a runway—a particularly difficult task because they had not brought along tools suitable for this work. With makeshift gear they did level off a runway. One plane was able to carry the men of both, and, using the pontoons for skis, they took off on June 15, flying back to Spitsbergen.

We have discussed the Nobile predicament of 1928. Amundsen was one of those who wanted to come to his help. As a passenger in a French seaplane piloted by a French naval officer, Captain Guilbaud, Amundsen flew from Tromsö, Norway, June 18th, bound for King's Bay, Spitsbergen. There was also a French crew of three and Dietrichson, a Norwegian who had piloted one of Amundsen's planes during the 1925 work. The weather was neither calm nor stormy but halfway between.

The world listened to the plane's radio. When the signals stopped, we knew there had been a forced landing. Ships began to cruise back and forth over the vicinity where the party must have descended but only wreckage of the plane was found—eventually.

Because Amundsen perished several hundred miles north of the Arctic Circle, it was repeated through the press frequently and with variations that he, the great conqueror of the Arctic, had finally been conquered by the Arctic; that the temporary master of the ice and snow had been mastered permanently by these inexorable forces. For the sake of rhetoric, or because they did not know, these commentators and sermonizers omitted mentioning that Amundsen's plane had come down in waters of the Gulf Stream. Not during thousands of years, probably not since the last Scandinavian Ice Age, has there been a floe or any piece of ice in the waters where Amundsen was lost.

Amundsen's descent was several hundred miles short of that ice pack which, at the very moment of his death, was keeping safe Nobile and the rest of the men whom the famous Norwegian explorer meant to help.

The contrast between a frozen and a liquid sea is basic. The pack gives you the amenities of land. You do not sink because ice is firm; you do not thirst, for sea ice is fresh if it is more than nine months old and there is fresh snow on much of it in any case (or fresh rain and thaw water in summer); your clothes keep you warm and dry, for they have been designed to repel air and rain; there are no waves and spray, for the hard surface is not stirred by the wind.

Arctic Flying Conditions

On the basic difference of a frozen from a liquid sea rested the presumption that Levanevsky and his companions were still living when the search for them began. If they failed to save themselves and if they failed to be saved by rescuers, then their lives would be the first to be lost of all those who have made forced or voluntary descents by airplane on the polar sea, whatever the weather and whatever the time of year.

For those who contend that lives have been lost by airplane in the polar sea can do it only by the specious reasoning that Amundsen was lost in the Arctic. True, he died within the Arctic Circle. But what we mean when we talk of Arctic conditions is at least that there shall be ice on water in January. Amundsen and his men died where the water has never felt ice. Definitely, no life had yet been lost in connection with airplanes in any icy part of the northern sea before Levanevsky took off from Moscow, though there had been thousands of flight miles and scores of descents.

But you could not go to the other extreme and take it for granted that Levanevsky was practically certain to have made a safe descent just because he was known to be one of the best flyers, careful and skillful, or because he was on a sea that never to that time had failed to give a safe landing to those who had descended upon it.

For, as we have previously said, Levanevsky was flying at the most dangerous time of year.

It has been found in millions of miles of Alaska flying, that ice can form on wing and propeller in very cold weather, for instance at —40° and —50°; and the like has been discovered in the old world. But this sort of thing in known to have happened only one day so far in Alaska flying—February 8, 1934—when several planes in different parts of the Territory were forced down, crusted with ice particles. The temperature at one of the localities was —8°. Since this "spicule fog" frosting is so rare in Alaska, it will probably occur only once in a long time over the polar sea. No one yet has had experience there with serious icing in very cold weather.

The most dangerous flying, in the north as elsewhere, is when temperatures hover between five degrees above and ten degrees below the freezing point. Most frosting on planes occurs between the temperatures of 27° and 36° Fahrenheit.

Out in the northern pack in summer you have fog perhaps every other day on the average during June and August, and some two days out of three during July. These fogs are liable to be of an icing temperature.

The Wilkins contention, with which most authorities now agree, that in the main body of the polar sea you find numerous patches of ice on which you can land, applies only to the cold part of the year. As late as May, or even the first part of June, emergency landing fields are still many and in good condition if you are far north, and especially if you are also far from land. But late in June, through arrival of air warmed over North America or Eurasia, the thaws become powerful even at a distance from land—even where most of the sun's light is reflected by snow before it has a chance to be converted into local heat. For there are comparatively dark surfaces, as of glare ice that has been broken and tilted up; there are bits of seaweed; there are tiny plants growing in the snow that are darker than the snow and capture sunlight, producing warmth and thawing. The snow becomes slush and rivulets trickle. Then it starts raining. Even from the vicinity of the North Pole Papanin's 1937 drift expedition reported summer rains, and we know that these spread throughout the polar basin.

Early in July rivulets of thaw and rain water are flowing over the surface of the previously level emergency landing fields. Late in that month the ditches cut by running water are two or three feet deep, and they form a network. By the 13th of August, when Levanevsky passed over the mathematical North Pole, the season is at its worst. There are few, if any, patches of ice on the whole polar sea that have not been spoiled, for aeronautical purposes, by the rain and the sun.

Put yourself in Levanevsky's place. You know all these things, and many others of a kind to give you a theoretical grasp of the situation below. You still have control over your plane and you have the necessary skill to guide it through the clouds. But you are 13,000 feet up in that obscurity and do not know whether there is a clear space even a few hundred feet between the lower side of the clouds and the ice. You do not know, then, whether you will ever be able to see anything before you strike ice or water, if you try coming down.

You know also, in the situation that is hypothetical to you but was real to Levanevsky, that what you are going to see, if there is a clear space between clouds and ice, will almost certainly prove hopeless. The previously level winter ice will be crisscrossed by summer ditches. There will be no smooth patch wide enough for an ordinary landing. Almost certainly you will have to pancake down and, for a minimum, the result will be the destruction of your landing gear—you will never be able to take off again.

Even in this merely hypothetical discussion you will feel the choice difficult. Ought you to keep aloft, though your wings and propellers are gathering frost, hoping to find warmer air that will melt the ice before the plane is out of control? Or should you make a precautionary landing, with the chance of saving your men, knowing that your plane will never fly again?

The best judges of polar conditions, and of the temperament of Levanevsky, believe that he decided in favor of a precautionary landing and that he came down with his plane still in control. It is, of course, possible that even if he made this decision to land his plane may have iced so rapidly as he came down through the cloud that it was out of control before he reached sea level. In that case he and his men were killed or maimed by the crash.

The search for Levanevsky which we are trying to explain, and shall later try to describe, was based on what some thought was an even chance, and others thought a chance in five or in ten, that he had pancaked down to a landing which completely destroyed his radio equipment but which nevertheless did not kill the men, or at least not all of them. The party, or some of it, would then be living on the ice. They might travel for land, though probably not, for they would know that a search would be made for them. Their best chance for rescue was to stay in that place where rescuers were most likely to look for them, which would be somewhere on the meridian that runs from the Pole to Fairbanks.

It is the tradition of exploration not to give up rescue work so long as there is any reasonable chance. The official search for Sir John Franklin, whose expedition was last heard from in 1845, continued until 1854. Private search, with hope of finding a survivor, was not given up for many years after that.

We know now that the search for Franklin started at least a year before the last of the 129 men died, and that some of his party might have been saved if the searchers had gone to place A, which they could have done just as easily as visiting places B, C, and D, where they did go. The official search was even continued for five years after John Rae had brought back evidence that at any rate most of the men were dead. It would seem to be a minimum, then, to search a year for Levanevsky.

Assuming that the Levanevsky party were alive, and not seriously injured, six hours after the descent, most authorities would agree that they could still be alive six months later. They had provisions for only three months; but they had rifles and ammunition; they were well clothed; they had the best of camping gear. Moreover, they believed in the so-called "friendly Arctic" view of the polar sea which, applied to their case, would mean that if they lived sensibly and made good use of every chance, then they could find food and fuel indefinitely. As to living quarters, they could be reasonably comfortable either in the tents which they carried or in snowhouses built Eskimo-fashion. That would mean only the use of such technique as Wilkins and Eielson, for instance, used when walking over a hundred miles of sea to Alaska.

Levanevsky knew that his compatriots, Papanin, Krenkel, Shirshov and Feodorov, of the Soviet drifting party, had confirmed the "friendly Arctic" view; for the newspapers not only of the Soviet Union but of the whole world carried on July 3, 1937, a radio dispatch from Papanin which said: ". . . the investigations . . . have disproved Nansen's conjecture that the central part of the Arctic ocean holds extremely little life. A net raised from a depth of 1,000 metres fairly teemed with diverse mollusca, larvae, medusae and crustacea." Other Papanin dispatches told of polar bear mothers with young cubs near the Pole, of seals swimming in leads eating shrimps, and of birds flying about.

It was the experience of the Canadian Arctic Expedition of 1913–18 when on the ice several hundred miles from land to the north of North America that polar bears can smell a camp from ten or more miles away and, so far as could be judged, every bear, on smelling a camp, walks right for it. There would be no excessive optimism in the hope that a bear would pass within ten miles to leeward of any sea ice camp on an average of once a month. These bears will average a thousand pounds, live weight, so that, if the Levanevsky party always stood guard, watch-and-watch sailor-fashion, and if the guard always looked down wind, then they would secure every bear visitor. For bears amble in without caution or haste.

Then you would think that the bears killed could have been supplemented by a few seals. Any bears or seals secured before the three months' provisions had been eaten would lengthen out the time of the provisioning. Altogether six months would seem a conservative estimate of the period during which the Levanevsky party would be reasonably safe, assuming that they were alive, not seriously injured, following the descent.

There has been much discussion of why no radio messages were received if the party were alive. To seek one of the possible answers to this we have studied equipment lists and plans of the expedition and have thought them admirable on the whole, but have found what appears a serious slip. There is seemingly no record that a spare hand radio set was carried. However, this may be a gap in our documentation and not in the equipment of the H-209, for the *Moscow Daily News* for August 14, 1937, in an account of Galkovsky, the radio operator, states: "Even at home, during his rest hours, he continued to work on an emergency radio apparatus."

Levanevsky may have been so confident of being able to cross the sea without a descent that he carried no radio except that which was attached to his plane's engine. At a minimum, the power plant and radio must have been destroyed by the descent, for no message, after the one we paraphrase, was ever received that for a certainty came from Levanevsky.

Radio messages did continue to be picked up for days following August 13 which seemed as if they might have come from the H-209. But we have had proof of a curious morbid psychology that grips the radio world when a heroine like Amelia Earhart, or a hero like Sigismund Levanevsky, disappears. The simulated Earhart messages had a devilish ingenuity so that a few of them are hard to dismiss even now. The same was true for messages which purported to come from Levanevsky. We still feel that some of them may really have come from him. Nothing was ever deciphered, however, that gave a clear geographical position for the senders; so that, even if genuine, these messages can prove no more than that the party were not all killed; that someone lived through who had at a partial grasp of radio technique.

That the messages gradually became weaker through several days, and finally died out, is perhaps the strongest argument for their being genuine. It was just as if storage batteries were gradually running down.

The Search

This, then, was the general picture when at eleven P.M., August 13, the Chargé d'Affaires of the Soviet Embassy in Washington, Constantine Oumansky, telephoned the Explorers Club. During the forenoon of the next day a program was adopted.

It was already known that the United States Government would cooperate in the search for the lost flyers through several of its departments. There was no doubt that Canada and other governments would help as and when needed. A coordinating agency was required. It was decided that the Explorers Club should take this role. The Club would advise and assist the Soviet Embassy, which would be in charge of all rescue efforts made from North America.

Upon nomination by the Club, the Embassy selected to command an American searching expedition Captain Sir Hubert Wilkins, who has most Arctic experience of those men available who are competent in aviation. Once embarked upon a search, he would be last to give up voluntarily; for he believes that a small group of men, resourceful and properly equipped, can secure anywhere on the polar sea enough wholesome food and suitable fuel to keep them alive indefinitely.

Wilkins was given free choice of men. He telegraphed to colleagues who had been with him on Antarctic work, Air Commodore Herbert Hollick-Kenyon, S. A. Chessman, and J. H. Lymburner. Lymburner was off on a flight in a remote mining region of subarctic Canada and did not receive his telegram until Kenyon and Chessman had accepted. Only two pilots were needed.

A quick survey of the United States and Canada showed but one type of plane that might be available and suited for the work. A flying boat was needed of 4,000-mile range. This would be such a craft as the Consolidated, used for long-range bombers by the United States Navy. Navy planes were out of the question, for they contained military secrets which makes it against both law and policy to turn them over to any foreign power; and, of course, airplanes used in the search would be the property of the Soviet Union.

There was in existence, however, one civilian plane of this type from which the military features had been sufficiently removed. This fortunately belonged to another member of the Explorers Club, Richard Archbold. He was about to start on a scientific expedition to New Guinea and refused to sell until he was convinced that his boat was the only one suitable, whereupon he immediately turned it over to the search at replacement cost. An example of the cooperation which the search was destined to receive from many individuals and industries, large and small, was an immediate offer by the Consolidated Aircraft Corporation of San Diego to put special overtime, without corresponding special cost, into making a duplicate craft for Archbold, so that the delay of his New Guinea expedition would be the least possible.

There were Government hurdles. Archbold had not been able to secure permission to leave the United States with his flying boat before November, 1937, and permission was needed to start within the week. No doubt with the knowledge and warm approval of the President, certainly with the cooperation of the State Department and all other pertinent departments of the Government, it was soon arranged through the Bureau of Aeronautics that the *Guba*, Archbold's plane, might leave when ready, on condition that at the end of her employment in the search she would be returned to the United States and would not be shipped abroad until November 1.

Now came the details of organization. Both for the safety of the men who were searching and for improvement of the prospects of finding Levanevsky, there had to be the most accurate possible weather forecasting. (You may be able to travel in fog, but there is no point in searching when the only report you could bring back would be of mileage and of invisibility.) The first step was that the United States Weather Bureau assigned two of its best forecasters to duty at Fairbanks, Alaska. There was a special concentration of weather information at Seattle for retelegraphing to Fairbanks. Canada would similarly help with weather reports, sending part of the information to Seattle, while that from its most northwesterly stations would go direct to Fairbanks. The Soviet Government would concentrate on Fairbanks its weather information from half a hundred stations in Arctic and subarctic Siberia and on the islands of the polar sea, while one of its meterorologists would proceed to Fairbanks to help with the interpretation of the Russian language information and in general with the forecasting.

Through these men and this service there resulted a weather forecasting of such accuracy that, on four long polar flights out of five, Wilkins found areas of fog and patches of clear out on the sea usually within fifty miles of where the limits had been set by the forecasts.

But these plans of the Weather Bureau would have been of no avail except for special cooperation from the United States Army through the Signal Corps, for the regular Alaska telegraphic facilities are insufficient for such a tremendous extra load. The Signal Corps facilities were doubled through assignment of special men and through other arrangements.

In order to prevent duplication of effort, to leave the scientific men free for their own work, and to see that those engaged in the search had everything they needed, Amtorg Trading Corporation, of New York, sent a coordinator to Fairbanks. He it was who attended to all details of supplies, equipment, and the like. To help in the interpretation of Russian signals at Point Barrow, the radio station of the United States Army, a Soviet radio technician was stationed there to cooperate with the Army's local representative.

Levanevsky had been overdue at Fairbanks the evening of Friday, August 13. The *Guba,* fitted by Archbold for tropical service, was refitted for Actic use so rapidly that on the 21st Wilkins, Kenyon, and Chessman in the *Guba* were on the north coast of Canada, ready to begin their research flying. With them were two members of the *Guba's* tropical crew, Radio Operator Raymond Booth and Mechanic Gerald D. Brown.

Between August 22 and September 21, these five men flew more than 10,000 miles over the polar sea. From the success of the weather forecasters in predicting conditions that were actually met on the flights, it would seem that they were right, too, when they said that during the rest of the time it was too foggy for useful flying. This means that the searchers were not having average weather; for, according to a compilation of available data, there ought to be not more than sixteen to eighteen foggy days in August and ten to twelve in September. (There should be four to five foggy days in October, one or two in November, and none from December to March inclusive.)

Thus through late August and through two-thirds of September, 1937, the *Guba* wrote one of the decisive chapters in the history of northern flying. She proved that aircraft of her type, managed by people like her crew, can deal successfully with the worst that the polar sea can offer. That she did not fly every day, with just time out for sleep and rest, was only because the purpose was not to make a record of sustained flying but to find a small black patch down on the sea ice—the hoped-for camp of Levanevsky pitched by the wreckage of the H-209. There was no use in taking the air when the chance for seeing down through the clouds was too small. It would have been merely tantalizing for Levanevsky to hear the engines of a plane flying over. That sound could have brought him no information except what he already knew, that a search was being carried forward with all the resources available. That search was from all sides of the polar basin, though we are telling here only the American part of the story.

We have said that the middle of August—the time of the Levanevsky flight—is the most dangerous of the whole year for making a safe descent with a plane mounted on skis, or on wheels as was the H-209. July is the foggiest month of the year, August the next foggiest; but these fogs are not quite so dangerous with regard to icing of wings and propellers as are those of late August and early September. To that extent the *Guba* was flying at a worse time than the H-209.

The 10,000 miles of the *Guba* over the polar sea in late August and through the first three weeks of September were a success in everything but the purpose for which they were made, to find Levanevsky. That search would now have to be carried on by a plane of another type.

Northern flying has to deal with a transition period between early September and middle or late October. The first week of September the days are still warm on the Arctic mainland, for the sun retains power and its beams change to heat when they strike black earth or green vegetation. Besides, a part of the 60° to 90° temperatures of midsummer has been stored in the soil, which can radiate its heat on cool nights; lakes have been warmed similarly, and they store heat better than the hard earth.

But out on the polar sea much of the sun's light is never converted into heat, but is instead reflected away by white surfaces. What heat is generated is neutralized constantly by the melting of ice, and there remains ice still unmelted. Ice in the water means that the whole surface of the polar sea is at, or just below, the freezing point of fresh water—perhaps at 29°. So the freeze-up and the winter that are delayed on the land come on schedule out at sea. Even in August a slush of ice, and perhaps a crust, may form upon leads in the pack. By the 1st of September, or at latest around the 10th, there will be so much ice on most leads that are far at sea that the hull of a flying boat would be injured upon descent. The same slush and crust would hinder a take-off.

The *Guba* started back for New York September 23 not because of ice forming at her Aklavik base in the Mackenzie delta but because of its formation out in the pack—so that, even were Levanevsky's camp discovered, the *Guba* would not be able to find water near him on which to settle for the rescue. It would be several weeks before there was enough ice on the rivers and lakes of the delta for the needs of a plane mounted on skis. Winter operations, therefore, could not start before some time in October or in early November.

The *Guba* was delivered at North Beach Airport, Long Island, on September 25, and was stored to await shipment to Leningrad when its export freedom should come on the first of November, 1937.

The plane now chosen for the continued search was a Lockheed Electra. Once more Government, corporations, individuals, worked together for speed and efficiency. The only suitable Electra ski undercarriage was owned by the Canadian Government and was intended for survey work toward opening the then projected trans-Canada air service. Upon the authority of the Minister of Transport, Trans-Canada Airways gave up this equipment and waited for replacement. We cite this merely as one of many examples of cooperation.

Before the northern ski season arrived the plane was ready. It flew by way of Edmonton and the Mackenzie River to Aklavik, about one hundred and fifty miles north of the Arctic Circle and one hundred miles south of the polar sea. Under Wilkins' command were still Kenyon and Chessman. Brown and Booth had been released for their tropical work with Archbold. In their place went S. R. Wilson and R. W. Cooke, radio engineers, who were to operate the expedition's radio stations at the Aklavik and Barrow bases. A. T. L. Dyne was the new mechanic.

November, though a good month far out on the polar sea, is rather bad on the shore, snowy and cloudy. With clearer skies a thousand miles away, taking off in thick weather is disagreeable rather than prohibitive. However, the return from such a clear area to the home base may be difficult, for at this season there is light only around noon and only a twilight then. So there ought to be a guiding radio at Aklavik. There should be a second guiding radio at Point Barrow, so that the plane could get its position, on the principles of triangulation, when far out at sea.

The establishment of two guiding radios was difficult, for suitable equipment was hard to get. With November so bad a month, the loss may not have been serious when delay with the radio establishment prevented flights.

In our chapter on Sir John Franklin we have pointed out that the many expeditions sent in search of him made as a by-product important contributions to geographical and other scientific problems. So it was, too, with the search for Levanevsky, particularly now in the winter flying of the Electra.

The usefulness of moonlight has been one of the debated problems, and the expedition hoped during December both to use the moon to rescue the drifting Soviet party and also to study moonlight for the benefit of aviation. It was heartbreaking, therefore, that forecasts made it seem unwise to use the December moon. The reports showed thick weather out over the searching area. The first flight that attempted for a thousand miles or more the exclusive use of moonlight would have to be done under favorable conditions.

From tropical experience you cannot understand the usefulness of the northern moon, for there is so much moisture and dust in the equatorial atmosphere as to reduce the moon's brightness appreciably. Then, striking the earth, the moonlight is absorbed by the blacks and greens of water, soil, and vegetation. In the forested Arctic, say the Yukon valley or the woods north of Great Bear Lake, there are many dark things to absorb the moonlight. It is only when you are out on the northern prairie, beyond the tree line, that you have approximately full use of the moon. You get a near perfection when you are on the polar sea, for there everything is white, except for some dark ribbons and patches where the ice breaks under the stress of currents and water shows through.

Because of the clearer atmosphere, the moon succeeds in delivering a litle more light at the earth's surface in the polar zones than elsewhere. This is in turn so fully reflected by the snow that its usefulness is nearly doubled—practically speaking, you have twice as much light from the moon in the Arctic winter as you ever have in the tropics. You can see farther by a half moon in the Arctic than by a full moon in the tropics. By a three-quarters moon in the Arctic you can see a mountain, no matter how far away, if it rises above the horizon. Even the moon's drawbacks have compensations. The light is less than that of the sun, but it is comfortable and effective; the sun's light is far more than you need, dazzling you when it is reflected by the snow. Your eyes feel constantly rested in the brightest moonlight. You go snowblind with Arctic sunlight.

January 14–15, 1938, Wilkins, with Kenyon at the controls, made the long awaited first extensive flight to depend wholly on moonlight. They flew a round-trip distance of 1,420 miles, turning back at 76° N. Lat., 140° W. Long., where they met thick weather. They found that both for operating the plane and for searching for men who are lost the moonlight was adequate. Had the Levanevsky camp been there, they would have seen it as far away by moonlight as by daylight. And they could have come down for one more Wilkins landing upon the Arctic sea; much the same kind of descent, too, as Kenyon had made again and again with Ellsworth on the Antarctic Continent in 1935. The moonlight was sufficient for that.

There was great hope of progress in the search by the full moon of February, for this is perhaps the clearest of all Arctic months; fogless, or nearly so, out at sea, and with few fogs on shore. It was tragic, therefore, that the plane injured one of her propellers while taxiing down the river on the take-off for the flight of January 14. Somebody had planted a stick upright in the snow that covers the ice of the Mackenzie River in front of the town of Aklavik; the propeller struck it, bending one of its tips. Those in the plane heard the noise; after the take-off they noticed that the left engine did not perform perfectly, but considered the trouble to be slight and temporary. Upon their return to Aklavik, the propeller tip was straightened and it was thought that there would be no further trouble. Due to unfavorable weather conditions the plane remained idle for some time following this and the seriousness of the injury was not discovered until February 6 when, upon warming up the motors, it was found the left engine was so badly injured that it would have to be replaced. Thus the precious full moon period of February was used up in coming several thousand miles south on a Mackenzie Air Service plane to get a new engine.

March 2–3 the Electra made some overland flights which we shall describe later.

The search over the ice of the polar sea was resumed on March 10 in a flight of 2,080 miles during eleven hours. Then on March 14 they took off on the final search, which carried them to a highest north of 87° 50′ N. Lat., 105° W. Long., where they turned homeward, landing at Aklavik after nineteen hours in the air. The distance was about 3,300 miles.

On March 15, Wilkins received orders from the Soviet Government that American participation in the search for Levanevsky was to be closed with the reception of that message.

Combining flying-boat and ski operations, Wilkins, with Kenyon or Chessman at the controls, had flown after leaving New York on August 19, 1937, about 45,550 miles, of which

33,970 were flown within the Arctic Circle. They had flown over and explored 170,000 square miles of the Arctic sea, of which at least 150,000 square miles had never been seen before. There had been only two slight accidents, the propeller injury we have described and a slight damage to a tail fin. There had been some trouble from icing during the summer flying-boat operation but none during the ski plane search, confirming that danger from ice on wings or propeller is negligible in winter. In summer icing trouble is about as serious over the Arctic as it is in late fall or early spring between New York and Chicago.

The foregoing is, of course, an oversimplified story. There was more to the search than we have told. For instance, the possibility could not be overlooked that Levanevsky might have reached the mainland, coming down somewhere in Alaska.

A small plane was hired from Mackenzie Air Service, Edmonton. Piloted by Robert Randall this plane descended the Mackenzie and carried on searching operations between August 15 and September 1. It traveled slowly west along 500 miles of the north coast, landing wherever people were sighted. Randall was not to ask direct questions; for, as said, the Eskimos, like most primitive people, have it as part of their ethics that they should tell the questioner only things that will please him. Randall was simply to gossip as to the happenings of the summer, what steamers had been around, what Eskimos had power launches in the neighborhood, what familiarity they had with airplanes, when they had last seen a plane, and so on.

Through this method Randall got only negative results, except in Barter Island. There he was told that on August 13 the people had been busy handling domestic reindeer in a corral. In their excitement they did not at first notice what they later took to be the noise of a power boat. Stopping to listen, they decided that there must be an airplane passing over, hidden by clouds, for many of these people own power boats and they all have seen and heard airplanes, most of them frequently, so that they can differentiate. The noise of the plane had begun seaward and had faded inland. If true, this would mean that Levanevsky had entered Alaska a little farther east than the meridian of Fairbanks, a slight deviation easily accounted for by the thick weather.

Randall secured no further information on his way to Barrow. A few days later he returned, flying a little inland and searching along the foot of the mountains from the Barter Island vicinity eastward. He saw nothing.

Acting upon the Randall clue, Joe Crosson, manager of Pacific Alaska Airways, made immediately a flight north from Fairbanks into the mountains. Thereafter during the next several weeks repeated flights were made by him and by others. Most of these were only to the mountains, triangulating different parts of them and the country to the south. But one flight was all the way to the Arctic coast.

There were reports of lights seen in the mountains, but apparently they were a result of vivid imaginations stirred by the Randall report.

During the fall operation the *Guba* made a flight to the Barter Eskimos, many of whom Wilkins knew through dealing with them in 1913–14. Some of the Barter group are particularly reliable, for instance, the sons of Thomas Gordon, a man well known to all who have been in northern Alaska during the last forty years. The reports were so convincing that Wilkins recommended further search in the Alaska mountains. He also made several searching flights himself in that region, first with the *Guba* but chiefly with the Lockheed Electra during the ski operations.

A notable overland Electra flight was from Aklavik, March 2–3. This was a westward search of more than 3,000 miles, flying the length of the Endicott and Brooks ranges several times and crisscrossing them at ten-mile intervals. No sign of the missing plane was found.

The chance of discovering mountain wreckage would be small. Had the men lived they could have walked out to some point of safety. Collision with a mountainside in a fog would have been followed by a burial of the plane by snow. The Endicotts are rugged and complicated south of Barter Island, where the plane was reported, and the wreckage, if it is there, may go decades without being discovered. For the only people who penetrate the mountains usefully are rare prospectors for gold and hunters that are almost equally rare now that mountain sheep are no longer numerous. Travelers who cross the mountains by sledge in winter or pack animals in summer naturally keep to the passes and would never find anything unless it happened to lie on their trail.

Much energy was spent with little success on summer operations from Point Barrow. First to arrive there was the American flyer Jimmie Mattern, whom, as we have said, Levanevsky rescued in Siberia. Mattern's equipment, however, was unsuitable, and he was inexperienced in northern work; so that the one excursion which he made out over the sea to the north or northeast of Barrow did no more than penetrate the fringe of the pack ice. It must have been in the neighborhood of a thousand miles short of the near edge of the district where a landing by Levanevsky was commonly thought to be most likely, north of Latitude 85°.

Longer flights were made from Barrow later in the year by Soviet planes. First was Vassili Zadkov, who flew with pontoons on September 5 to the supply ship and icebreaker *Krassin* which was then located at 72° 36′ N., 147° 12′ W. Zadkov went some distance beyond the *Krassin* on a reconnoitering flight, then descended in a lead beside the ship to await favorable weather for a northern flight to the vicinity of the Pole. Unfortunately, on September 8 the ice began to crowd and crush through wind or current pressure and the plane was lost. This type of difficulty with ice is serious on the edge of the pack, or even fifty miles within it, but not serious if you are one hundred or more miles from open water, for then you can usually haul a pontoon plane out upon safely solid ice.

At this time the *Krassin* was working in the edge of the pack, the thought being to find a level floe and set out upon it one of the airplanes which the ship carried. However, the ice was not suitable, for reasons which we have described. The *Krassin's* planes were of small range in any case—they were just craft which had happened to be available in northeastern Siberia.

By reputation and experience the several pilots involved with the *Krassin* were good men, but they really had no chance. A good man with a moderate chance was Graziansky who arrived at Barrow after thousands of miles of flying across Soviet territories and then across Bering Strait and along the north coast of Alaska. He had an American S-43 amphibian which, in spite of its many good qualities, is not very well suited for this type of work. For one thing, its clearance on wheels is so slight that practically it can take off only from a prepared landing field. The nearest thing to that at Barrow is a beach running to the northeast from the village. You might find this level on a given occasion, or you could level it for a particular take-off with the help of Eskimos; but waves, or ice pushed up by pressure, might roughen it again any time.

At first Graziansky operated his amphibian from water and made several flights to the north and northeast, one of them up to 76° N. Lat. When the freeze-up came the low clearance of his plane began to give him trouble. The S-43 finally got so banged up that he had to take it to Fairbanks for repairs. Then he flew it back to Siberia.

We have discussed only search operations on the American side of the Pole. There were operations from the Eurasian side—chiefly by several airplanes of various sizes which either were already at the world's most northerly air base, Rudolf Island, or had been flown there on purpose. This base is in the Franz Josef group, about five hundred miles from the North Pole—a thousand miles nearer the Pole than the Electra's base at Aklavik.

Before an assembled Soviet publication of the Levanevsky operations from the Eurasian side, we can speak of it only in very general terms.

It was not logical to do much flying from Eurasia while it seemed probable that Levanevsky was either on the ice several hundred miles on the American side of the Pole or else (if the Eskimo reports were correct) somewhere within the territory of Alaska—in that case probably victim of a fatal crash. It had always been likely that after descending, perhaps near 88° or 86° on the Fairbanks meridian, the party would begin drifting back toward the North Pole and thus toward the Atlantic. When it was seen how rapidly the contemporaneous Papanin expidition was drifting—there or four miles per day instead of the half-mile daily average predicted by most authorities—there was increased evidence of the definiteness of the drift in which the Levanevsky floe encampment should be moving, as well as of its direction and speed.

It was logical, then, to conduct the summer operation from the American side and also most of the autumn search. Midwinter would theoretically bring Levanevsky to the old-world side of the Pole, whereupon the main operations should be on that side. There was an added factor, that equipment manufactured in the Soviet Union was strong in planes on wheels and on skis, but was not (in 1937) strong in long-range flying boats, such as those of the United States Navy, adapted for summer work.

Old-world operations began, however, while still (theoretically speaking) Levanevsky was a considerable distance on the Alaska side of the Pole. We know there must have been several flights for every one that was mentioned in the press. A notable journey was on October 7 when Mikhail V. Vodopyanov flew the five hundred miles from the Rudolf Island base to the North Pole and about one hundred miles on the Alaska side, with a good deal of crisscross search flying added. This made history in that it was the first long flight in the vicinity of the North Pole made wholly with the sun below the horizon. Seemingly Vodopyanov depended more on what daylight there still was than on moonlight. The distance has not been announced, but it must have been as much as twelve hundred miles and probably was a good deal more.

When the sun returned in 1938, the Levanevsky camp or wreckage should have been well on the old-world side of the North Pole, northwesterly or westerly from the Rudolf

Island air base—in the direction of Greenland. Systematic flying now began, on which nothing has been published beyond some newspaper mention. We take, therefore, only as a sample the flight of March 31 by Y. D. Moshkovsky west from Rudolf Island, and his search by crisscross flying in the vicinity of latitudes 82° and 84°, to the east of northeast Greenland. That distance was given as 1,250 miles. Much of this and no doubt a considerable part of the other flights was over districts never traversed by man, therefore a discovery flight as well as a search flight. Expectations were confirmed in that no new islands were found to the east or northeast of Greenland.

Soviet operations from Rudolf Island appear to have continued well into the spring.

Officially the search lasted for exactly a year. It was closed on the anniversary of Levanevsky's final message, on August 13, 1938.

The Possibilities

In the beginning, it was the consensus of Soviet and American opinion that Levanevsky probably came down between one and three hundred miles from the Pole, on the Alaska side.

Gradually, as the months passed, it developed that on one point there was some differences of opinion between the authorities of the two countries. The Soviet geographers apparently felt certain that the ice upon which Levanevsky descended must have commenced immediately to drift toward the Atlantic, and at a speed comparable to, though perhaps somewhat less than, that of Papanin—which averaged more than three miles a day, increasing as he neared the open Atlantic. Apparently the Soviet assumption has been that Levanevsky would have drifted, with an initial speed of a mile or two per day, toward the Atlantic.

This may not have been 100 per cent the Soviet view; the American view did not agree to more than perhaps 90 per cent. We would have said that the chances were four to one that Levanevsky's drift was toward the Atlantic, and at an average speed for the first month of one or two miles per day. We feel, however, that there could be a Y in the current somewhere not far on the Alaska side of the probable Levanevsky descent and that he may have descended at this Y or even south of it.

If he came down at the bifurcation of the current he might have found himself in more or less of an eddy, such as the one which carried the Storkerson party of the 1913–18 Canadian expedition back and forth so much that, during six months of drifting about two hundred miles north of Alaska, and during more than four hundred miles of zigzag movement, they traveled only ninety miles in a direct line.

Or, again some authorities feel there might be near the Levanevsky point of descent such an extreme eddy as the one we know about north and west of Point Barrow, where a ship caught in the ice has disappeared to the north of Barrow and has returned months later, coming in from the southwest making this circuit and reappearing once or oftener each year for several years before finally escaping from the eddy.

In other words, some Americans feel that there was perhaps one chance in ten either that Levanevsky's floe would mill around for a long time near where he descended or else that it would start southeast toward Borden Island, swerve south and southwest parallel to the trend of Prince Patrick and Banks Island at a distance of one or two hundred miles, then turn west along the north coast of Alaska two or three hundred miles from shore, and finally arrive in the North Atlantic to be dissolved there by Gulf Stream warmth, four to seven or eight years later.

It is also a possibility that at some point or other the party may have decided to make for an island. With this in mind, some of the likeliest Canadian islands were searched by Wilkins.

We have seen in a previous chapter that in 1846–48 there were still numerous survivors of the Franklin party; but in a place where nearly everyone thought they could not be. If the like has happened to the crew of the H-209, these six

Russians may yet come through, as did the "four Russian sailors" who were stranded on an island off Spitsbergen in 1743, and of whom Scoresby writes: "Three out of the four survived on resources (except a few pounds of flour and a little tobacco) entirely provided by themselves, during a period of six years and three months, whilst unheard of and assumed to have perished, and were then rescued and, enriched with the results of their hunting and fishing, restored in health to their friends."

As he left New York City for the Antarctic in August, 1938, Wilkins said he still had some hope that the Levanevsky party would eventually come through safe to an inhabited Arctic land. The chances against that marvel are high, but not prohibitive. They might be reckoned up in some such way as this:

Original chance of death or crippling injury, through a bad landing, 50 per cent—because of summer icing of wings and summer corrosion of ice.

Chance, after a safe landing, of being able to live by food and fuel secured on the ice, or on an uninhabited Arctic island, 50 per cent. The chance that the party were still alive one year from a descent upon the pack is, therefore, 25 per cent.

If they landed where commonly supposed, *and if they drifted in the same direction as the Papanin group* and at a comparable speed, they would have died by drowning before the end of the summer of 1938, the ice on which they drifted melting under them. The chance of their being alive on January 1, 1939, will then be zero—unless, just conceivably, they left the ice as it was passing Peary Land or farther southeast. In that case they have a tiny chance to reach the Norwegians in northeast Greenland.

But if they drifted toward Borden Island and Alaska, the chance of living through the winter of 1938–39, either on the ice or on one of the Canadian islands, is again 50 per cent. Half of a quarter is 12½ per cent.

If the party should live through the second year they would live indefinitely—like the Russian sailors of Spitsbergen who had much trouble the first year on meat exclusively, little the second and none during the remaining four years till they were picked up.

But, we said, the chances are at least ten to one that the Soviet judgment is right: that Levanevsky's party, dead or alive, drifted with the ice in the same direction as Papanin—toward the Gulf Stream warmth and a sinking to the Atlantic's bottom when their floe melted.

If the Barter Island people really heard a plane coming from the north August 13, 1937, then Levanevsky crashed in the Alaska mountains and the chance of survival is zero.

The Soviet decision to close the search on the anniversary of the H-209's leaving Moscow was, in practice, right. If the drift was toward the Atlantic his camp site has melted under him; if the drift was some other, we have no idea where to look.

The final chance that one or more members of the Levanevsky party win through is only perhaps one in a hundred.

But it is not unknown for a hundred-to-one chance to win. There is still a ray of hope for Levanevsky up to four or five years after his disappearance. Inside that time, men would surely leave whatever camp they had, on drifting ice or uninhabited island, and travel toward a settlement. If they fail to reach a settlement by 1943, six years after their disappearance, all reasonable hope will be gone.

The Compensations

If hope completely disappears, Levanevsky will have joined Franklin among those who have succeeded through failure.

By their disappearance, both Franklin and Levanevsky caused a search of the Arctic where several nations cooperated in a humanitarian effort which of itself had value in promoting better understanding.

The Franklin search brought cooperation chiefly between Great Britain and the United States, whose relations were a bit strained then by animosities which dated from the American Revolution. There was world sympathy toward Britain in addition, and notable cooperation by other nations, particularly the French.

In the Levanevsky case the cooperation was chiefly between three nations: the Soviet Union, the United States, and Canada. But there was a helpful attitude by Great Britain, and there were offers of help by the Scandinavian countries.

But an equally striking comparison, and a more readily measured benefit, is through the increase of knowledge which followed the disappearance of Franklin and of Levanevsky.

The Franklin search revealed much of the Canadian archipelago and added greatly to knowledge of the Canadian mainland. It brought many advances in departments of science other than geography, and was responsible for notable progress in the technique of polar exploration.

It is still too early for judging what may be the chief contributions to science from the Levanevsky search. We can, however, name some with confidence.

From a cooperation in weather forecasting on behalf of the Consolidated and Lockheed flights, which was carried on chiefly between the Soviet, United States and Dominion governments, there came a speed-up in general cooperation between these weather bureaus—the United States and Canada are certainly receiving now (1938) far more weather news from the Soviet Union than they would have obtained so soon in normal course. The United States Weather Bureau has stated through its chief, Dr. Willis R. Gregg, that by the early part of 1938 there was already a substantial improvement in the accuracy of weather forecasting for the entire United States which had resulted directly from the Levanevsky search. The benefit was greatest, he said, in Alaska and in the western states but could be felt all the way to the Atlantic seaboard.

In the routine of the search the Consolidated flying boat, suited for descents upon open leads in the Arctic during summer, and the Lockheed Electra, suited for descents upon the pack ice in winter, did together more miles of flying over the polar sea than had been done by all non-Soviet nations combined since the first Arctic trial of the airplane.

There is no doubt that the total polar sea flying by Soviet-built aircraft in the Levanevsky search greatly exceeded the Wilkins flights. But we have not the figures yet.

The American part of the Levanevsky search, taken with the Chkalov, Gromov flights and with the known part of the Levanevsky flight itself, confirmed that Arctic fogs average lower than usual fogs, and can be avoided more often and more easily than the North Atlantic by high flying. It was shown by the boat operation that frosting on planes can usually be eliminated, even within the cloud, by either rising higher or dropping lower—methods which are in routine use on certain scheduled air lines of the United States and Europe.

The Soviet flyer Vodopyanov, and perhaps others, demonstrated that flying is comparatively easy in the latitudes immediately around the North Pole (from 82° N. on the Soviet side past the Pole to 86° N. on the Alaska side) by that twilight which lasts some weeks after the disappearance of the sun in autumn—therefore, also through that twilight which begins some weeks before the return of the sun in spring.

By Wilkins and Kenyon there was satisfactory trial of the belief that the Arctic moon, which does not set for several days around the full (does not set for two weeks each month at the exact North Pole) gives light enough not merely for flying but for searching out comparatively small things like a camp on the ice and for making any necessary intentional or forced descents within the pack.

These are only a few of the contributions. It may, therefore, be said of Levanevsky, as it was of Franklin, that by failing in his own expedition he promoted both international good relations and the purposes of science more than he could have done by succeeding.

Bibliography

Bibliography

Disappearance of the Greenland Colony

BERTELSEN, ALFR., "Sanitation and Health Conditions in Greenland," *Greenland* (ed. by M. Vahl, G. C. Amdrup, L. Bode, Ad. S. Jensen), Vol. III. Copenhagen, 1929.

EGEDE, HANS, *Det gamle Grönlands nye Perlustration, eller Naturel-Historie* . . . Kjöbenhavn, 1741.

Flatey Book and Recently Discovered Vatican Manuscripts Concerning America as Early as the Tenth Century. Norroena Society, London-Stockholm-Copenhagen-Berlin-New York, 1906.

HÖYGAARD, ARNE, *Some Investigations into the Physiology and Nosology of Eskimos from Angmagssalik in Greenland: A Preliminary Statement.* Oslo, 1937.

—Letter dated June 29, 1938.

ISACHSEN, GUNNAR, and ISACHSEN, FRIDTJOF, "Hvor Langt mot Nord Kom de Norröne Grönlendinger på sine Fangstferder i Ubygdene," *Norsk Geografisk Tidsskrift,* Bind 4, Hefte 1-3. Oslo, 1932.

JONSSON, FINNUR, *Graenlendinga Saga.* Copenhagen, 1899.

—"The Icelandic Colonization of Greenland," *Greenland,* Vol. II. Copenhagen and London, 1928.

MELDORF, GUSTAV, "Om den gamle islandsk-grönlandske Kolonis Undergang," *Det Grönlandske Selskabs Aarskrift.* Odense, 1906.

NANSEN, FRIDTJOF, *In Northern Mists.* New York, 1911.

—*Klimat-Vekslinger I Nordens Historie.* Oslo, 1925.

NÖRLUND, POUL, *De Gamle Nordbobygder Ved Verdens Ende, Skildringer fra Grönlands Middelalder.* Copenhagen, 1935.

RASMUSSEN, KNUD, *Myter og Sagn fra Grönland.* Copenhagen, 1925.

ROCHEFORT, C. DE, *Histoire Naturelle et Morale des Isles Antilles de l'Amérique,* Rotterdam, 1658.

Sundt, Eilert, *Egedes Dagbog i Udtag*, Christiania, 1860.

Thomas, Wiliam A., "Health of a Carnivorous Race: A Study of the Eskimo," *Journal* of the American Medical Association, Chicago, May 14, 1927.

Thorhallesen, E., *Efterretning om Rudera*, etc. Kjöbenhavn, 1776.

Those interested in the documentation of Greenland history can find it brought down fairly well to date in the 130-page introduction to *The Three Voyages of Martin Frobisher*, by Vilhjalmur Stefansson with the collaboration of Eloise McCaskill, London, 1938.

The Lost Franklin Expedition

Arctic Expeditions: *Return to an Address of the Honourable The House of Commons*, dated 21 March 1848. . . . Ordered by The House of Commons, to be Printed 13 April 1848.

—*Report of the Committee Appointed by the Commissioners of the Admiralty . . . together with the Minutes of Evidence taken before the Committee and papers connected with the Subject*, London, 1852.

—*Return to an Address of the Honourable the House of Commons dated 20 February 1852 for Papers in Connection with the late Arctic Expeditions, or with any which may be in preparation*. Ordered by the House of Commons to be printed 27 February 1852.

—*Papers Relative to the Recent Arctic Expeditions in Search of Sir John Franklin and the crews of H.M.S. Erebus and Terror*, London, 1854.

—*Return to an Address of the Honourable the House of Commons dated 17 March 1854*. Ordered by the House of Commons to be printed 24 March 1854.

—*Further Papers Relative to the Recent Arctic Expeditions*. Presented to both Houses of Parliament by Command of Her Majesty, January, 1855.

—*Further Papers Relative to the Recent Arctic Expeditions . . . Including the Reports of Dr. Kane and Messrs. Anderson and Stewart; and Correspondence relative to the *adjudication of £10,000 as a Reward for ascertaining the fate of the crews of H.M.S. Erebus and Terror.* London, 1856.

ANONYMOUS, *A Brave Man and His Belongings.* London, 1874.

—Review of H. D. Traill's "Life of Sir John Franklin," *Blackwood's Magazine,* Edinburgh, Feb., 1897.

—Review of John Franklin's "Narrative of a Second Journey to the Shores of the Polar Sea," *Quarterly Review,* London, 1828.

—"The Arctic Expeditions," *Littell's Living Age,* Boston, Feb. 17, 1849.

—"The Search for Sir John Franklin," *Littel's Living Age,* May 21, 1853.

—"The Search for Sir John Franklin," *Eclectic Magazine,* London, March, 1851.

—"Sir John Franklin and the Arctic Regions," *North American Review,* New York, July, 1850.

—"The Search for Sir John Franklin," *Quarterly Review,* London, 1853.

—"The Search for Franklin," *Cornhill Magazine,* London, Jan., 1860.

—"Expeditions to the North Pole," *Hours at Home,* New York, June, 1868.

—"Thirty Years' Search for Franklin," *Chambers's Journal,* Edinburgh, Feb. 26, 1881.

—"Sir John Franklin and His Crews," *Household Words* (conducted by Charles Dickens), London, 1855.

—"Food of the Arctic Regions—Franklin's Expedition," *Chambers's Edinburgh Journal,* Feb., 1852.

BACK, GEORGE, *Narrative of the Arctic Land Expedition to the Mouth of the Great Fish River.* London, 1836.

—*Narrative of an Expedition in H.M.S. Terror.* London, 1838.

BEESLY, A. H., *Sir John Franklin.* London, 1894.

BELL, BENJAMIN, ed., *Lieut. John Irving, R.N., of H.M.S. Terror: A Memorial Sketch with Letters.* Edinburgh, 1881.

BROWN, JOHN, *The North West Passage and the Plans for the Search for Sir John Franklin,* 2nd ed. with *Sequel.* London, 1860.

BROWNE, JAMES A., *The Northwest Passage and the Fate of Sir John Franklin.* Woolwich, 1860.

BURWASH, L. T., *Canada's Western Arctic.* Ottawa, 1931.

Cassell's Illustrated Family Paper, London, Dec. 2, 1854

ELLIOTT, HENRY, "Sir John Franklin," *The Nineteenth Century,* London, July, 1892.

FINDLAY, A. G., "On the Probable Course Pursued by Sir John Franklin's Expedition," Paper Read Before the Royal Geographical Society, London, Jan. 28, 1856.

FRANKLIN, JANE, *Letter to Viscount Palmerston, K.G.,* 2nd ed. with Appendix and Chart. London, 1857.

FRANKLIN, JOHN, *Narrative of a Journey to the Shores of the Polar Sea in the Years 1818–20–21–22.* London, 1824.

—*Narrative of a Second Expedition to the Shores of the Polar Sea in the Years 1825–1826–1827 . . . including an Account of the Progress of a Detachment to the Eastward by John Richardson.* London, 1828.

FYFE, H. HAMILTON, *The Triumphs of Invention and Discovery.* London, 1861.

GIBSON, WILLIAM, "Sir John Franklin's Last Voyage," *The Beaver,* Winnipeg, June, 1937.

—"Some Further Traces of the Franklin Retreat," *Geographical Journal,* London, May, 1932.

GILDER, WILLIAM H., *Schwatka's Search: Sledging in the Arctic in Quest of Franklin Records.* New York, 1881.

HALL, CHARLES FRANCIS, *Narrative of the Second Arctic Expedition,* ed. by Prof. J. E. Nourse, U.S.N. Washington, 1879.

HUISH, R., *The Last Voyage of Captain Sir John Ross . . . compiled from authentic informations and original documents transmitted by William Light, Purser's Steward through the Expedition.* London, 1834.

KING, RICHARD, *The Franklin Search from First to Last.* London, 1855.

LIVINGSTON, PETER, *Poems and Songs with Lectures,* 10th ed., Dundee, 1864.

M'CLINTOCK, LEOPOLD, *Voyage of the Fox.* London, 1859.

MANGLES, JAMES (collector and arranger), *Papers and Despatches relating to the Arctic Searching Expeditions of 1850–51–52,* 2nd ed. with copious additions. London, 1852.

MARKHAM, ALBERT H., *Life of Sir John Franklin.* London, 1891.

MARKHAM, CLEMENTS R., *Franklin's Footsteps.* London, 1853.

NOURSE, J. E., *American Explorations in the Ice Zones,* 3rd ed. (copyright 1884). Boston.

OSBORN, SHERARD, *Stray Leaves from an Arctic Journal.* London, 1852 and 1865.

PARRY, REV. EDWARD, *Memoirs of Rear Admiral Sir W. Edward Parry, Kt.* London, 1857.

PARRY, WILLIAM EDWARD, *Journal of a Voyage for the Discovery of a North-West Passage . . . performed in the years 1819–20 in H.M.S. Hecla and Griper.* London, 1821.

—*Journal of a Second Voyage for the Discovery of a North-West Passage . . . performed in the Years 1821–22–23 in H.M.S. Fury and Hecla.* London, 1824.

RAE, JOHN, "The Lost Arctic Voyagers," *Household Words* (conducted by Charles Dickens), March, 1855.

—*Narrative of an Expedition to the Shores of the Arctic Sea in 1846–47.* London, 1850.

RASMUSSEN, KNUD, *The Netsilik Eskimos.* Copenhagen, 1931.

RICHARDSON, JOHN, *Journal of a Boat Voyage Through Ruperts Land and the Arctic Sea in Search of the Discovery Ships under Command of Sir John Franklin.* London, 1851.

—*The Polar Regions.* Edinburgh, 1861.

ROSS, JOHN, *Narrative of a Second Voyage in Search of a North-West Passage, and of a residence in the Arctic Regions during the Years 1829–30–31–32–33; with Appendix.* London, 1835.

SIMMONDS, P. L., *The Arctic Regions.* London and New York, 1875.

SKEWES, J. HENRY, *Sir John Franklin: The True Secret of His Fate,* 2nd ed. with supplement. London, 1890.

Traill, H. D., *Life of Sir John Franklin, R.N.* London, 1896.

The Strange Fate of Thomas Simpson

Back, George, *Journal of the Arctic Land Expedition.* London, 1836.

—*Narrative of an Expedition in H.M.S. Terror.* London, 1838.

Ballantyne, R. M. *Hudson's Bay, or Everyday Life in the Wilds of North America.* Edinburgh, 1848.

Bryce, Rev. George, *Mackenzie, Selkirk, Simpson.* Toronto, 1905.

—*Remarkable History of the Hudson's Bay Company.* New York, 1900.

Connon, John R., *Elora.* Ontario, 1930.

Cowie, Isaac, *Company of Adventurers.* Toronto, 1913.

Crouse, Nellis M., *Search for the Northwest Passage.* New York, 1935.

Ellesmere, Earl of, *Essays on History, Biography, Geography, Engineering &c. Contributed to the Quarterly Review.* London, 1858.

Franklin, John, *Narrative of a Journey to the Shores of the Polar Sea in the Years, 1819, 20, 21 and 22.* London, 1824.

—*Narrative of a Second Expedition to the Shores of the Polar Sea in the Years 1825, 1826 and 1827.* London, 1828.

Greely, A. W., *True Tales of Arctic Heroism in the New World.* New York, 1912.

Hargrave Correspondence, 1821–1843, ed. with Introduction and notes by G. P. de T. Glazebrook. Toronto, 1938.

Huish, Robert, *The Last Expedition of Captain Sir John Ross . . . to the Arctic Regions.* London, 1835.

I., W. E., "Red River Tragedy." *Winnipeg Free Press,* June 11, 1935.

King, Richard, *The Franklin Expedition from First to Last.* London, 1855.

—*Narrative of a Journey to the Shores of the Arctic Ocean,* London, 1847.

McArthur, Alex., "A Prarie Tragedy: The Fate of Thomas Simpson, the Arctic Explorer." Paper read before the Historical and Scientific Society of Manitoba, *Transaction No. 26*, Winnipeg, 1897.

McDonald, Archibald, *Canoe Voyage from Hudson's Bay to the Pacific by the late Sir George Simpson in 1828: Journal of the late Chief Factor Archibald McDonald, who accompanied him,* ed. with notes by Malcolm McLeod. Ottawa, Montreal, and Toronto, 1872.

MacKay, Douglas, *The Honourable Company.* Indianapolis and New York, 1936.

—and Lamb, W. Kaye, "More Light on Thomas Simpson." *The Beaver,* Winnipeg, Sept. 1938.

McLean, John, *Notes of a Twenty-five Years Service in the Hudson's Bay Territory,* London, 1849.

Mark, Frederick, *Fur Trade and Empire.* Cambridge, Mass., 1931.

Mountain, G., *The Journal of the Bishop of Montreal during a visit to the Church Missionary Society's North-West America Missions.* London, 1845.

Pinkerton, Robert E., *The Hudson's Bay Company.* New York, 1931.

Rae, John, *A Narrative of an Expedition to the Shores of the Arctic Sea in 1846 & 1847.* London, 1850

Report from the Select Committee on the Hudson's Bay Company; together with the Proceedings of the Committee, Minutes of Evidence, Appendix and Index, ordered by the House of Commons to be printed 31 July and 11 August, 1857.

Richardson, John, *The Polar Regions,* Edinburgh, 1861.

Ross, Donald, Unpublished letters from Thomas Simpson and others (MS. consulted through the kindness of Will E. Ingersoll and The Macmillan Company of Canada).

Scott, S. F., *From Franklin to Nansen.* London, 1904.

Sibley Papers in the Minnesota Historical Library, St. Paul, Minn. (unpublished). (The papers contains depositions on the Simpson case, etc., made before Henry H. Sibley, Justice of the Peace in 1840.)

Simpson, Alexander, *Life and Travels of Thomas Simpson.* London. 1845.

Simpson, George, *Narrative of a Journey Round the World during the years 1841 and 1842.* London, 1847.

Simpson, Thomas, *Narrative of Discoveries on the North Coast of America.* London, 1843.

Stevenson, John A., "The Unsolved Death of Thomas Simpson, Explorer." *The Beaver,* Winnipeg, June, 1935.

Willson, Beckles, *The Great Company.* Toronto, 1899.

—*Lord Strathcona: The Story of His Life.* Toronto, 1902.

Young, Egerton, *Apostle of the North.* New York, 1899.

How Did Andrée Die?

Ahlmann, Hans Wm., Letter dated Sept. 14, 1938.

Andersson, Gunnar, *S. A. Andrée: Hans Följeslagare och Hans Polarfärd, 1896-1897.* (A memorial volume published through the Swedish Society for Anthropology and Geography.) Stockholm, 1906.

Andrée, S. A., *Förslag till Polarfärd med Luftballong.* Stockholm, 1895.

—*Kutdlartausiap assinga Polarballoon.* (Circular distributed among Greenland Eskimos by the Danish Government showing Andrée's balloon and asking them to help him if he got into their country.)

—"Letters from the Andrée Party," *McClure's Magazine,* New York, March, 1898.

—*Andrée's Story: The Complete Record of His Polar Flight 1897,* ed. by Swedish Society for Anthropology and Geography (transl. from Swedish by Edward Adams-Ray). New York, 1930.

—"Andrée's polarexpeditionen," *Norsk Geografiske Selskabs Aarbog,* Vol. VII, 1895–1896, Kristiania, 1896.

—"The Finding of Andrée," *Week End Review,* London, Aug. 30, 1930.

—*Fynden På Vitön; Minnesutställning over S. A. Andrée, Nils Strindberg och Knut Fraenkel anordnad i Liljevalchs Konsthall January 1931.* Stockholm, 1931.

ARNASON, ARSAELL, *Andrée Polfari og Felagar Hans.* Reykjavik, 1931.

BYRD, REAR ADMIRAL RICHARD E., *Little America.* New York, 1930.

COTTER, H. M. S., "Tried for North Pole by Balloon," *The Beaver*, Winnipeg, July, 1921.

DAHL, KAI R., *The Teddy Expedition.* New York, 1925.

DE VEER, GERRIT, *The Three Voyages of William Barents to the Arctic Regions*, 2nd ed. London, 1876.

HANSON, MALCOLM P., Letter dated Aug. 25, 1938.

LACHAMBRE, HENRI, and MACHURON, ALEXIS, *Andrée and His Balloon.* Westminster, 1898.

LEWIS, LEON, *Andrée at the North Pole: With Details of His Fate.* New York, 1899.

NANSEN, FRIDTJOF, *Farthest North.* Westminster, 1897.

NATHORST, A. G., *Tva Somrar i Norra Ishafvet.* Stockholm, 1900.

PALLIN, H. N., *Andréegåtan.* Upsala, 1934.

PELLHAM, EDWARD, *Gods Power and Providence: Shewed, In the Miraculous Preservation and Deliverance of eight Englishmen, left by mischance in Green-land Anno 1630.* London, 1631.

PUTNAM, GEORGE PALMER, *Andrée: The Record of a Tragic Adventure.* New York, 1930.

STADLING, JONAS, *Genom Siberien: På Spaning efter Andrée.* Stockholm, 1901.

STEFANSSON, VILHJALMUR, "An Arctic Mystery," *Saturday Review of Literature*, New York, Jan. 3, 1931.

—"How Andrée Lived and Died," *The Sphere*, London, Oct. 11, 1930.

STORY, ALFRED T., "Mr. Andrée's Balloon Voyage to the North Pole," *Strand Magazine*, London, 1896 (pp. 76-91).

SWEDISH SOCIETY OF ANTHROPOLOGY AND GEOGRAPHY, *Med Ornen mot Polen.* Stockholm, 1930.

WELLMAN, WALTER, "On the Way to the North Pole," *Century Magazine*, New York, Feb., 1899.

The Missing Soviet Flyers

This chapter is based largely on personal knowledge, including conversations with many of those concerned. Apart from these, the sources are files of the United States and Canadian newspapers, some dispatches to the *New York Times* which were received direct from its radio department, and files of the *Moscow Daily News*.